Pressure and Power: Organized Interests in American Politics

The *New Directions in Political Behavior* Series

GENERAL EDITOR
ALLAN J. CIGLER
University of Kansas

PRESSURE AND POWER: ORGANIZED INTERESTS IN AMERICAN POLITICS

Anthony J. Nownes

UNIVERSITY OF TENNESSEE, KNOXVILLE

Houghton Mifflin Company   Boston   New York

Editor-in-Chief: *Jean Woy*
Sponsoring Editor: *Mary Dougherty*
Assistant Editor: *Jennifer DiDomenico*
Project Editor: *Florence Kilgo*
Editorial Assistant: *Cecilia Molinari*
Senior Production/Design Coordinator: *Jill Haber*
Senior Manufacturing Coordinator: *Sally Culler*
Senior Marketing Manager: *Sandra McGuire*

Cover design: Harold Burch, Harold Burch Design, NYC
Cover image: JAMES RICHARDSON/NGS Image Collection

Printed in the U.S.A.

Library of Congress Catalog Number: 00-133850

ISBN: 0-395-95150-X

123456789-HAP- 04 03 02 01 00

Preface

As its title suggests, this book is about organized interest groups—what I call *organized interests*—in American politics. However, *Pressure and Power: Organized Interests in American Politics* differs from most other books on interest groups in its comprehensive treatment of the full range of politically active organizations in the United States. During my first decade of university teaching, I became convinced that students, journalists, and scholars alike often overlook large segments of the organizational world when they discuss the politics of organized interests. Specifically, many people mistakenly believe that broad-based membership groups such as the American Civil Liberties Union (ACLU), the Christian Coalition, the National Rifle Association (NRA), and the Sierra Club comprise the bulk of organized interests. Nothing could be further from the truth. As this book documents in its first few chapters, broad-based membership groups make up only a small fraction of the universe of organized interests in the United States. Broad-based membership groups actually operate alongside tens of thousands of corporations, governments, labor unions, political action committees, professional associations, trade associations, and "think tanks," among other types of organizations. In short, the universe of organized interests is much more diversified than it may appear at first glance, and this book conveys this simple yet crucial fact.

The organizing concept of this book is what I call the paradox of organized interests. On the one hand, most Americans *fear* organized interests. Polls consistently show, for example, that Americans feel that organized interests are "out of control." On the other hand, most Americans *support* organized interests. Vast majorities of Americans join or otherwise support some type of organized interest, and Americans participate in group endeavors at far higher rates than do citizens of other countries. The organizing theme of the paradox helps students examine their own, often conflicting opinions about organized interests, and encourages them to move beyond stereotypes to critically engage with the political reality of organized interests.

The turn of the millenium is an especially appropriate time to take a fresh look at organized interest politics in the United States. All available evidence suggests that organized interests are more copious, more active, and more resourceful than ever before. Indeed, one of the enduring themes in the literature on organized interests in the United States is that organized interest politics changes rapidly, unpredictably, and unrelentingly. One major goal of this book is to explain how organized interest politics has changed over time. Chapters 1 through 3, for example, pay special attention to how the composition of the universe of organized interests has changed over the last 35 years. In a similar vein, Chapters 4 through 8 highlight and explain the evolution of lobbying activities since the "advocacy explosion" of the 1960s.

No book on organized interests would be complete without a serious look at what I call "the influence question"—the question of how much influence organized interests exert over public policy outcomes. Chapter 9 is devoted solely to this question, examining what we have learned about the nature and extent of organized interest power, without offering a simplistic answer to the influence question. The bulk of the evidence suggests that organized interest influence is situational—that is, influence varies according to context. Chapter 9 offers an accessible model for students that engages and stretches critical thinking and analytic skills about the complex reality of organized interests in the United States.

To further assist students in engaging with and accessing resources on organized interests, I have included exercises at the end of Chapters 1-9. The exercises are designed to get students started with their own research on organized interests. In addition to a set of exercises, these chapters contain a section entitled *Research Resources*. Each *Research Resources* section contains a list of published and internet resources pertaining to the chapter topic. While publications remain useful, the World Wide Web offers unprecedented access to a great deal of information on organized interests. I have provided URLs for the most current and helpful Internet sites. One web resource that will prove especially useful is the *Pressure and Power* web site, located at http://college. hmco.com. This web site will be updated periodically, and will provide additional information on how to research organized interests on the web.

Finally, I must acknowledge my debts to the many people who have helped make this book possible. First and foremost, I must recognize the help and support of my mentor, Dr. Allan J. Cigler. Much of what is good about this book can in one way or another be traced back to him. I would also like to thank the only two people not officially involved in this project who read earlier versions of the book: my wife Elsa Nownes, and her mother Jilda MacMillan. Neither of these wonderful women wavered in their support of this book, nor were they afraid to confront me with its problems.

Intellectually, I also owe debts to the following: Mike Bath, William K.

"Bubba" Cheek, Jeffrey Berejikian, Regis Boyle, David Elkins, Frankie Sue Howerton, Kennith Hunter, Garrett Johnson, Paul Johnson, Debbie McCaulley, Emil Nagengast, Bryan Schmiedeler, Kurt Thrumaier, and Karen Ye.

I would also like to extend special thanks to those scholars who provided useful suggestions for the development of this text: Joanne Connor Green, Texas Christian University; Sara A. Grove, Shippensburg University; Marjorie Hershey, Indiana University; Kevin W. Hula, Loyola College in Maryland; Philip H. Pollock III, University of Central Florida; Margaret Trevor, University of Iowa; Darrell West, Brown University; Graham Wilson, University of Wisconsin, Madison; and Laura R. Woliver, University of South Carolina.

Over the years, I have also benefited from the help of a number of University of Tennessee, Knoxville, students including Robert M. Alexander, Sina Bahadoran, Matthew Bax, Shari Garber Bax, Clint Cantrell, Chris Cooper, Steve Graziano, Angela Lewis, Jennifer Murray, Mark Schwerdt, and Walter Williams. Finally, for inspiration I would like to thank Jason Falkner, and Chris at the Java House.

A.J.N.

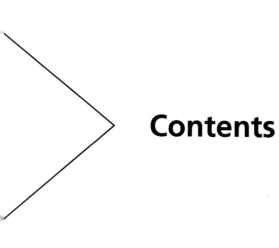

Contents

Organized Interests
in the United States

Washington, D.C.
February 12, 1999

Two months after the House of Representatives approved two articles of impeachment against President Bill Clinton, the Senate puts the articles to a vote. In approving the articles, the House had alleged that in the course of his attempt to conceal an affair with White House intern Monica Lewinsky, the president lied to a federal grand jury and obstructed justice. On the first article of impeachment (perjury), the Senate votes 55–45 against removal. On the second (obstruction of justice), the Senate deadlocks at 50–50. President Clinton is spared removal from office.

In late 1998 and early 1999, President Clinton's impeachment dominated the American political agenda. At the center of the drama were President Clinton and the members of Congress who decided his fate. Yet the president and his congressional accusers were far from the only players. Also active were large numbers of interest groups—groups that in this book we refer to as *organized interests*. For example, on one random weekday before the House impeachment vote, Jesse Jackson's PUSH Coalition led an anti-impeachment march and prayer vigil on the west steps of the Capitol building. Simultaneously on the east steps of the Capitol building, the Christian Defense Coalition led a pro-impeachment prayer vigil.[1]

Throughout the impeachment saga, pro- and anti-Clinton forces battled relentlessly. On one side was a coterie of liberal organized interests that worked to save Clinton's presidency. The group that spearheaded the pro-Clinton campaign was People for the American Way, which placed pro-Clinton advertisements in national newspapers, encouraged its members to contact members of Congress, and sent professional lobbyists directly to Capitol Hill. On the eve of the House impeachment vote, People for the American Way spent over $75,000 on a four-city pro-Clinton radio advertising campaign targeted at eleven undecided House Republicans.[2] People for the American Way was at the forefront of the pro-Clinton campaign, but it was not alone. The AFL-CIO (American Federation of Labor-Congress of Industrial Organizations) and the Communications Workers of America used their Internet web sites to encourage union members to oppose impeachment and removal. The International Union of Brick Layers and Allied Craftworkers contacted its 92,000 members and asked them to call their senators to express opposition to removal.[3] A number of other liberal groups, including the National Organization for Women, the Rainbow/PUSH Coalition, and the American Federation of State, County, and Municipal Employees, got into the act as well.

An impressive array of pro-impeachment groups lined up on the other side of the issue. Foremost among them was the Christian Coalition, which used its extensive network of grass-roots organizers to gather over a quarter of a million signatures on a pro-removal petition. The Christian Coalition's efforts were buttressed by those of the Conservative Caucus, which sent out 1 million pieces of anti-Clinton mail in 1998 alone. The group generated tens of thousands of pro-impeachment letters to members of Congress.[4] Other conservative groups that joined the fray included the Family Research Council, the John Birch Society, and Concerned Women for America.

THE PARADOX OF ORGANIZED INTERESTS

Impeachment battles are once-in-a-lifetime phenomena. In fact, President Clinton is only the second president in U.S. history to be impeached.[5] Thus, it is certainly not the case that the battle over the impeachment represented business as usual in the nation's capitol. Yet in one way, the impeachment battle *did* embody business as usual: *It took place among a backdrop of furious and frenzied organized interest activity.* For better or worse, in Washington, D.C., as well as in other cities and states across America, organized interests can be found wherever government policy is made.

Organized interests worry many Americans. Lobbyists, the people who represent organized interests in front of government officials, are not popular. Public opinion polls show that most Americans hold them in slightly lower esteem than telemarketers, used-car salesmen, and daytime talk show hosts. Organized interests themselves are similarly scorned by the public. While the military, the police, churches, and even governmental institutions get relatively high marks from citizens, organized interests generally do not. Ordinary Americans are not the only ones who disdain organized interests. Politicians scorn them as well. Hardly a day passes without some high-ranking public official decrying the impact of "special interests" on government policy. Presidents have proven especially contemptuous of organized interests. Every president

For sale? The fear that our government is controlled by powerful "special interests" is, and always has been, widespread. This fear is manifest in this editorial cartoon, which implies that both major political parties are "for sale" to wealthy corporate interests. *Bob Engelhart, The Hartford Courant.*

since George Washington has taken time out from his busy schedule to take potshots at lobbyists and the organizations they represent. Even before the Constitution was ratified, for example, future president James Madison warned that organized interest groups posed a danger to the republic because they worked to gain advantage for themselves at the expense of others.[6] Similarly, upon retiring from office, President Eisenhower warned of the pernicious influence of powerful organizations representing the "military-industrial complex." Two of Eisenhower's successors, Lyndon Johnson and Richard Nixon, frequently complained about radical "hippie" groups that fanned the flames of dissent by protesting American involvement in Vietnam. More recently, in the 1980s, President Ronald Reagan made it a point to attack "liberal special interests" every chance he got. And throughout his troubled presidency, President Clinton denounced conservative groups that dredged up allegations of philandering and fund-raising improprieties.

But apparently just as many Americans *support* organized interests as abhor them. Numerous studies indicate that most Americans belong to organized interests of some sort.[7] One recent study, for example, reports that 65 percent of all adult Americans belong to at least one politically active organization.[8] In addition, few of us can deny that there are organized interests working on our behalf. For example, as the vignette that opened this chapter attests, both pro- and anti-impeachment Americans were well represented by organized interests during the impeachment battle. As it turns out, so were people who simply wanted the whole thing to go away. The upstart organization Move On urged the Senate to censure Clinton and move on to other business.[9]

The theme of this book is that there is something paradoxical about the way Americans view organized interests. On the one hand, most of us belong to or identify with some organized interests. We live in a country that values political freedom, liberty, and equality, and we jump at the chance to make our voices heard. On the other hand, most of us are uneasy about the role organized interests play in American politics. To put it briefly, we worry that powerful "special interests" dominate policymaking and drown out the voices of ordinary citizens. Why the contradiction? What explains this paradox—a paradox I call the *paradox of organized interests*? Is there a solution to this paradox? Or is it an inevitable epiphenomenon of American democracy?

Before we begin to explore this paradox, it is worth noting that we are hardly the first to recognize it. James Madison, who wrote most of the Constitution, identified the crux of the paradox of organized interests over two hundred years ago. In Federalist No. 10, he correctly predicted that if the Constitution was ratified and the United States of America became a sovereign nation, citizens would organize themselves into groups (which he referred to as "factions") to further their common interests.[10] This was a problem, Madison averred, because a powerful "faction" could conceivably run roughshod over other interests in society, thus threatening the representative government created by the Constitution. Madison concluded that the most obvious solution to this problem would be to prevent people from joining "factions." This would prevent any single "faction" from dominating American politics and despotizing other citizens. Madison, however, summarily dismissed this solution, for two reasons. First, he regretfully conceded that the desire to achieve one's selfish interests was innate—"sown in the nature of man," he said.[11] As a free society evolves, Madison pointed out, different social classes and political groupings emerge. Eventually these differences naturally manifest themselves in competition among various societal groupings. Madison concluded that in the end, the selfish desire to organize into "factions" to protect common interests was universal, inevitable, and unstoppable, so any efforts to prevent factionalization were destined to fail. Second, Madison dismissed the prohibition of membership in factions because he recognized that the ability of people to organize and pursue their selfish interests was the cornerstone of a free society. The very essence of liberty, Madison argued, was the ability to pursue one's dreams, goals, and aspirations. To deprive people of this ability would be antithetical to the ideals of American constitutional government.

Madison recognized that a paradox lay at the heart of American politics. On the one hand, factions—which are very much akin to what we call "organized interests"—are potentially divisive, destructive, and malignant forces that threaten the integrity of American popular government. On the other hand, factions are an integral part of American democracy. The obvious solution to the potentially destructive problem of faction is off-limits in a society that values individual political freedom. So what to do? Madison offered an ingenious solution to the paradox of organized interests. Writing before the Constitution was ratified, he argued that a republican form of government as embodied by the U.S. Constitution would check the worst effects of faction. First, governmental decisions would be made by representatives elected by ordinary citizens. Madison argued that these representatives, who were likely to be more cosmopolitan and better educated than other citizens, would have to weigh the demands of many different factions and groups in society and thus could resist the demands of any single impassioned faction. Second, the new country governed by the Constitution would cover an immense territory, encompassing a large and diverse population. Diversity ensured that the new country would be home to numerous factions representing dozens of discrete interests. Madison argued that the United States would be so large and diverse that no one faction could dominate government. Third, the new country would divide power among various branches of government (separation of powers) and levels of government (federalism). This would make it exceedingly difficult for any faction to take control of the entire government. In the end, Madison concluded that the system of government created by the Constitution would act as a check on the most deleterious effects of faction. A representative government with built-in "checks and balances," he argued, could weigh the demands of the numerous factions in America and make policies for the common good.

Over the years, scholars and political observers of all stripes have revisited the paradox that Madison identified. Many have agreed with him that American constitutional government does a good job of keeping factions in check. For example, in the 1950s and 1960s, a group of political scholars called pluralists argued that the American governmental system did a reasonably good job of solving the paradox of organized interests. They concluded that just as Madison had hoped, representative government coupled with a natural diversity of interests rendered organized interests in the United States more or less benign.[12] In his 1961 book, *Who Governs?* political scientist Robert Dahl made an eloquent case for pluralism. Dahl, hoping to answer the question that was the title of his book, examined policymaking in the city of New Haven, Connecticut. After studying how decisions were made in three different policy areas, he reached a number of conclusions about who exerted influence over policy decisions. His most important finding was that in each of the three policy areas he studied, *different* groups were active and influential. In other words, no single faction dominated New Haven politics. Instead, power was widely dispersed among various factions and individuals. Although Dahl recognized that a few groups were left out of the decision-making process altogether, he also determined that any group of people who wished to be heard by government *was* heard by government. According to Dahl, in most policy battles, many different points of view were represented, and government officials made decisions after considering these various points of view. This ensured that political decisions were reasonably fair and representative and that no single faction dominated the political process.

In sum, pluralists concluded that organized interests were active and influential but neither malignant nor dominant. Although pluralism reached the height of its popularity in the mid-1960s, it continues to resonate with some scholars who view organized interests as more or less benign by-products of popular government.[13]

Not surprisingly, not everyone accepts pluralism's sanguine view of organized interests. A number of scholars have concluded that decision making in America is dominated by a small group of wealthy and well-connected leaders who ignore ordinary citizens. In the 1950s, for example, sociologist C. Wright Mills argued that America was ruled by a "power elite"—a small stratum of affluent and privileged individuals who ignored the wishes of regular people.[14] Few other scholars or laypeople accept Mills's radical critique of American government, but many observers of American politics have agreed with him that pluralism's uncritical view of organized interests is off base. Longtime political analyst Theodore Lowi, for example, concludes that organized interests are far from harmless. Some organized interests, he argues, have much better access to government officials than others do.[15] Government officials are eager to please those organized interests that are most vocal and active, and thus they generally give in to their demands. This, of course, leads to policy outcomes that are skewed toward specific favored organized interests and away from the interests of the population at large. In the end, Lowi concludes that not all interests are equally represented before government, and thus some interests have a disproportionate amount of influence over policy outcomes.

In one form or another, the jousting between pluralists and their critics continues to this day. Some scholars maintain that pluralists are more or less correct in their conclusion that organized interests are influential but neither dominant nor malevolent. Others counter that organized interests are both dominant and malevolent. In short, the argument over organized interests is far from settled, and the paradox of organized interests is far from solved. The primary goal of this book is to have you ponder and understand this paradox. Why does the paradox of organized interests exist? Why do laypeople and scholars alike express ambivalence about organized interests? Why do most ordinary Americans both support *and* fear organized interests? Why do some scholars view organized interests as important and beneficial aspects of representative government, while others view them as heinous and destructive manifestations of selfishness? Is there a resolution to the paradox of organized interests? Or is this paradox destined to remain unresolved? The answers to all of these questions, I believe, lie in the complicated nature of organized interest politics in the United States. To address these questions, it is necessary to understand precisely what organized interests are, where they come from, how they operate, and to what extent they influence the decisions of government officials. Ultimately the goal of this book is to provide the foundation of knowledge necessary for you to weigh in on the paradox of organized interests.

The remainder of this chapter provides the foundation necessary to deal with the rest of this book. We begin with definitions of essential terms and key concepts in order to identify as quickly as possible the types of organizations that are the focus of this book. As you will see, there is considerable confusion among scholars and laypersons alike about exactly what kinds of groups constitute organized interests. A full understanding of organized interest politics requires a sharp awareness of precisely what organized interests are. Next, we proceed to examine the major types of organized interests active in the United States today. The brief tour of the universe of organized interests is designed to breathe life into the generic definition of organized interest. As you will see, my deceptively simple definition of *organized interest* belies the complexity and diversity of the universe of organized interests. This introductory chapter ends by spelling out the plan for the rest of this book.

WHAT IS AN ORGANIZED INTEREST?

This book uses the term *organized interests* rather than the more common *interest groups* to describe political organizations that are active in American politics. This is the case because the term *interest group* conjures up a narrow and misleading view of the universe of politically active organizations in the United States.[16]

What is wrong with the term *interest group*? For starters, it is imprecise. When most people think of an interest group, an organization like the Sierra Club, the Christian Coalition, or the National Rifle Association comes to mind. That is, they think of a membership organization with political goals. But this is a narrow view, and it overlooks the bulk of organizational activity that occurs in the United States. More important, it fails to acknowledge the vast numbers of nonmembership organizations active in politics. It appears to exclude, for example, corporations, many of which are extremely active politically. In addition, this narrow view implies that all politically active organizations consist of individuals. In fact, some of the largest and most powerful political organizations in America do not consist of individuals. The U.S. Chamber of Commerce, for example, which has an annual budget of $75 million, employs 1,000 people, and has dozens of registered lobbyists on its payroll, consists of corporations, not individuals.[17] Finally, this narrow view implies that a political group's members, if it even has members, share goals. This, it turns out, is not always true. Research on why people join political organizations has found that in many organizations, members do not share the goals of their fellow members. Many people who join the American Association of Retired Persons (AARP), for example, do so not because they share the goals of other members but because they value the hotel, rental car, and insurance discounts that come with membership.

This book therefore discards the misleading and inaccurate term *interest group* in favor of the more accurate and precise *organized interest*. We define an organized interest as *any organization that engages in political activity*.[18] There are two components to this definition: organization and political activity. To say that a group is *organized* is to say that it has a budget, employees, and an office. Groups that are not organized are not considered organized interests. Women as a group, for example, although they share several traits and may even share some ideas about government policies, do not constitute an organized interest because not all of them belong to the same organized group that engages in political activity. The National Organization for Women (NOW), in contrast, *is* an organized interest. In other words, women as a group are not organized, but NOW is.

The second component of the definition, political activity, is important because the main difference between organized interests and other types of organizations is that the former engage in political activity. What constitutes political activity? The short answer is *lobbying*, which we define as *attempting to influence government decisions*.[19] As you will see in Chapters 5 through 8, organized interests use a startlingly large variety of activities to influence government policy. For now, it shall suffice to say that all such activities constitute lobbying. Unfortunately, determining if a group is politically active is not always easy. Organizations like the American Heart Association and the American Red Cross, for example, dedicate most of their time and energy to helping people but nonetheless spend some of their time trying to influence government decisions. Are these organizations considered organized interests? Our answer is an emphatic yes.

Table 1.1 shows the differences between organized interests and other types of groups. It lists groups that are not organized and organized groups that do not engage in political activity. One particularly noteworthy entry in the table is "college students." Although often people talk about college students as if they comprise an organized interest, the reality is that they are not. College students as a group are not organized. Certainly some specific groups of college students are organized, but the mass of college students throughout the United States is not.

The term *organized interest* is the most important one in this book. Nevertheless, there are some other terms that will be useful. One of them is *political party*. At first glance, political parties seem to fit the broad definition of organized interest. After all, they are organized, and virtually all of them engage in political activity. Yet it is crucially important to recognize that political parties are *not* organized interests, and organized interests are *not* political parties. The precise definition of *political party* is as follows: *an organized group of individuals that nominates candidates for election to public office and proposes*

TABLE 1.1 Selected Groups That Are Not Organized Interests

Group	Reason the Group Is Not an Organized Interest	What Is It Then?
Association of Coffee Mill Enthusiasts	Has no interest in government policy	Hobby club
Beach Boys Fan Club	Has no interest in government policy	Fan club
Beer of the Month Club	Has no interest in government policy	Hobby club
College students	Not organized	Unorganized group
Environmentalists	Not organized	Unorganized group
Farmers	Not organized	Unorganized group
Sequoyah Square Condominium Association	Does not try to influence government policy	Homeowners' association

Sources: *Encyclopedia of Associations: National Organizations of the U.S.* (34th ed.) (Detroit: Gale Research, 1999); *State and Regional Associations of the United States* (11th ed.) (Washington, DC: Columbia Books, 1999).

policies for implementation. The crucial difference between political parties and organized interests is that the former nominate candidates for election while the latter do not. This is not to say that organized interests are not involved in election campaigns. Many are. But organized interests do not nominate candidates for office. One other factor that distinguishes political parties from organized interests is that the former tend to have a much broader focus than the latter. Both major parties, for example, take positions on literally hundreds of issues, whereas most organized interests take positions on only one or a handful of issues.[20]

Another term useful throughout this book is *interest.* In the most general sense, an interest refers to any attitude, value, or preference. However, political scientists are concerned only with interests that have some relevance to government policy. As political scientist Robert Salisbury puts it:

> It is the perceived or anticipated effects of policy—government action or inaction including all its symbolic forms as well as more intangible allocations—upon values that create politically relevant interests. Similarly, interested behavior expresses policy-related purpose, sometimes very broadly defined and sometimes highly specific and detailed.[21]

Following Salisbury's lead, we define the term *interest* as *an attitude, value, or preference with some relevance to public policy.* This definition has two important implications. First, interests in society may be represented by organized interests to varying degrees. In other words, some interests have large, powerful, and perhaps multiple organizations working on their behalf, while others have either very few or no organizations working on their behalf. Second, both individuals and institutions have interests. While most of us recognize that groups of individuals have interests, few of us stop to think that institutions also have interests. Here, we define an *institution* as *a nonmembership organization*. Corporations, governmental entities, and colleges and universities are examples of institutions. Institutions are distinguished by the fact that they have interests separate from the interests of the individuals who comprise them.[22] Corporations, for example, have interests separate from those of the people who work for them. And colleges and universities have interests that are distinct from those of the students, administrators, faculty, and staff who comprise them. We will have much more to say about institutions later in this chapter.

One final useful term is *lobbyist*. A lobbyist is defined as *an individual who represents an organized interest before government*. In the broadest terms, every time you contact a public official to express your opinion, you are lobbying. Does this make you a lobbyist? No. We reserve the term *lobbyist* for an individual who represents an organized interest when he or she lobbies. There are two types of lobbyists: *professional lobbyists,* who lobby for a living, and *amateur lobbyists,* who lobby voluntarily. Many organized interests use volunteer lobbyists because professional lobbyists are expensive. We have much more to say about lobbyists in Chapters 5 through 8.

Let us conclude this section with a term that will *not* come in handy in subsequent chapters. That term is *special interest*. Any discussion of organized interests inevitably turns to the topic of so-called special interests, which are sometimes referred to as "narrow special interests" or "selfish special interests." Generally *special interest* is used pejoratively to imply that a certain organized interest has goals antithetical to the *public interest*, which is defined as *an interest held in common by all members of society*.[23] There is a huge problem with the term *special interest*. The problem is that to call a specific organized interest a "special interest" is to say that it has goals antithetical to the public interest and, by implication, antithetical to the interests of virtually everyone in society. Consider an example. Each time labor unions push for a higher federal minimum wage, they face opposition from business groups. Thus, they are not working for the public interest if by "public interest" we mean an interest held in common by all members of society. This is rather silly. Simply because labor unions face opposition does not mean that they are working against the interests of every man, woman, and child in the United States. It means only that they are active on an issue about which there is no public consensus. In America today, there are many issues about which there is no public consensus.

My point here is this: the term *special interest* is fraught with baggage and is not useful for an academic discussion of organized interests. Rather, it is a term that is useful primarily to pundits, politicians, and organized interest "spinmeisters" who wish to demonize their enemies. As such, we will eschew the use of this term for the remainder of this book.

THE UNIVERSE OF ORGANIZED INTERESTS

The universe of organized interests consists of the myriad organizations that fit our definition of *organized interest*. No one knows for sure how many organized interests there are in the United States, but conservative estimates put the number at over 200,000. What are all these groups, and whom do they represent? We answer this question by examining the thirteen major types of organized interests active in the United States today: corporations, trade associations, labor unions, professional associations, citizen groups, think tanks, domestic governmental entities, churches, foreign governmental entities, universities and colleges, coalitions, charities, and political action committees.

Corporations

Corporations are business enterprises that exist primarily to make money. Nevertheless, many have an abiding interest in politics and government and thus constitute organized interests.[24] It is easy to see why many business firms take an interest in politics. Companies across the country are profoundly affected by public policy. Every time Congress and the president raise the minimum wage, for example, every business firm in the United States must change the way it operates.

A company that wishes to lobby has two options: it can hire a lobbying firm or do its own lobbying. Companies that can afford to do so generally do their own lobbying and form separate public affairs or governmental relations divisions to do so. The majority of Fortune 500 companies, for example—firms like Atlantic Richfield (ARCO), IBM, Procter and Gamble, Eastman Kodak, Ford Motor Company, and Boeing—have their own lobbyists.[25] Companies that cannot afford to have large-scale public affairs divisions hire lobbying firms.[26] Not surprisingly, many foreign corporations also lobby in the United States. British Aerospace (a British company), Nissan Motor Co. (a Japanese firm), and Bayer (a German company), for example, have large American business operations and are quite active in American politics.

Trade Associations

Some business lobbying is conducted not by individual corporations but by trade associations. A *trade association* is an organized group of businesses.[27] There are two types of trade associations: *peak associations*, which represent broad business interests, and *single-industry trade associations,* which represent businesses in a specific industry.

The biggest and best-known trade associations in the United States are the National Association of Manufacturers (NAM), which consists of over 13,000 manufacturing firms, and the U.S. Chamber of Commerce, both of which are peak associations. NAM and the Chamber of Commerce have massive memberships and work on issues that affect businesses of all kinds and sizes.

Single-industry trade associations are far more numerous than peak associations. Practically every industry you can think of has its own trade association. Companies that refine asphalt products, for example, belong to the Asphalt Institute, pesticide manufacturers belong to the National Agricultural Chemicals Association, and makers of frozen food belong to the American Frozen Food Institute. Some single-industry trade associations have names that border on the comical. But while groups like the Association of Nonwoven Fabrics Industry, the Beer Institute, the Glutamate Association, and the Society for Protective Coatings may provoke snickers, they take their political activity quite seriously.

Few other sectors of the American economy are home to more trade associations than the agricultural sector. The best-known and largest agriculture group in the United States is the American Farm Bureau Federation (AFBF), a peak association with over 3.5 million members in all fifty states. Some influential single-industry trade associations in the agricultural sector are the National Association of Wheat Growers, the National Corn Growers Association, and the National Cattlemen's Association.[28]

Trade associations lobby government for the same reason that individual companies do: because government activity affects business interests. Government activity is of such interest to corporate America, in fact, that many business firms lobby on their own *and* belong to trade associations. An example illustrates this point. Eli Lilly and Company, the manufacturer of Prozac, is one of the nation's largest pharmaceutical companies, with nearly $10 billion in annual revenue. Lilly has a large Washington, D.C., office, complete with dozens of staff people and its own in-house lobbyists. It also contracts with several prominent lobbying firms. In addition, it belongs to trade associations, including the Business Roundtable, the Chemical Manufacturers Association, the National Association of Manufacturers, and the Pharmaceutical Research and Manufacturers Association. And Lilly has separate lobbying operations in its Alabama, California, Colorado, Georgia, Illinois, Minnesota, New York, Ohio, Pennsylvania, Texas, and Washington state offices.[29]

Labor Unions

A *labor union* is a group of workers joined together for the purpose of collective bargaining with employers.[30] Although labor unions are not organized primarily to influence government policy, most are nonetheless heavily involved in politics. Traditionally, manufacturing industries like steel, rubber, and automobiles were the most heavily unionized in the United States. Today the largest and most powerful labor unions represent public sector employees—people who work for the government. The National Education Association, for example, which represents teachers, has 2 million members and an annual budget of over $145 million. Other prominent public sector unions represent postal workers, prison guards, and sanitation workers. A number of old-line labor unions are also powerful. The Teamsters Union, which represents over 1 million workers engaged in transportation and trucking, demonstrated its strength in a successful 1997 strike against United Parcel Service (UPS). Autoworkers, steelworkers, and garment workers also remain politically powerful.

The best-known labor union in the United States is not really a labor union at all. The AFL-CIO, which is often called a labor union, is actually a federation of labor unions—sort of a peak association of labor unions. The AFL-CIO has a membership consisting of over one hundred individual unions. It uses some of the dues it collects from member unions to engage in political activity on their behalf.

Professional Associations

A *professional association* is an organization that represents the interests of people in a specific profession.[31] Unfortunately, there is no good definition of *profession*, and the line between a "profession" and an "occupation" is not at all clear. As a result, we are left to define *professional* by example. Generally doctors, lawyers, nurses, and other relatively highly paid, well-educated workers are considered professionals.

Two of the largest and most powerful professional associations in the United States are the American Medical Association, which represents doctors, and the American Bar Association, which represents lawyers. Each of these groups represents the broad interests of individuals in one profession and provides goods and services to members. Although many professional associations are active in Washington, most concentrate their efforts at the state level because the licensing of professionals is for the most part a state government responsibility.

Citizen Groups

A *citizen group* is defined as an organized interest that is open to any citizen.[32] Citizen groups often refer to themselves as "public interest groups." The citizen group universe is incredibly varied and contains groups representing environmentalists, proabortion and antiabortion activists, pro- and anti-gun control activists, consumers, taxpayers, the elderly, the disabled, children, and myriad others. Citizen groups are what most people think of when they think of interest groups: they are explicitly political in nature, consist of individual members, and have meetings, rallies, and social events.

The largest citizen group in the United States is the AARP. At first glance, you may not think that the AARP fits our definition of citizen group because not anyone can join: members must be at least fifty years old. But because all of us, barring bad luck, will eventually reach age fifty, the AARP is considered a citizen group. The AARP, which represents the interests of the people over fifty, is a massive organization. It has 32 million members, 30 lobbyists in Washington alone, a Washington staff of almost 2,000 people, and an annual budget approaching half a billion dollars. Other large and powerful citizen groups are the National Rifle Association (NRA), the Sierra Club, the National Wildlife Federation (NWF), the National Association for the Advancement of Colored People (NAACP), and the National Right to Life Association.

Think Tanks

A *think tank* is a nonprofit institution that conducts and disseminates research.[33] (In lay terms, a think tank is a group of smart people organized to study things.) Think tanks have no members per se, but rather consist of scholars (sometimes called fellows) who conduct research designed to affect government policy. Some of the best-known think tanks in the United States are the American Enterprise Institute, the Brookings Institute, and the Heritage Foundation. Virtually all think tanks have an explicit ideology that is reflected in their work. The American Enterprise Institute, for example, acknowledges its free-market conservative ideology and publishes only research that supports this ideology.[34] Citizens for Tax Justice is a liberal think tank that publishes research which supports its ideology.

Domestic Governmental Entities

Domestic governmental entities are organized interests that lobby one layer of American government on behalf of another.[35] Several thousand states, counties, cities, school districts, water districts, and townships lobby in Washington. All fifty states, for example, lobby in Washington, as do most major cities and many counties. In addition, many cities, counties, special districts, and school districts lobby state governments. Governments lobby other governments because one level of government is often affected by the policies of others. State governments, for example, take a keen interest in federal government policies on such issues as highway funding, environmental regulation, and defense spending. Similarly, cities, counties, and special districts are very interested in state government policies that affect the way they operate.

Churches

A *church* is an organized group of worshippers. Many of the largest religious denominations in the United States have their own ecclesiastical governments that make church policy, run church programs, and recruit members. Many of these church governments also lobby government. Catholics, Jews, and several other major denominations, for example, have national organizations that engage in lobbying. The Catholic church, for example, is active on issues including disaster relief, public housing, food stamps, and health care. Other less hierarchical denominations also lobby. Many community Baptist churches, for example, are active on issues such as civil rights, abortion, and religious expression.

Foreign Governmental Entities

A *foreign governmental entity* is a governmental body that lobbies American government on behalf of the government of another country. Many foreign governments have lobbyists in the United States representing their interests. Not surprisingly, large countries are better represented than small ones. China, for example, retains several lobbyists in Washington, while Burkina Faso retains none. Foreign countries have an interest in U.S. politics because a variety of policies made here affect them. Trade pacts and treaties, for example, are negotiated with other countries.

Universities and Colleges

Universities and colleges are institutions of higher learning. Universities and colleges exist, of course, to educate people. Nonetheless, because they are affected by government policies, many hire lobbyists. The political issue of most interest to colleges and universities is funding. All public colleges and universities receive some of their money from the government. The University of Tennessee (where I work), for example, is funded partially by state tax revenues. Universities and colleges receive other forms of government support as well. The federal government, for example, through institutions such as the National Endowment for the Humanities, the National Science Foundation, and the National Aeronautics and Space Administration, provides grants for university- and college-based research. Moreover, the federal government's student loan programs indirectly provide money to colleges and universities.

Coalitions

A *coalition* is a loose collection of organizations and individuals that cooperates to accomplish common objectives.[36] Most coalitions are short-term entities that rise up to deal with a particular issue. For example, when Congress was debating President Clinton's sweeping health care reforms in 1993 and 1994, a group of business-organized interests that opposed reform formed the Coalition for Health Care Choices to coordinate their efforts. Similarly, when the

Clean Air Act of 1990 was being hammered out on Capitol Hill, environmental groups that supported the bill formed the Clean Air Coalition, while industry groups formed their own opposition coalition, the Clean Air Working Group.[37] Most coalitions include organized interests of various types. The Clean Air Working Group, for example, consisted of both individual companies and trade associations.

Charities

A *charity* is defined as an organized interest engaged in free assistance to the poor, the suffering, or the distressed.[38] Charities exist primarily to help people. Many, however, are also active politically. Among the best-known politically active charities in the United States are the American Red Cross, the American Heart Association, and the American Lung Association. Charities typically lobby on issues of social justice and, like churches, are often active in health care and disaster relief.

Political Action Committees

A *political action committee* (PAC) is an organization set up solely to collect and spend money on electoral campaigns.[39] Federal tax laws, as well as tax laws in many states, forbid organized interests other than PACs from making direct monetary contributions to candidates for public office.[40] Thus, organized interests such as corporations, trade associations, professional associations, and citizen groups that wish to make such contributions must set up PACs. PACs that are set up by other organized interests are called *affiliated PACs*. Most of America's largest corporations have affiliated PACs, as do many of the nation's largest labor unions, trade associations, professional associations, and citizen groups. *Unaffiliated PACs* are PACs that are not affiliated with other organized interests. Currently there are approximately 3,778 PACs registered with the Federal Election Commission.[41] During the 1997–1998 election cycle, these PACs contributed $219.9 million to federal candidates.[42] Several thousand other PACs operate at the subnational level.

THE PLAN FOR *PRESSURE AND POWER*

We have now covered the basics: definitions of important terms (including the most important one, *organized interest*) and an introduction to the varied universe of organized interests in the United States. To help demonstrate this point about variety, Table 1.2 lists some interesting-sounding organized interests.

Representing turkeys in Washington The universe of organized interests is incredibly diverse. Turkeys do not have their own organized interest, but turkey growers, breeders, processors, and distributors do—it's called the National Turkey Federation. Every year on the day before Thanksgiving, the Federation presents a turkey to the president. In this picture from 1995, President Clinton is presented with a 75-pound turkey, as the chairmain of the National Turkey Fe16deration looks on. When the National Turkey Federation is not presenting huge turkeys to public officials, it is busy lobbying on behalf of its (human) members. *AP/Wide World Photos.*

TABLE 1.2 Some Interesting-Sounding Organized Interests

Adhesive and Sealant Council

Alaska Crab Coalition

Allied Underwear Association

American Association of Grain Inspection and Weighing Agencies

Anti-friction Bearing Manufacturers Association

Beyond Beef

Chimney Safety Institute of America

Coalition for Non-violent Food

Committee for Thorough Agricultural Political Education of Associated Milk Producers

The Formaldehyde Institute

Garage Door Council

Headwear Institute of America

International Association of Heat and Frost Insulators and Asbestos Workers

Japanese Frozen Food Association

Marine Cooks and Stewards Voluntary Federal Political Fund

National Spotted Swine Record

Pressure Sensitive Tape Council

Prescription Footwear Institute

Rubber Pavements Association

Sources: *Washington Representatives* (23rd ed.) (Washington, DC: Columbia Books, 1999); *Encyclopedia of Associations: National Organizations of the U.S.* (34th ed.) (Detroit: Gale Books, 1999); *National Trade and Professional Associations of the United States* (34th ed.) (Washington, DC: Columbia Books, 1999).

What's Next

Chapter 2 examines the evolution of organized interests in the United States. First, it documents the recent explosion in the number of politically active organized interests. Then it addresses two related questions: Why are there so many organized interests in the United States? and Why are there so many more organized interests in the United States today than there used to be? Chapter 3 addresses a question that has long puzzled scholars of organized interests: Why are some interests better represented by organized interests than others? This question speaks directly to the nature of American democracy and deserves serious attention.

Chapters 4 through 8 examine what organized interests actually do. Throughout most of our history, lobbyists have been portrayed as sleazy "fixers" who bribe public officials, procure sexual companionship for political elites, and regularly lie, cheat, and steal to get what they want. These chapters show instead that lobbying is actually quite pedestrian and that among the many things that lobbyists do, few involve bribery, drinking, procuring, or lying.

Chapter 9 asks perhaps the most important question of all: How influential are organized interests in American politics? Through an examination of contemporary theories of organized interest influence, the chapter illustrates the difficulties inherent in ascertaining the extent and nature of group influence. These difficulties notwithstanding, Chapter 9 concludes with a delineation of the circumstances under which organized interests are most likely to influence policy outcomes. Finally, Chapter 10 is a broad overview of the politics of organized interests in the United States. It attempts to resolve the paradox of organized interests and then asks: Are organized interests good or bad for American democracy?

This book takes a holistic approach to the study of organized interests. That is, whenever possible, it examines organized interests everywhere they operate in America—in cities, towns, counties, and states, as well as in Washington, D.C. Unfortunately, there is a tendency in the media and academia to focus solely on Washington organized interests despite the fact that organized interests operate at all levels of government. This is the case mostly because we know far less about organized interests in states and localities than we do about organized interests in Washington. Nonetheless, organized interests are important players in state and local as well as national politics. As such, throughout this book I provide a well-rounded picture of organized interests in the whole United States.

CONCLUSION: WHY STUDY ORGANIZED INTERESTS?

It would be an exaggeration to say that organized interests are at the very center of American politics. After all, as the battle over President Clinton's impeachment illustrates, public officials—the elected and appointed leaders who represent us in government—are at the center of most political storms. And this is as it should be, for the founders of this country designed a democratic republic in which most authoritative decisions are left to elected representatives. Yet the impeachment battle also shows that public officials are hardly the only players in the American political process. As the storm brewed around President Clinton and the members of Congress who would decide his fate, all sorts of organized interests became involved. They lobbied officials, mobilized citizens, advertised on television and radio, circulated petitions, and held protests and rallies. Some even asked for divine inspiration and intervention. What all these organized interests had in common is this: they participated in the American political process. This is why we study organized interests: because they are important players in the American political process.

EXERCISES

1. Choose one of the organized interests listed in Table 1.2, and investigate it using one or more of the directories listed in the Research Resources section (which follows). Answer the following questions: What type of organized interest is it? Does the organization have members? If so, what kinds of members? What are the goals of the organized interest? In what types of political activities is the organization involved? What are the potential benefits and drawbacks of these activities for the population at large?
2. Select a public policy issue that is currently receiving a great deal of attention in Congress or the news. Identify and describe at least two organized interests that are politically active on the issue. Compare and contrast the goals and activities of the organizations you choose.

RESEARCH RESOURCES

At the end of Chapters 1 through 9, you will find a list of research resources designed to help you conduct research on organized interests. They are also designed to help you with the exercises that appear at the end of each chapter. There are two things to keep in mind as you peruse these lists of resources. First, the lists are by no means exhaustive. They are intended only to help you get started. Second, the lists are cumulative in the sense that some of the resources listed in the early chapters are also of great use in completing the exercises in subsequent chapters. For example, Chapter 1 is the only one that explicitly mentions Internet search engines as important web resources, although search engines will prove helpful in completing exercises at the end of subsequent chapters. When you complete the exercises for any specific chapter, I suggest you consult the list of research resources at the end of previous chapters as well as those at the end of the chapter at hand.

Publications

Organized interest directories. Some of the most useful published directories of organized interests are: *The Annual U.S. Union Sourcebook* (an index of labor unions), *The Encyclopedia of Associations* (an index of nationally active membership organizations), *The Encyclopedia of State and Regional Organizations* (an index of state and local membership organizations), *The National Directory of Corporate Public Affairs* (an index of corporate lobbying and public affairs operations), *National Trade and Professional Associations of the United States* (an index of trade and professional groups), *Public Interest Profiles* (an index of citizen groups), and *Washington Representatives Index* (a directory of lobbyists, foreign agents, political consultants, public affairs and governmental relations representatives, and legal advisers active in Washington).

Web Resources

Web directories. Several sites contain access to on-line directories of organized interests. The best way to locate such directories is to search for them using an Internet search engine—for example, *www.altavista.com, www.lycos.com, www.yahoo.com,* and *www.google.com.*

Organized interest web sites. Many organized interests have their own web sites. To locate an organization's web site, insert the name of the organization in the Search For box that appears when you arrive at an Internet search engine.

Congressional web sites. To find out what Congress is doing, check out the web site for the House of Representatives, *www.House.gov,* or the Senate, *www.Senate.gov.*

The Pressure and Power *web site.* Additional web resources for each chapter can be found at http://college.hmco.com.

Notes

1. Stacey Zolt, "Activists on Both Sides to Rally at Capitol," *Roll Call*, December 17, 1998, p. 1.

2. Aaron Zitner, "By Phone and E-mail, Public Lobbies Hard," *Boston Globe*, December 15, 1998, p. A1.

3. Peter H. Stone, "Left, Right, Battle for Jurors' Attention," *National Journal*, January 16, 1999, p. 139.

4. Ibid.

5. The first was Andrew Johnson (1868), who was also spared removal from office.

6. See James Madison, "Federalist #10," in Randall B. Ripley and Elliot E. Slotnick, eds., *Readings in American Government and Politics* (3rd ed.) (Needham Heights, MA: Allyn and Bacon, 1999).

7. For a summary of these studies, see Frank R. Baumgartner and Beth L. Leech, *Basic Interests: The Importance of Groups in Politics and in Political Science* (Princeton, NJ: Princeton University Press, 1998), pp. 89–93.

8. Sidney Verba, Kay Lehman Schlozman, and Henry E. Brady, *Voice and Equality: Civic Voluntarism in American Politics* (Cambridge, MA: Harvard University Press, 1995), pp. 81–82.

9. Zitner, "By Phone and E-mail, Public Lobbies Hard," p. A1.

10. Madison, "Federalist #10."

11. Ibid., p. 20.

12. See, for example, Robert A. Dahl, *Who Governs?* (New Haven, CT: Yale University Press, 1961); David Truman, *The Governmental Process: Political Interests and Public Opinion* (New York: Knopf, 1951).

13. See, for example, William P. Browne, *Groups, Interests, and U.S. Public Policy* (Washington, DC: Georgetown University Press, 1998).

14. C. Wright Mills, *The Power Elite* (New York: Oxford University Press, 1956).

15. Theodore J. Lowi, *The End of Liberalism* (2nd ed.) (New York: Norton, 1979).

16. Baumgartner and Leech, *Basic Interests: The Importance of Groups in Politics and in Political Science* (Princeton, NJ: Princeton University Press, 1998), pp. 26–28.

17. U.S. Chamber of Commerce, "About Us," accessed at *http://www.uschamber.com*, August 24, 1999.

18. Paraphrased from Kay Lehman Schlozman and John T. Tierney, *Organized Interests and American Democracy* (New York: Harper and Row, 1986), p. 10.

19. Ibid.

20. Burdett A. Loomis and Allan J. Cigler, "Introduction: The Changing Nature of Interest Group Politics," in Allan J. Cigler and Burdett A. Loomis, eds., *Interest Group Politics* (5th ed.) (Washington, DC: Congressional Quarterly Press, 1998), p. 17.

21. Robert Salisbury, "Interest Representation: The Dominance of Institutions," *American Political Science Review* 78 (March 1984): 65.

22. Ibid., pp. 64–70.

23. This is paraphrased from William H. Riker, *Liberalism Against Populism* (Prospect Heights, IL: Waveland Press, 1982), p. 291.

24. *The National Directory of Corporate Public Affairs* (17th ed.) (Washington, DC: Columbia Books, 1999).

25. Ibid.

26. Richard Harris, "Politicized Management: The Changing Face of Business in American Politics," in Sidney Milkus, ed., *Remaking American Politics* (Boulder, CO: Westview Press, 1992), pp. 261–288.

27. Schlozman and Tierney, *Organized Interests and American Democracy*, p. 10.

28. See William P. Browne and Allan J. Cigler, eds., *Agriculture Interests* (Westport, CT: Greenwood Press, 1991).

29. *Government Affairs Yellow Book* (Washington, DC: Columbia Books, Summer 1997), Vol. 3, No. 2, p. 150.

30. Schlozman and Tierney, *Organized Interests and American Democracy*, p. 42.

31. Ibid., p. 44.

32. Jack L. Walker, "The Origins and Maintenance of Interest Groups in America," *American Political Science Review* 77 (June 1983): 393.

33. Andrew Rich and R. Kent Weaver, "Advocates and Analysts: Think Tanks and the Politicization of Expertise," in Cigler and Loomis, eds., *Interest Group Politics*, 5th ed., pp. 236–237.

34. James G. McGann, "Academics to Ideologues: A Brief History of the Public Policy Research Industry," *PS* 4 (September 1992): 733–740.

35. Schlozman and Tierney, *Organized Interests and American Democracy*, pp. 55–57.

36. Alan Rosenthal, *The Third House: Lobbyists and Lobbying in the States* (Washington, DC: Congressional Quarterly Press, 1993), p. 150.

37. Clyde Wilcox, "The Dynamics of Lobbying the Hill," in Paul S. Herrnson, Ronald G. Shaiko, and Clyde Wilcox, eds., *The Interest Group Connection: Electioneering, Lobbying and Policymaking in Washington* (Chatham, NJ: Chatham House, 1998), pp. 89–99.

38. Baumgartner and Leech, *Basic Interests: The Importance of Groups in Politics and in Political Science* (Princeton, NJ: Princeton University Press, 1998) pp. 91–93.

39. Schlozman and Tierney, *Organized Interests and American Democracy*, p. 221.

40. In some cases, however, other types of organized interests may contribute money to candidates for state and local office. This is the case because campaign finance laws vary from place to place. These issues are discussed in Chapter 7.

41. Federal Election Commission, "FEC Issues Semi-Annual Federal PAC Count," July 20, 1999, p. 1, accessed at *http://www.fec.gov/press/pcnt799*, July 29, 1999.

42. Federal Election Commission, "FEC Releases Information on PAC Activity for 1997–98," July 8, 1999, p. 1, accessed at *http://www.fec.gov/press/pacye98*, July 29, 1999.

The Evolution of Organized Interests in the United States

Washington, D.C.
July 1999

The Center for Responsive Politics releases its second annual lobbying report, *Influence Inc.: The Bottom Line on Washington Lobbying.*[1] The report, based on lobbying disclosure reports filed under the Lobbying Disclosure Act of 1995, places the number of Washington lobbyists at 20,512 and the number of organized interests active in Washington at 15,705.[2] These numbers, the report notes, represent a vast increase from years past. A spokesman for the center warns, however, that the figures may actually underestimate the number of lobbyists and organized interests active in Washington, for the complexities and vagaries of the Lobbyist Disclosure Act allow some lobbyists and organizations to escape registration.

The number of organized interests in the United States is enormous. In Washington, D.C., alone, over 15,000 organized interests actively lobby government. Outside Washington, in states and localities across the country, the number of organized interests probably exceeds 200,000.[3] Political scientists agree that there are more organized interests in the United States today than at any other time in American history.[4] In fact, it is safe to say that there are more organized interests active in the United States today than there ever have been in any one place, at any one time, in the history of the world.

Why does this country have so many organized interests? Why are there so many more organized interests active today than ever before? These are the questions addressed in this chapter. We begin by placing the contemporary universe of organized interests in historical perspective by examining trends in organized interest representation over time. Next, we examine how America's unique political system has fostered the proliferation of organized interests. Finally, we explain how social, economic, and political changes have contributed to a tremendous explosion of organized interests over the past forty years.

A HISTORY OF ORGANIZED INTEREST ACTIVITY

From the very beginning, organized interests have been active in American politics. Labor unions, for example, are as old as the republic itself.[5] And within twenty years of ratification of the Constitution, Alexander Hamilton founded what is believed to be the country's first organized interest to represent business interests: the Philadelphia Society for the Promotion of National Industry.[6]

Historical documents tell us that throughout this country's earliest years, organized interests of all kinds pressed their demands on government. In the 1820s, for example, temperance groups throughout the United States urged state and local governments to ban the sale of alcohol. Also in the 1820s, a variety of business organized interests led by the Pennsylvania Society for the Encouragement of Manufacturers and the Mechanical Arts lobbied strenuously for tariffs on foreign goods.[7] Organized interest activity was so pronounced in the first half of the nineteenth century that James Buchanan wrote to his friend Franklin Pierce:

> The host of contractors, speculators, stockjobbers, and lobby members which haunt the halls of Congress, all desirous *per fas aut nefas* [whether within the realm of the law or not] and on any and every pretext to get their arms into the public treasury are sufficient to alarm every friend of his country. Their progress must be arrested.[8]

Organized interest activity continued unabated throughout the latter half of the nineteenth century. For example, in the decades before the Civil War, abolitionist citizen groups appealed to lawmakers in Washington to end slavery. And in the decades immediately following the Civil War, several organized interest powerhouses, including the National Rifle Association (1871), the American Bankers Association (1875), and the American Federation of Labor (1886), were born.

THE ADVOCACY EXPLOSION

Although organized interests have always been active in American politics, pronounced organized interest growth is largely a twentieth-century phenomenon, with the numbers of organized interests beginning to grow dramatically around the turn of the century.[9] Not only did existing organizations such as the NRA and the AFL gain in stature, but a number of new organized interests, including such now-well-known groups as the National Audubon Society (1905),

Young crusaders While organized interests have always been active in American politics, pronounced organized interest growth is largely a twentieth-century phenomenon. Numbers of organized interests began growing dramatically around the turn of the century. Here, children march on behalf of prisoners held for violating speech codes passed during World War I. *Library of Congress, LC-H234-A4380.*

the National Association for the Advancement of Colored People (1909), and the U.S. Chamber of Commerce (1912), came on the scene. By 1920, organized interests had become major political players. Organized interest proliferation continued between 1920 and 1960, as the number of Washington-based organized interests doubled from about 300 to about 600.[10] Although data on subnational organized interests are spotty, it seems clear that organized interest proliferation at the state and local levels was also pronounced during this period.[1]

Figure 2.1 illustrates the growth of organized interests over the past one hundred years. The number of organized interests active in Washington grew steadily from 1900 to 1960. After 1960, steady growth gave way to massive proliferation. It is hard to overstate the magnitude of this shift. From 1960 to 1980, the number of nationally active organized interests in this country more than quadrupled. One recent study estimates that over half of all extant nationally active organized interests did not exist before 1960.[12] Numbers on

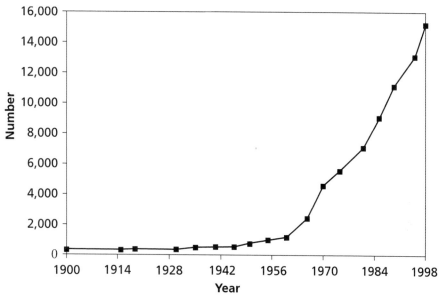

FIGURE 2.1 Trends in the Number of Washington-based Organized Interests, 1900–1998

Sources: John R. Wright, *Interest Groups and Congress: Lobbying, Contributions, and Influence,* chap. 2; *Washington Representatives* (Boston, MA: Allyn and Bacon, 1996); Mark P. Petracca, "The Rediscovery of Interest Group Politics," in Petracca, ed., *The Politics of Interests: Interest Groups Transformed* (Boulder, CO: Westview Press, 1992), pp. 3–31.

specific types of organized interests illustrate the true expanse of organized interest proliferation. The number of Washington-based citizen groups, for example, has grown from fewer than 100 in the mid-1970s to over 2,400 today.[13] Similarly, the number of nationally active PACs rose from 100 in the mid-1970s to approximately 3,800 today, and the number of corporations with Washington offices has grown from 50 in 1960 to over 3,000 today.[14]

THE DIVERSIFICATION OF ORGANIZED INTERESTS

As the universe of organized interests has grown, it has also become much more diverse. For most of our history, trade, professional, and labor organizations constituted the bulk of the organized interest universe.[15] Although we have no accurate baseline, it appears that before 1950, these three types of groups composed well over three-quarters of all organized interests active in American politics. This began to change around the turn of the twentieth century, as citizen groups became more prominent in national politics. In the decades after the Civil War, for example, several powerful veterans' groups formed and pressed Congress for more and better pension benefits.[16] Nonetheless, pronounced diversification did not begin until the early 1960s. The degree of this diversification has been startling.

Political scientists Frank Baumgartner and Beth Leech recently concluded that "the past 35 years have seen remarkable changes in the nature of the American interest-group [organized interest] system."[17] We have already noted the pronounced growth of PACs and corporations; their numbers have increased exponentially since 1960. The most important change, however, has been the tremendous ascendance of citizen groups.[18] To illustrate just how pronounced this growth has been, Baumgartner and Leech examined the growth of one type of citizen group: the environmental group. The number of environmental groups, they found, "almost tripled in the three decades from 1960 to 1990."[19] "Whereas the beginning of the 1960s saw 119 environmental groups with a combined staff of only 316 active at the national level," they note, "the beginning of the 1990s saw almost 3,000 staffers working for more than 300 groups."[20] Although no one has studied other specific types of citizen groups in such depth, overall numbers suggest that consumer, civil rights, civil liberties, elderly, taxpayer, religious, gun control, and antiabortion and pro-choice citizen groups have also proliferated massively since 1960.[21]

Along with PACs, corporations, and citizen groups, other types of organized interests have become more prominent in recent decades as well. Think tanks, for example, were virtually nonexistent before 1960. Today there are several thousand of them.[22] The figures on colleges and universities, coalitions, and domestic and foreign governmental entities are sketchy, but there is evidence that they too have become much more prominent since 1960.

The results of diversification are obvious in Figure 2.2, which illustrates the makeup of the contemporary Washington, D.C., organized interest universe. As has always been the case, trade, professional and labor groups comprise a substantial proportion of this universe—together, perhaps as much as 20 percent.[23] However, Figure 2.2 clearly shows that the Washington organized interest universe is no longer dominated by trade, professional, and labor organizations.

In sum, although the United States has always been home to large numbers of organized interests, today organized interests are more prevalent than ever before. In the twentieth century, and especially since 1960, the number of organized interests in the United States exploded. With this growth has come diversity. The universe of organized interests is now as diverse as it is vast. PACs, corporations, citizen groups, governmental entities, think tanks, coalitions, and other types of organizations now flesh out an organized interest universe once dominated by trade, professional, and labor groups. Although data on the diversification of organized interests in states and localities are hard to come by, all indications are that a similar diversification has taken place there as well.[24]

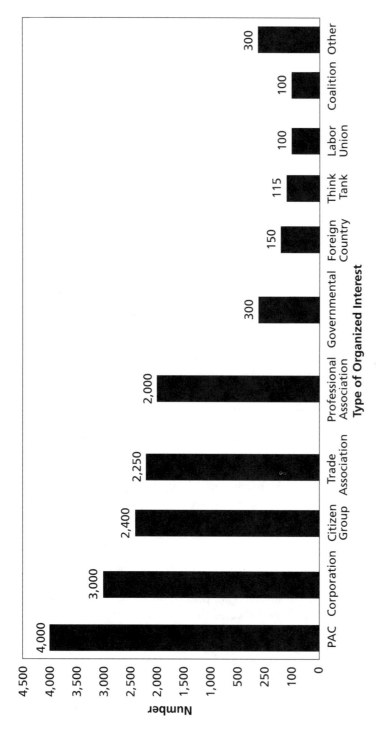

FIGURE 2.2 The Makeup of the Washington Universe of Organized Interests, 1995

Sources: John R. Wright, *Interest Groups and Congress: Lobbying, Contributions, and Influence,* chap. 2; *Washington Representatives* (Boston, MA: Allyn and Bacon, 1996); and Mark P. Petracca, "The Rediscovery of Interest Group Politics," in Petracca, ed., *The Politics of Interests: Interest Groups Transformed* (Boulder, CO: Westview Press, 1992), pp. 13–21.

THE UNITED STATES AS ORGANIZED INTEREST INCUBATOR

There are very few comprehensive studies of organized interests in other countries. Nevertheless, comparative studies show that the number of politically active organized interests in most other countries is relatively limited.[25] All in all, it is safe to conclude that America is home to more organized interests than any other country. What is it about the United States that makes it such an ideal place for the formation and survival of organized interests? The answer is four-fold: diversity, constitutional freedoms, federalism, and the separation of powers. Each of these factors contributes to this country's unique status as what I call an *organized interest incubator*.

Diversity

There is no question that America's diversity contributes to its favorable climate for organized interest formation and survival. On virtually all dimensions, America is amazingly diverse.

Consider religion. One recent estimate suggests that there are thirty-eight religious denominations in this country with at least 50,000 adherents. From Adventists and Baha'is, to Roman Catholics and Universalist Unitarians, virtually every religion on earth is practiced in this country.[26] The United States is also ethnically and racially diverse. Although the majority of Americans (about 74 percent) are Caucasian, this country is home to a large number of African Americans (11 percent), Hispanics (8 percent), Asian Americans (2.5 percent), and Native Americans (1 percent).[27] Finally, the United States is economically diverse. Whereas many other countries are dominated by one or a handful of essential industries, the United States produces everything from oil and coal to sorghum and sod. Just to give you an idea of how diverse our economy is, consider that in 1998, the United States ranked among the world's leaders in the production of automobiles (first), fish (first), corn (first), copper (second), and filmed and recorded entertainment (first), among other things.[28]

How does diversity contribute to organized interest formation and survival? Most important, diversity creates societal cleavages—differences of opinion about social, economic, and political matters. Political scientists Burdett Loomis and Allan Cigler have noted the importance of cleavages in creating a climate for organized interest growth. "Substantial cleavages among a society's citizens," they note, "are essential for [organized interest] development."[29] Think of it this way: in a society where everyone is the same color, has the same religious views, does the same work for a living, and lives in the same conditions, the number of societal cleavages is likely to be small. In contrast, a society with lots of differences is likely to have many societal cleavages.

Constitutional Freedoms

Constitutional freedoms also make the United States an ideal place for organized interest proliferation. As one study of organized interest proliferation points out, "Guarantees of free speech, association, and the right to petition the government for redress of grievances are basic to [organized interest] formation."[30] The First Amendment guarantees the right to free speech and assembly, as well as the right "to petition the Government for a redress of grievances." Although the Constitution does not explicitly mention the freedom of association, the Supreme Court has consistently ruled over the years that the Constitution protects this freedom. For example, it has ruled that the freedom to associate serves other essential rights such as the freedom of speech.[31] In addition, "general liberty as protected by the Fifth and Fourteenth Amendments," according to numerous Supreme Court decisions, often extends to the right to associate freely.[32]

America is not unique in the freedoms it affords its citizens to join and participate in groups, but it is unusual. In most totalitarian systems, for example, lobbying and other forms of political participation are more or less prohibited. Anyone who remembers or has read about Tiananmen Square, a place in Beijing, China, where in 1989 over 5,000 prodemocracy protesters were killed by the Chinese government, recognizes that not all the world's peoples have the right to express themselves politically. Even in Western democracies such as Canada and the United Kingdom, relatively strict lobbying laws constrain the activities of organized interests.[33]

Federalism

The United States has over 80,000 governments: 1 national government, 50 state governments, over 3,000 county governments, over 35,000 municipal and town governments, and over 45,000 special districts. This is the case because this country has a federal system of government—one in which power is divided between a central national government and numerous state and local governments. The opposite of a federal system is a unitary system—a system of government in which all power resides in a central government. What distinguishes a federal system from a unitary system is that in the former, a number of different and distinct governments make decisions that affect people's lives.

Federalism both allows and encourages organized interest activity. It encourages organized interest activity because it provides organized interests with numerous points of access to government. In my community, for example, if an organized interest is unhappy with government policy, it has manifold outlets to express its dissatisfaction. One option is to contact an official in the federal government—the president, the vice president, a senator, or perhaps a

House member. Another is to contact someone in state government—perhaps the governor or a state senator. Yet another is to contact someone in local government. The group could, for example, talk to the mayor, a member of city council, or a county commissioner. In short, in a federal system like ours, organized interests have many options. This encourages organized interest activity by making lobbying relatively easy and affordable.

Separation of Powers

Finally, the separation of powers helps make the United States an ideal place for organized interest growth. In this country, numerous actors at each level of government share governmental power. At the national level, for example, power is shared by the president, Congress, the bureaucracy, and the judiciary. All fifty state governments have similar arrangements, in which the governor, state agencies, the state legislature, and state courts share power. Even local governments are characterized by a separation of powers. Most city governments, for example, divide power between the city council and the mayor.

Much like federalism, the separation of powers increases the number of access points for organized interests. For example, a business lobbyist who thinks that the president is an enemy of business can take his or her case to Congress, a federal agency, or federal court. Political scientists Burdett Loomis and Allan Cigler point out that the separation of powers and federalism work together to encourage organized interest development. "The decentralized political power structure in the United States," they note, "allows important decisions to be made at the national, state, or local levels. Within each level of government there are multiple points of access. For example, business-related policies such as taxes are acted upon at each level, and [organized interests] may affect these policies in the legislative, executive, or judicial arenas."[34]

America's History of Organized Interest Activity: A Summary

In sum, America's unique governmental system, together with constitutional freedoms and diversity, make it an ideal place for the proliferation of organized interests. Thus, not surprisingly, America has always been home to a great many organized interests.

EXPLAINING ORGANIZED INTEREST PROLIFERATION

Political scientists have identified two phenomena in particular as significant causes of massive organized interest proliferation since 1900, and especially since 1960: societal change and governmental growth. In this section, we take a closer look at these two factors.

Societal Change

In his now-classic book *The Governmental Process* (1952), political scientist David Truman explicated a general theory of organized interest proliferation: *disturbance theory*, which holds that societal change is responsible for organized interest proliferation. According to the theory, as American society evolves and becomes more complex and differentiated, new interests emerge and multiply.[35] For example, economic change leads to the creation of new economic interests. This is what happened, Truman notes, in the late nineteenth century as America evolved from a simple agrarian country to an urban industrial one, and new industries, such the automobile industry and the oil industry, were born. Similarly, social change leads to the creation of new social interests. This is what happened, Truman notes, early in the twentieth century as the United States evolved from a relatively homogeneous country to an incredibly heterogeneous one. Finally, technological change makes it easier for people to band together to form organized interests. Truman points out that early in the twentieth century, technological innovations such as the radio, the telephone, and the telegraph made it easier for people to communicate with one another and thus to identify others who shared their interests.

Because Truman was writing in 1952, he did not examine the post-1960 proliferation of organized interests. Nonetheless, his disturbance theory helps explain this proliferation. The theory's logic implies that organized interests have proliferated since 1960 because of pronounced and substantial societal change. This is undoubtedly true. Clearly, part of the reason that organized interests have proliferated since the 1960s is that American society has changed substantially since then. First, America has undergone substantial economic change. The postindustrial revolution, for example, has reshaped the national economy. In the last few decades, new scientific and high-tech industries have become prominent in the economy. This economic shift has given rise to new industries such as the computer industry and the wireless telecommunications industry, which have organized to protect their interests. In addition, this country has become much more affluent since World War II. Even after adjusting for inflation, the median income in the United States doubled between 1947 and 1972.[36] The rise of affluence has contributed to organized interest proliferation in two ways. First, it has allowed many Americans to think about issues other than "bread-and-butter" economic issues for the first time. For example, as many Americans began to feel economically secure, they became more interested in quality-of-life issues such as the environment, consumer safety, and women's rights, and moral issues such as abortion, homosexual rights, and euthanasia.[37] In addition, affluence has made it easier and cheaper for Americans to join organized interests.[38]

Along with economic change has come social change. For example, cultural, racial, and religious diversification has continued as a new round of immigrants, especially Hispanics and Asians, have become part of the American melting pot.

Finally, further advances in communications technology have made it easier for organizations to form and survive.

A crucial assumption of disturbance theory is that as new interests emerge, they organize and press their demands on government. New industries, for example, organize and appeal to the federal government for protection from foreign competitors. Similarly, disturbance theory assumes that as more and more people become concerned about an issue, they band together and appeal to the government to pass laws concerning that issue. According to Truman, the reason that new interests organize and appeal to government for help is that the government has the power to make and enforce societal rules.

Government Growth

There is a certain amount of logic in Truman's contention that when new interests emerge, they organize and press their demands on government. Truman underestimated, however, the extent to which the government itself could contribute to organized interest proliferation. A number of studies show that government growth has been an important cause of organized interest proliferation in this country, especially since 1960. Before we examine how government growth has contributed to organized interest proliferation, it is important to acknowledge just how much the government has grown since the 1930s.

For the first one hundred years of our history, the federal government did little more than deliver the mail and fund the armed forces. Since about the turn of the twentieth century, however, the size and scope of the federal government have increased substantially. During the Progressive Era, for example, the federal government began regulating railroads and breaking up monopolies. Later, in the 1930s, New Deal Democrats passed laws that regulated banking, stock trading, broadcasting, and air travel, among other things. And in 1935, the federal government created income security programs including social security and welfare (Aid to Families with Dependent Children). Government growth continued gradually throughout the 1940s and 1950s and then in the 1960s gave way to rapid and massive growth. As part of Lyndon Johnson's Great Society, the federal government levied substantially more regulations on businesses and created a number of new income assistance programs. Among the more important programs were Medicare and Medicaid and the food stamp program.

To get an idea of how much the federal government has grown since 1960, consult Figure 2.3, which illustrates how federal budget outlays have exploded in the past forty years. The rise in federal spending reflects the massive increase in the size and scope of the federal government. Figures on state and local government spending are less reliable, but research indicates that these governments have grown tremendously as well in recent decades.

Government growth contributes to organized interest proliferation in two principal ways. First, new government programs and initiatives create new interests. To use a simple example, consider the case of the Regulatory Affairs Professionals Society (RAPS). RAPS, founded in 1976, is a professional association consisting of health care regulatory professionals in industry and government. In government, these are the people who write or enforce health care regulations. In industry, these are the people who are in charge of making sure their companies comply with government regulations. Without government initiatives to regulate health care, RAPS would not exist because the health care regulatory profession would not exist.

Government growth also contributes to organized interest proliferation as organized interests mushroom around new policy initiatives.[39] This mushrooming occurs because government initiatives and programs entail costs and benefits for various groups in society and thus provide incentives for groups to organize. An example illustrates this point. Slowly but surely since the social security program was created in 1935, the federal government has increased the benefits it provides to the elderly. Today benefits to the elderly account for one-third of all federal government spending.[40] The most important way that government programs for the elderly have contributed to organized interest proliferation is by providing powerful incentives for the recipients of these benefits—the elderly—to organize to protect these benefits. And organize they have. The main organized interest concerned with protecting the interests of the elderly, the American Association of Retired Persons (AARP), was founded in 1958 and is now the country's largest membership organization other than the Catholic church. Government programs for the elderly have also contributed to organized interest proliferation by providing incentives for service deliverers to organize to protect their interests. For example, the number of service deliverers that have organized around Medicare and other health care programs for the elderly is startling. One study notes that in the health care sector, service deliverers ranging "from professional associations of doctors and nurses to hospital groups to the insurance industry to suppliers of drugs and medical equipment" have organized to protect their interests.[41]

Spurs to Organized Interest Proliferation: A Summary

In sum, the massive proliferation of organized interests in the United States since 1960 can be attributed primarily to two factors: societal change and government growth. Since 1960, the American economy has created new economic interests and unprecedented affluence. In addition, cultural, religious, and social changes have accelerated since 1960, and technological changes have been swift. Finally, the government has grown tremendously since 1960.

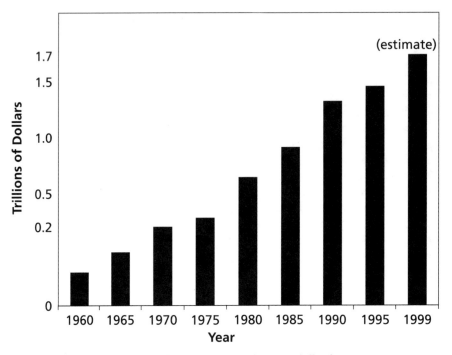

FIGURE 2.3 Annual Federal Outlays, 1960–1999 (in 1999 dollars)

Sources: Office of Management and Budget, *Budget of the United States Government, Fiscal Year 1997, Histori-cal Tables* (Washington, DC: Government Printing Office, 1996), pp. 23–24; Office of Management and Budget, *Mid-Session Review, Budget of the United States Government, Fiscal Year 2000* (Washington, DC: Government Printing Office, 1999), p. 15.

Together, these factors help to account for the unprecedented organized inter-est proliferation of the last thirty to forty years.

CONCLUSION: THE EVOLUTION OF ORGANIZED INTERESTS IN THE UNITED STATES

It is safe to say that there are more organized interests in the United States to-day than there ever have been in any one place, at any one time, in the history of the world. One of the reasons that America is home to so many organized interests is that it provides an ideal climate for organized interest formation and survival. The combination of diversity, constitutional freedoms, federal-ism, and the separation of powers helps make the United States a virtual incu-bator for organized interests. Although America has always been an ideal place for the proliferation of organized interests, only recently have organized inter-ests proliferated massively. Two broad phenomena in particular have contributed to this massive proliferation of the last thirty to forty years: societal change and government growth.

At this point, it is tempting to ask: What has been the effect of this immense organized interest proliferation on American politics? There are two schools of thought on this question. Some argue that organized interest proliferation has been a good thing, because more viewpoints than ever before are now represented before government. Others argue that organized interest proliferation has been a bad thing, because huge numbers of organized interests interfere with the government's ability to get things done and make it impossible for government officials to serve the "public interest." Unfortunately, we are not yet in a position to answer this important question. Why not? Because we do not yet know enough about what organized interests do and how much influence they exert over policy outcomes. If we find, on the one hand, that organized interests do very little and have little influence over policy outcomes, then we might conclude that organized interest proliferation has had little or no effect on American politics. If, on the other hand, we find that organized interests do a great deal and have a great deal of influence over policy outcomes, then we might conclude that organized interest proliferation has had a large impact on American politics. But in fact, we have much more to learn before we are in a position to weigh in on the effects of organized interest proliferation.

What's Next

In the next chapter, we explore the question of which interests are represented before government. As you will see, despite the massive organized interest proliferation and diversification, it turns out that some interests are better represented before government than others. For example, some interests have large and well-funded organizations working on their behalf, while others are represented by small ragtag operations. Furthermore, some widely shared interests are not represented by organized interests at all. Which interests are well represented by organized interests? Which are not so well represented? Why? These are the questions we tackle in Chapter 3.

EXERCISES

1. Choose two countries from the following list: Australia, Austria, Belgium, Brazil, Canada, France, Germany, Italy, Japan, Luxembourg, New Zealand, Portugal, Spain, Switzerland. Compare and contrast the laws and regulations that govern lobbying in the two countries you have chosen to those that govern lobbying in the United States. In what country are the laws more restrictive? In what country are laws less restrictive?

2. Choose and research one federal government program created since 1960. Identify and investigate at least three organized interests that formed around this program. Based on the information you have found, how would you characterize the relationship between these organized interests and the federal government? Is the relationship cooperative? Is it antagonistic? And how closely do the organized interests work with government officials?

RESEARCH RESOURCES

Publications

Books. The best place to start when researching organized interests in other countries is the library. Here are some recent books on organized interests in other countries: Claude Ake, *Democracy and Development in Africa* (Washington, D.C.: Brookings Institute, 1995); Russell J. Dalton, *The Green Rainbow: Environmental Groups in Western Europe* (New Haven, Conn.: Yale University Press, 1994); Wyn Grant, *Pressure Groups and British Politics* (New York: St. Martin's Press, 2000); Frank J. Schwartz, *Advice and Consent: The Politics of Consultation in Japan* (London: Cambridge University Press, 1998).

Chamber of Commerce. The local chamber of commerce is a good source for information on organized interests active in your community. To find out how to contact your local chamber, look in the business pages of the local telephone book.

Newspapers and magazines. Prominent national newspapers such as the *New York Times,* the *Washington Post,* and the *Wall Street Journal,* as well as prominent national magazines such as *Time, Newsweek,* and *U.S. News and World Report,* often have articles on organized interests at home and abroad. More specialized political magazines such as the *National Journal, Congressional Quarterly Weekly Report,* and *Campaigns and Elections* are also good sources for stories on organized interests.

The Yellow Pages. The Yellow Pages of the local telephone book is an excellent source for information on local organized interests. Look under "Political Organizations" or "Community Organizations."

Web Resources

Federal government web sites. The federal government has a number of web sites for gathering information on specific federal programs and policies. To locate these sites, enter the name of a specific agency or government program into the Search For box of any Internet search engine. The University of Michigan Documents Center also offers a gateway to federal government resources at *henry.ugl.lib.umich.edu/libhome/Documents .center/federal.html.*

State and local government web sites. Visit the federal government's directory of state and local government sites, organized by state, category, and topic area at *www.statelocal.gov.*

Notes

1. Allan Shuldiner and the Center for Responsive Politics, *Influence Inc.: The Bottom Line on Washington Lobbying* (Washington, DC: Center for Responsive Politics, 1999).

2. Bill McAllister, "Special Interests: A Record Year for Lobby Shops," *Washington Post,* July 29, 1999, p. A27.

3. Tyra Phillips, ed., *Encyclopedia of Associations: Regional, State, and Local Organizations* (9th ed.) (Detroit: Gale Research, 1999); Jeffrey M. Berry, Kent E. Portney, and Ken Thomson, *The Rebirth of Urban Democracy* (Washington, DC: Brookings Institution, 1993); Clive S. Thomas and Ronald J. Hrebenar, "Interest Groups in the States," in Virginia Gray and Herbert Jacob, eds., *Politics in the American States: A Comparative Analysis* (6th ed.)(Washington, DC: Congressional Quarterly Press, 1996); Alan Rosenthal, *The Third House: Lobbyists and Lobbying in the States* (Washington, DC: Congressional Quarterly Press, 1993), pp. 2–5.

4. For details, see Burdett A. Loomis and Allan J. Cigler, "Introduction: The Changing Nature of Interest Group Politics," in Allan J. Cigler and Burdett A. Loomis, eds., *Interest Group Politics* (5th ed.) (Washington, DC: Congressional Quarterly Press, 1998), pp. 1–32; Rosenthal, *The Third House, Lobbyists and Lobbying in the States* (Washington, DC: Congressional Quarterly Press, 1993), pp. 2–5; Jack L. Walker, *Mobilizing Interest Groups in America: Patrons, Professions, and Social Movements* (Ann Arbor: University of Michigan Press, 1991), pp. 1–3.

5. John R. Commons et al., *History of Labor in the United States* (New York: Macmillan, 1918).

6. Karl Schriftgiesser, *The Lobbyists: The Art and Business of Influencing Lawmakers* (Boston, MA: Little, Brown, 1951), p. 6.

7. Ibid., pp. 6–7.

8. Ibid., p. 7.

9. Margaret Susan Thompson, *The Spider Web: Congress and Lobbying in the Age of Grant* (Ithaca, NY: Cornell University Press, 1985).

10. Mark P. Petracca, "The Rediscovery of Interest Group Politics," in Mark P. Petracca, ed., *The Politics of Interests: Interest Groups Transformed* (Boulder, CO: Westview Press, 1992), pp. 13–18.

11. Phillips, ed., *Encyclopedia of Associations*; Rosenthal, *The Third House: Lobbyists and Lobbying in the States* (Washington, DC: Congressional Quarterly Press, 1993), pp. 1–5.

12. See Robert H. Salisbury, "The Paradox of Interest Groups in Washington—More Groups, Less Clout," in Anthony King, ed., *The New American Political System,*

Second Version (Washington, DC: American Enterprise Institute, 1991), pp. 203–230.

13. Jeffrey Berry, *Lobbying for the People* (Princeton, NJ: Princeton University Press, 1977), pp. 11–17; Ronald G. Shaiko, "Lobbying in Washington: A Contemporary Perspective," in Paul S. Herrnson, Ronald G. Shaiko, and Clyde Wilcox, eds., *The Interest Group Connection: Electioneering, Lobbying, and Policymaking in Washington* (Chathan, NJ: Chatham House, 1998), pp. 37–51; John R. Wright, *Interest Groups and Congress: Lobbying, Contributions, and Influence* (Boston, MA: Allyn and Bacon, 1996), p. 27.

14. M. Margaret Conway and Joanne Connor Green, "Political Action Committees and the Political Process in the 1990s," in Allan J. Cigler and Burdett A. Loomis, eds., *Interest Group Politics* (4th ed.) (Washington, DC: Congressional Quarterly Press, 1995), pp. 155–174; Salisbury, "The Paradox of Interest Groups in Washington—More groups, Less clout," in Anthony King, ed., *The New American Political System,* Second Version (Washington, DC: American Enterprise Institute, 1991), p. 205.

15. Loomis and Cigler, "Introduction," pp. 1–5; Wright, *Interest Groups and Congress: Lobbying, Contributions, and Influence* (Boston, MA: Allyn and Bacon, 1996), pp. 20–30.

16. Thompson, *The Spider Web,* pp. 259–263.

17. Frank R. Baumgartner and Beth L. Leech, *Basic Interests: The Importance of Groups in Politics and in Political Science* (Princeton, NJ: Princeton University Press, 1998), p. 102.

18. Ibid., p. 104.

19. Ibid., p. 108.

20. Ibid.

21. Jeffrey M. Berry, *The New Liberalism: The Rising Power of Citizen Groups* (Washington, DC: Brookings Institution Press, 1999), chap. 1.

22. See R. Kent Weaver, "The Changing World of Think Tanks," *PS* 3 (September 1989): 563–578.

23. Baumgartner and Leech, *Basic Interests: The Importance of Groups in Politics and in Political Science* (Princeton, NJ: Princeton University Press, 1998), p. 109.

24. Rosenthal, *The Third House: Lobbyists and Lobbying in the States* (Washington, DC: Congressional Quarterly Press, 1993), pp. 2–5.

25. See, for example, Naomi Chazan, "Engaging the State: Associational Life in Sub-Saharan Africa," in Joel S. Migdal, Atul Kohli, and Vivenne Shue, eds., *State Power and Social Forces* (New York: Cambridge University Press, 1994), pp. 255–292. See also Sylvia Bashevkin, "Interest Groups and Social Movements," in Lawrence LeDuc, Richard G. Niemi, and Pippa Norris, eds., *Comparing Democracies: Elections and Voting in Global Perspective* (Thousand Oaks, CA: Sage, 1996), pp. 134–159.

26. *The World Almanac and Book of Facts, 1999* (Mahwah, NJ: World Almanac Books, 1999), pp. 684–685.

27. Ibid., p. 375.

28. Ibid., pp. 121–144.

29. Loomis and Cigler, "Introduction: The Changing Nature of Interest Group Politics," in Allan J. Cigler and Burdett A. Loomis, eds., *Interest Group Politics* (5th ed.) (Washington, DC: Congressional Quarterly Press, 1998), p. 5.

30. Ibid.

31. George Kateb, "The Value of Association," in Amy Gutman, ed., *Freedom of Association* (Princeton, NJ: Princeton University Press, 1998), p. 35.

32. Ibid.

33. Canada, Department of Justice, "Lobbying Registration Act (SOR/95–579)," accessed at *http://canada.justice.gc.ca,* March 24, 2000; Department of Justice, Canada, "Lobbyists' Code of Conduct," accessed at *http://strategis.ic.gc.ca/SSG /lr01044,* March 24, 2000; Philip Norton, "The United Kingdom: Parliament Under Pressure," in Philip Norton, ed., *Parliaments and Pressure Groups in Western Europe* (London: Frank Cass, 1999), pp. 36–38.

34. Loomis and Cigler, "Introduction: The Changing Nature of Interest Group Politics," in Allan J. Cigler and Burdett A. Loomis, eds., *Interest Group Politics* (5th ed.) (Washington, DC: Congressional Quarterly Press, 1998), p. 6.

35. David Truman, *The Governmental Process: Political Interests and Public Opinion* (2nd ed.) (New York: Knopf, 1971), chaps. 3, 4.

36. U.S. Bureau of the Census, *Historical Statistics of the United States, Colonial Times to 1970* (Washington, DC: Government Printing Office, 1976), p. 297.

37. Loomis and Cigler, "Introduction: The Changing Nature of Interest Group Politics," in Allan J. Cigler and Burdett A. Loomis, eds., *Interest Group Politics* (5th ed.) (Washington, DC: Congressional Quarterly Press, 1998), pp. 18–19.

38. Robert Salisbury, "An Exchange Theory of Interest Groups," *Midwest Journal of Political Science* 13 (1969): 1–32.

39. Loomis and Cigler, "Introduction: The Changing Nature of Interest Group Politics," in Allan J. Cigler and Burdett A. Loomis, eds., *Interest Group Politics* (5th ed.) (Washington, DC: Congressional Quarterly Press, 1998), p. 12.

40. Office of Management and Budget, "A Citizen's Guide to the Budget, Budget of the United States Government, Fiscal Year 2000," accessed at *http://www.access.gpo .gov/usbudget/fy2000/guide02.html#spending,* Chart 2–6, August 12, 1999.

41. Loomis and Cigler, "Introduction: The Changing Nature of Interest Group Politics," in Allan J. Cigler and Burdett A. Loomis, eds., *Interest Group Politics* (5th ed.) (Washington, DC: Congressional Quarterly Press, 1998), p. 12.

The Formation and Maintenance of Organized Interests

Washington, D.C.
May 5, 1999

The House of Representatives passes a new bankruptcy reform bill, 313-108. The bill, if it passes the Senate and the president signs it, will vastly change the consumer bankruptcy system in the United States. The bill is complex and confusing, but the bottom line is fairly simple: the new bill will make it harder for many consumers who wish to declare bankruptcy to do so. The bill was subject to fierce lobbying on both sides. On one side was a powerful array of organized interests representing creditors. Led by the National Consumer Bankruptcy Coalition—a coalition led by Master-Card, Visa, the National Retail Federation, and the American Bankers Association—these creditor organizations spent more than $13 million lobbying for the bill. On the other side was a loose coalition of labor unions and consumer citizen groups. The opponents of the bill spent only a fraction of the amount spent by its supporters, but their voice was clearly heard. In fact, Henry Hyde, the powerful Republican chair of the House Judiciary Committee, declared his support for the opposition even as the bill sailed through the House.

Interestingly, one voice was silent during the House debate over bankruptcy: the voice of the bankrupt. Every year in the United States, approximately 1.4 million people declare bankruptcy. Thus, at any given time, hundreds of thousands of people are in the midst of declaring bankruptcy, hundreds of thousands of others are seriously contemplating doing so, and tens of millions of others have recently done so. Yet notably absent during the battle over bankruptcy reform was a group representing these people—the very people most affected by the bankruptcy bill. In fact, not a single organized interest in the United States represents the interests of the bankrupt.[1]

A close look at the universe of organized interests uncovers numerous examples like this one—cases in which the composition of the universe of organized interests does not reflect the distribution of interests in society as a whole. There are many instances of bias in the system of organized interest representation in the United States. In short, some interests are better represented by organized interests than others. This chapter asks why this is so.

We begin by delineating the barriers to organized interest formation and survival in order to demonstrate that organized interest formation and survival cannot be taken for granted. In other words, just because an interest exists does not mean that an organized interest will form in its wake. From here, we explore how organized interests overcome the barriers to formation and survival. Finally, we examine how these barriers have manifested themselves in unequal organized interest representation—the tendency for some interests to be better represented by organized interests than others. Ultimately this chapter seeks to explain unequal organized interest representation wherever it exists.

DEFINING *FORMATION* AND *SURVIVAL*

The terms *formation* and *survival* seem straightforward, but they are not. The term *formation,* for example, has different meanings for different types of organized interests. For organizations that consist of individual citizens and are created with an explicit political purpose, *formation* means coming into existence. For example, Common Cause—a "good government" citizen group—was formed as an organized interest in 1970 when a man named John Gardner collected enough money to get the group off the ground. For some organized interests, however, formation is not synonymous with coming into existence. Many businesses, for example, do not become active in politics until many years after they come into existence. In cases like these, we say that the businesses were formed as organized interests when they became active in politics, not when they were originally incorporated. The point here is this: When scholars speak of the formation of an organized interest, they are referring to the point at which that organization becomes politically active. For many organizations, this means the point at which they come into existence. For many others, it simply means the point at which they begin to lobby government.

As for *survival,* it means the ability to remain in business as an organized interest over the long haul. Like *formation,* the term *survival* means different things for different types of organized interests. For organized interests that are initially formed for a political purpose, groups like Common Cause, survival means staying in business. For organizations that exist for nonpolitical purposes yet still engage in political activity—corporations, for example—survival as an organized interest means maintaining political activity.

In sum, the terms *formation* and *survival* are not as straightforward as they seem. Both have different meanings for different types of organized interests.

THE BARRIERS TO ORGANIZED INTEREST FORMATION AND SURVIVAL

Disturbance theory, which we encountered in the last chapter, has a straight-forward explanation for why some interests are better represented by organized interests than others. It posits "that elements of society possess common needs and share a group identity or consciousness, and that these are sufficient conditions for the formation of effective [organized interests]."[2] In other words, disturbance theory holds that as society evolves and new interests emerge, groups of individuals realize that they share interests and band together to protect these interests. This cause-and-effect logic implies that objective societal conditions determine which interests are best represented by organized interests, and thus why some interests are better represented by organized interests than others.

Despite its considerable appeal, there are two major problems with the logic of disturbance theory. First, at numerous points in American history, organized interests have not emerged when societal changes and disturbances would appear to have demanded it. For example, for most of our history, African Americans suffered enslavement, lynchings, and rampant discrimination. Yet from 1789 to 1900, African Americans did not band together on a large scale to protect their shared interests. Similarly, throughout American history, homosexuals have been subject to all sorts of harassment and persecution—not only general societal disapproval but prosecution under state and local sodomy laws. Yet not until the 1960s did homosexuals band together on a large scale to protect their shared interests. Examples like these contradict the cause-and-effect logic of disturbance theory.

Second, even now, in a time of organized interest ubiquity, organized interest representation does not reflect the distribution of opinions and interests in American society. The example at the beginning of this chapter attests to this, and there are numerous other examples as well. Consider how poorly organized interest representation reflects the interests of Americans who support the death penalty. Recent polls show that approximately 80 percent of adult Americans support the death penalty.[3] Despite this overwhelming support, *The Encyclopedia of Associations,* a directory of membership organized interests, lists only seven nationally active organized interests whose primary interest is the death penalty.[4] Together these groups represent well under 1 million people. Perhaps more shocking than this relative lack of organized interest representation is the fact that only one of these seven groups supports the death penalty. All the others want to abolish it. To say the least, these numbers do not reflect the interests of the millions of Americans concerned with the death penalty. Cases like this one in which the composition of the universe of organized interests does not reflect the distribution of interests in society as a whole augur against disturbance theory.

In his landmark book *The Logic of Collective Action* (1965), economist Mancur Olson exposed the flaws in the cause-and-effect logic of disturbance theory.[5] Although he accepted the notion that increased societal complexity caused the emergence of new interests, he questioned the notion that the emergence of new *interests* necessarily leads to the creation of new *organized interests*. Olson concluded that shared interests alone are not sufficient to cause the formation of organized interests. In other words, according to Olson, just because a group of people shares an interest does not mean they will organize to protect that interest. The reason is that there are substantial barriers to organized interest formation and survival. According to Olson, three barriers in particular hinder the formation and survival of organized interests: cost, the free-rider problem, and the political efficacy problem.

Cost

According to Olson, cost is one reason that individuals who share an interest may not band together to address their concerns. Simply sharing an interest does not pay the bills. Any unorganized group of people that wishes to form an organized interest, Olson argues, must raise a lot of money to get the group off the ground. Moreover, once an organized interest successfully forms, it must continually raise money to stay in business.

Money is not the only cost in forming and maintaining an organized interest. Time and effort are also costs. Organizing meetings, recruiting members, and holding rallies, for example, require the time and effort of numerous people. These costs may not seem important, but they are when you consider that most people do not enjoy dedicating their free time to political activity—even if they feel strongly about a political issue. Most of us prefer to invest our extra time and effort in more rewarding activities like earning more money, spending time with family and friends, watching television, or going on vacation. In sum, one of the reasons that shared interests do not necessarily lead to the formation of organized interests is that this activity is costly.

Free-Rider Problem

The free-rider problem refers to the tendency for individuals not to join organized interests that work on their behalf. Why would an individual choose not to join an organized interest that works on his or her behalf? Let us follow Olson's logic. First, Olson assumes that an individual will join an organized interest only when the benefits outweigh the costs. (It is important to reiterate here that not all membership organized interests consist of individual members. Trade associations, for example, consist of corporations. Olson's analysis applies to all types of membership organizations, not just those consisting of individuals.)

Next, Olson notes that virtually all organized interests lobby government for *collective benefits*—benefits that accrue to an organized interest's members as well as to nonmembers. An example will clarify what Olson means by collective benefits. Consider the case of the National Rifle Association (NRA), whose primary political goal is the prevention of gun control legislation. This is a collective benefit: If it is achieved, it accrues to all individuals who oppose gun control, not just members of the NRA. From here, Olson argues that individuals often choose not to join organized interests that work on their behalf because they can enjoy the collective benefits that these organized interests provide without joining. In essence, Olson concludes that most of us do not want to pay for something we can get for free.

To see the free-rider problem at work, assume for a moment that you oppose gun control. Clearly you support the NRA's political goals, but you also realize that the NRA is working to achieve collective benefits. In other words, you know that if the NRA succeeds in preventing gun control, all people who oppose gun control, not just NRA members, will benefit. Therefore, according to Olson, it is rational for you not to join the organization. In essence, you can get a "free ride" by letting others join the NRA and pay for the collective benefits you value. Political scientists Burdett Loomis and Allan Cigler sum up Olson's free-rider logic like this: "Rational individuals choose not to bear the participation costs (time, membership) because they can enjoy the group [collective] benefits (such as favorable legislation) whether or not they join."[6]

Political Efficacy Problem

The third major barrier to the formation and survival of organized interests, according to Olson, is the *political efficacy problem*. This problem flows from the widespread *tendency for people to think that one person cannot make a difference*. Who among us has not at some point looked inward and asked, "I would like to do something about that problem, but what can one person do?" Olson argues that this tendency manifests itself in the reluctance of individuals to join organized interests.

To see how the political efficacy problem works, let us again assume that you support the political goals of the NRA. The political efficacy problem means that although you support the organization's political goals, you realize that neither its multimillion-dollar budget nor its political efforts will substantially suffer if you decide not to join. Surely you realize, Olson argues, that a group with millions of dollar and thousands of members does not really need your annual dues of thirty-five dollars. The political efficacy problem means that when confronted with the decision of whether to join the NRA, you ask yourself, "What difference can my contribution make?" and answer, "Not a whole heck of a lot." You decide not to join.

The Barriers to Formation and Survival: A Summary

In sum, together, cost, the free-rider problem, and the political efficacy problem represent substantial barriers to organized interest formation and survival. These barriers, economist Mancur Olson argues, explain why shared interests do not necessarily lead to the formation of organized interests. It is hard to underestimate the importance of Olson's insights. The recognition that there are barriers to organized interest formation and survival has two hugely significant implications. The first is that some large segments of the population will remain unorganized and thus unrepresented by organized interests. For example, the young, the homeless, and the poor are segments of society that have been unable to overcome the barriers to organized interest formation. The second implication is that the organized interests that *do* exist are not necessarily representative of the different interests that make up society.

HOW UNORGANIZED CONSTITUENCIES BECOME ORGANIZED

Mancur Olson did not preclude the possibility that organized interests could form and survive. He simply noted that barriers must be overcome if a group of people is to form and maintain an organized interest. To understand how organized interests form and survive, Olson argued, we must understand how they overcome these barriers.

According to Olson, there are two primary ways that organized interests can overcome the barriers to formation and survival: providing selective benefits and coercing people to join. Writing after Olson, other political scientists identified one other way that organized interests overcome the barriers to formation and survival: procuring patron support. Each of these methods of overcoming the barriers to organized interest formation and survival deserves a close look.

Providing Selective Benefits

One way an organized interest can overcome the barriers to formation and survival is to provide *selective benefits*—those that accrue only to an organized interest's members. Because many people will not join organized interests for collective benefits, Olson argues, they must be offered inducements they cannot receive unless they join. There are three basic types of selective benefits: *material benefits,* which have tangible economic value (e.g., magazines, discounts, inexpensive insurance, hats, stickers, and newsletters); *solidary benefits,* which are social rewards (e.g., meetings, outings, and group gatherings); and *expressive benefits,* which are intangible benefits derived from working for a cause.[7] One example of an expressive benefit is the good feeling you get when you work for a cause you believe in. Another is the avoidance of guilt for not having "done your part."[8]

To understand how selective benefits induce people to join organized interests, let us consider the case of the American Association of Retired Persons

A solidary benefit The AARP is the largest citizen group in the United States, with a membership of over 32 million. One of the benefits the AARP offers its members is the ability to interact with other seniors. Here, a group of AARP members known as "fraud fighters" work together to raise citizen awareness of fraudulent mail and telephone schemes. *AP/Wide World Photos.*

(AARP), the massive organization that represents the interests of the elderly. The primary collective benefits that the AARP seeks are programs and policies that ensure financial security for older Americans. These benefits are collective because if they are obtained, they accrue to all elderly Americans—not just members of the AARP. The leaders of the AARP long ago realized that collective benefits are not enough to induce membership, so they offered members a number of selective benefits: discounts on hotel rooms, rental cars, vacations, and prescription drugs, as well as a bimonthly magazine, *Modern Maturity*. These are all selective material benefits. The group also provides its members selective solidary benefits in the form of meetings, outings, and on-line chat rooms on the Internet. Finally, the AARP provides its members with a sense of well-being associated with political activism. This constitutes a selective expressive benefit. Table 3.1 lists the collective and selective benefits offered by

TABLE 3.1 Two Organized Interests and Their Collective and Selective Benefits

Organized Interest	Collective Good Sought	Selected Selective Benefits Offered	
American Association of Retired Persons	Legislation that guarantees "income security" for the elderly	*Material*:	Hotel, car rental, and insurance discounts Low-cost home delivery of prescriptions Bimonthly magazine, *Modern Maturity* Monthly newspaper Low-cost pharmacy service
		Solidary:	Local chapter meetings Annual convention
		Purposive:	"Involvement in politics" Feeling of "doing your part"
National Rifle Association	Legislation that guarantees "gun owners' rights"	*Material*:	Monthly magazine, *American Rifleman* Low-cost gun insurance Firearms Information Service Shooting clinics and competitions
		Solidary:	Local chapter meetings Annual convention
		Purposive:	"Having a voice in Washington" A good feeling from "pitching in"

Source: Each group was contacted and asked to describe both the collective benefits and selective incentives they offered. Phrases and sentences in quotes are direct quotations from organized interest representatives.

two citizen groups: the AARP and the NRA. As you can see, the variety of selective benefits organized interests use to entice members is quite remarkable.

Providing selective benefits helps overcome all three barriers to organized interest formation and survival. First, it overcomes the desire to free-ride by making some benefits unavailable to free riders. Second, it renders the political efficacy problem moot by delivering something tangible to members in return for their support. Third, it helps overcome the cost barrier by providing money for the organization by levying membership dues on people who wish to join.

Coercing People to Join

Another way that organized interests overcome the barriers to formation and survival is by coercing people to join. Coercion is most common in labor unions. In some states, in some industries, labor unions are allowed under the law to compel individuals to support them financially as a condition of employment. In 1935, the federal government passed the National Labor Relations Act (NLRA). Political scientist Paul Johnson explains the effect of the NLRA: "The NLRA allowed labor unions to sign 'security agreements' with employers, stipulating that all employees had to pay union dues as a condition of employment."[9] In short, a business that operated under a security agreement with a specific labor union agreed not to hire nonunion employees. Thus, a person who wished to work for a business that had a security agreement with a specific union was, in essence, forced to join the labor union in order to do so. Security agreements were allowed in all states until 1947, when the Taft-Hartley Labor-Management Relations Act was passed. Taft-Hartley allowed states to adopt "right-to-work" laws that could forbid security agreements. Today twenty-one states have right-to-work laws that make it very difficult for labor unions to coerce people to join. In the twenty-nine states without right-to-work laws, a person may be required to pay union dues as a condition of employment if the collective bargaining agreement contains a union security clause that requires all employees either to join or pay union dues. In short, there are still places where people are coerced into joining labor unions as a condition of employment. Thus, coercion as a means of overcoming the barriers to organized interest formation and survival is alive and well.

None of this is to say that unions have an easy time forming and surviving. Before a labor union wins the right to represent a group of workers for collective bargaining purposes, it faces a serious barrier to formation: it must convince a majority of workers at a site to affiliate with it. To overcome this problem, labor unions generally emphasize the selective material benefits of labor union membership such as health insurance, life insurance, employment security, and seniority perquisites.[10] Nonetheless, coercion was instrumental in making labor unions strong in the late 1930s and early 1940s, and coercion continues to help some labor unions overcome the barriers to collective action.

Many PACs also practice coercion, though more subtly than labor unions do. Specifically, many corporate PACs "strongly encourage" corporate managers and executives to contribute. Over the years, many disgruntled corporate managers and executives have reported that "encouragement" often amounts to coercion. In one high-profile case from the early 1990s, a Prudential Securities executive charged that his firm fired him when he refused to contribute 5 percent of his salary to the corporation's PAC.[11] Finally, many state bar associations also practice coercion. In thirty-two states, attorneys must join the state bar association to practice law.[12]

Coercion, like the provision of selective benefits, helps organized interests overcome all three barriers to formation and survival. First, it makes free-riding an impossibility. Second, it renders the political efficacy problem moot. Finally, it guarantees a steady flow of income for the organized interest in question.

Relying on Patrons

Another way to overcome the barriers to formation and survival is to find a patron. A *patron* is defined as an individual or organizational benefactor that contributes substantial resources to an organized interest.

Thousands of individuals and institutions give away money to organized interests. *Private foundations,* for example, are nonprofit institutions that exist solely to make grants to individuals and nonprofit organizations. Private foundations get their money primarily from wealthy individuals. They then use this money to fund other organizations. High-profile foundation patrons include the Ford Foundation, the MacArthur Foundation, and the Sarah Scaife Foundation. Every year private foundations provide hundreds of millions of dollars to organized interests. The bulk of this money goes to citizen groups and think tanks. One study suggests that over 80 percent of all citizen groups received some type of private foundation support during their initial start-up.[13]

Corporations are also important sources of patronage. Every year, corporate America donates billions of dollars to organizations across the country. The vast majority of this money goes to organizations that are not politically active, such as local United Way chapters, schools, museums, and symphonies. However, a fraction of each year's corporate support—in fact, hundreds of millions of dollars—finds its way into the coffers of organized interests. According to one recent study, think tanks and citizen groups receive the bulk of corporate patronage.[14] Many conservative think tanks, for example, rely heavily on corporate support to survive.

The federal government provides patron support as well. Government patronage usually comes in the form of contracts for services. An environmental citizen group, for example, may be hired to conduct a study of environmental quality. Similarly, an organization that represents the elderly may be given a government grant to provide legal services for the indigent elderly.

Organized interests themselves also act as patrons. Many trade associations, for example, contribute money to think tanks and citizen groups. Similarly, some labor unions support think tanks, coalitions, and citizen groups. Finally, wealthy individuals sometimes pump large amounts of money into organized interests. The annual reports of most large citizen groups, for example, contain the names of individual patrons who have been especially generous.

Of course, locating a patron willing to donate large sums of money is not always easy. Some organized interests have an easier time attracting patron support than others, and few organized interests are totally dependent on patronage. Nonetheless, patrons have been instrumental in the formation and survival of thousands of organized interests.

Overcoming the Barriers to Formation and Survival

In sum, Mancur Olson, the preeminent analyst of organized interest formation and survival, argues that organized interests must find a way to overcome substantial barriers if they are to form and survive. The reason some interests are better represented by organized interests than others, he argues, is that some have an easier time overcoming the barriers to formation and survival than others. All this, of course, begs the following question: Which organized interests are in the best position to overcome the barriers to formation and survival? We have established how organized interests can overcome these barriers but still have not looked at which types of organized interests are in the best position to use the solutions we have discussed. This is the next order of business.

EXPLAINING UNEQUAL ORGANIZED INTEREST REPRESENTATION

Now we will move beyond the generic conclusion that some interests are better represented than others by organized interests and describe which types of organized interests are most plentiful and why. Specifically, we examine why institutions, the affluent, the intense, and groups of individuals with strong leaders are better represented by organized interests than other segments of society are.

Institutions

Institutions—nonmembership organized interests like corporations, governments, foreign countries, and colleges and universities—are ideally suited to overcoming the barriers to organized interest formation and survival. Why? Because two of the barriers—the free-rider problem and the political efficacy problem—have virtually no relevance to them. Think of it in this way: an organized interest without members does not have to worry about either free riders or individuals who do not feel politically efficacious. Institutions do, of course, face one major barrier: cost. Where do institutions get the resources they need to form and maintain organized interests? The answer to this question varies by type of institution. Corporations get the money they need to form and maintain organized interests by selling products and services. Shoe giant Nike, for example, hires lobbyists and joins trade associations with some of the money it earns selling athletic equipment. Governmental entities and foreign countries use tax dollars to form organized interests. When Californians, for example, pay their taxes, they are indirectly funding the state's lobbyist corps. Similarly, when citizens in China pay taxes, they are indirectly supporting their country's lobbying efforts in Washington.

In short, when it comes to forming and surviving, institutions face a tremendous advantage over membership organized interests: they face neither the free-rider problem nor the political efficacy problem. Their only significant barrier is cost. This is not an insubstantial factor, but it turns out that many institutions have an advantage in overcoming this barrier as well: lots of resources at their disposal. Corporations, for example, generally have huge sums of money in their treasuries. So do some colleges and universities, governments, and foreign countries. The reason that institutions often have money at their disposal is that most of them exist for some nonpolitical purpose. Corporations, for example, exist to make money, universities exist to educate people, and local governments exist to deliver services to residents. The political activities of these institutions are secondary or even tertiary to their main purposes. This is important because an organized interest that exists for a nonpolitical purpose has an advantage over explicitly political organizations in overcoming the cost barrier. Instead of asking or begging people or patrons for money, it can meet the costs of organized interest formation and survival by diverting some resources as a result of its primary activities and investing them in political activity.

The ease with which institutions can form and maintain organized interests has manifested itself in what political scientist Robert Salisbury calls "the dominance of institutions," defined as the awesome and overwhelming presence of institutions in the universe of organized interests.[15] In the biggest study yet of institutional representation before government, Salisbury concluded that despite the preoccupation of the public and the media with "conventional membership [organized interests]," it is "institutions, especially those of business, which clearly dominate" interest representation in Washington.[16] In his detailed study of national agricultural policy, Salisbury concluded that only one-sixth of the organized interests active on agricultural issues were traditional "individual membership groups."[17] The bulk of active organized interests, he found, were corporations.

Figure 2.2 buttresses Salisbury's claims. As you can see, institutions vastly outnumber individual membership organizations in Washington. This is the case in states and localities as well. Not surprisingly, the most prominent institutions are corporations. Clearly business dominates the world of organized interest representation. As Figure 2.2 shows, of the approximately 15,000 organized interests active in Washington, about one-fifth are corporations and one-seventh are trade associations. Together, they comprise over one-third of all the organized interests in Washington. Furthermore, over half of all PACs are associated with either corporations or trade associations, and on average corporate and trade association PACs account for well over half of all PAC money contributed to federal candidates.[18] All told, corporations, trade associations, and business PACs account for well over 50 percent of the organized interests in Washington.[19] There is ample evidence that business is equally dominant in states and localities.[20]

In the most general sense, this dominance of institutions means that in most policy battles, the interests of institutions are much better represented by organized interests than the interests of individuals—even individuals who use or are affiliated with these institutions. The dominance of institutions means, for example, that in making higher education policy, state governments hear much more from organized interests representing colleges and universities than they do from organized interests representing students. Similarly, it means that in policy battles that affect business interests, there are likely to be many more organized interests representing businesses than there are representing consumers. In making health care policy, for example, the federal government hears much more from organized interests representing the health care industry than from organized interests representing patients. None of this means, of course, that institutions always get what they want from government. For one thing, not all institutions share the same interests. Businesses, for example, often disagree among themselves about what constitutes good public policy. In addition, the interests of groups of individuals are seldom completely ignored. Labor unions, citizen groups, professional associations, and other organized interests that represent the interests of individuals rather than institutions are still major players in organized interest politics. In the end, however, the dominance of institutions means that in most major policy battles, the interests of America's most prominent institutions are likely to be well represented by organized interests.

Groups of Affluent Individuals

For many institutions, organizing is simply a matter of desire. But what about groups of individuals? Why do some groups of individuals have large and powerful organized interests working on their behalf while others have either small operations or no organized interest representation at all? Why, for example, are the bankrupt not represented by any organized interests? Why are death penalty opponents so much better represented by organized interests than death penalty supporters?

Contrary to disturbance theory, the sheer number of people who share an interest does not determine to what extent groups of individuals are represented by organized interests. What, then, does determine the extent to which groups of individuals who share an interest are represented by organized interests? The short answer is this: their ability to overcome the barriers to organized interest formation and survival. Groups of individuals that have the easiest time overcoming the barriers to organized interest formation and survival are likely to be better represented by organized interests than groups of individuals that struggle to overcome these barriers. Which groups of individuals have the easiest time overcoming the barriers to organized interest formation and survival? There are two answers to this question.

One answer is groups of affluent individuals. No matter what interest they may have in common, groups of affluent individuals have an easier time overcoming the barriers to organized interest formation and survival than groups of nonaffluent individuals. The reasons are numerous. First, the affluent have an easier time paying the costs of organized interest membership. Second, they are less susceptible than the nonaffluent to the political efficacy problem. Studies have shown, for example, that income is highly correlated with education and that education increases an individual's level of efficacy—the feeling that one person can make a difference.[21] Third, affluent people are more likely to have effective leaders in their midst than nonaffluent people. By effective leaders, we mean individuals who are capable of doing what is necessary to get a group off the ground—raise money, design packages of selective incentives to attract members, organize meetings, hold rallies—and make sure it survives. The importance of effective leaders in overcoming the barriers to organized interest formation and survival cannot be overestimated. Political scientist Robert Salisbury has pointed out that virtually all organized interests—like business firms—require leadership, both at their founding and throughout their existence.[22] Salisbury likens the people who start and run organized interests to business entrepreneurs. Research on leadership shows that organized interest founders and leaders tend to be much more educated and affluent than the average American. Thus, the affluent have more and more skilled potential leaders in their midst than the needy do.[23]

It is worth mentioning that the crucial importance of leadership provides yet one more advantage to institutions: virtually all institutions have at least some capable leaders. Corporations, for example, are likely to have dozens of capable and effective leaders. These individuals—though they may not be political leaders—are likely to possess the skills necessary to get an organized interest off the ground, which in this case means figuring out a way to divert some of the institution's resources into political activity.

The evidence that the affluent dominate individual membership organized interest representation is overwhelming. First, studies show that upper-income individuals join membership groups at a much higher rate than lower-income Americans. One recent study, for example, compared two income groups at the extremes—those with annual family incomes below $15,000 and those with annual family incomes above $75,000—and found that 73 percent of people in the highest income bracket were affiliated with a political organization, compared to only 29 percent of people in the lowest income bracket.[24] A similar study found that individuals in the highest income bracket were over twice as likely to belong to more than one political organization than individuals in the lowest income bracket.[25] Second, case studies show that membership groups, even those that claim to represent the public at large, tend to draw their members from the upper circles of American society. For example, in an exhaustive study of the "good government" group Common Cause, Andrew McFarland found that the median Common Cause member "had a family income of about $37,000 at a time when the national average family income was about $20,000 per year." Members were also highly educated: close to 50 percent had earned graduate or professional degrees.[26] Similarly, a study of contributors to Christian Right political action committees found that 63 percent had incomes over $50,000 per year at a time when the median was around $20,000, and 75 percent were college graduates.[27] Finally, a number of studies show that when membership groups recruit members, they focus most of their efforts on the affluent. Not surprisingly, their memberships are dominated by affluent Americans.[28]

The advantage of affluence has several implications. First, and perhaps most important, it means that constituencies, no matter how large they are, that consist wholly or mostly of lower-income Americans are likely to be poorly represented by organized interests. There are, of course, organized interests working on behalf of lower-income Americans. In Washington alone, for example, dozens of labor unions represent the interests of working people, and hundreds of citizen groups represent the interests of the homeless, the poor, the uneducated, and the indigent. Not surprisingly, however, these groups tend to have rather limited resources compared to organized interests representing the interests of upper- and middle-income Americans. Second, the affluence advantage means that even organized interests that do represent the interests of lower-income Americans are likely to be formed and maintained by upper- and middle-class Americans. Studies of organized interest leadership have consistently found that with a few exceptions, organized interests working on behalf of America's most disadvantaged citizens tend to be formed and maintained by upper- and middle-class Americans.[29] Finally, the affluence advantage means that in any policy battle, the views of the affluent are likely to be well represented by organized interests. This is true whether the affluent are united on a particular issue—say, for example, if 80 percent of upper-income Americans believe that capital gains taxes should be lowered—or divided—say, for example, if 50 percent of affluent Americans supported abortion rights and 50 percent opposed them. In the first case, the view that capital gains taxes should be decreased will most likely be better represented than the view that capital gains taxes should be increased. In the second case, which side is better represented by organized interests is likely to be determined by something other than how the opinions and views of affluent Americans are distributed.

In the end, of course, none of this means that the affluent always get what they want from government. For one thing, as you will see in Chapter 9, policymakers do not make all their decisions based solely on what organized interests want. Second, lower-income people do participate in politics in other ways—mainly by voting, though at a much lower rate than higher-income people. And most public officials who run for office know that they cannot ignore the views of lower-income Americans.

Groups of Intense Individuals

Another answer to the question of which groups of individuals have the easiest time overcoming the barriers to organized interest formation and survival is groups of individuals who feel intensely about an issue. Political scientists have found that no matter what interest they may have in common, groups of intense individuals have an easier time overcoming the barriers to organized interest formation and survival than less intense individuals. The reason is simple: people who feel intensely about an issue are more willing to bear the costs of organized interest membership than people who do not feel intensely. The intense are also more likely to see pitching in as their duty.

Intensity can mitigate the effects of the free-rider and political efficacy problems. The tendency of the intense to participate in collective endeavors explains why organized interest representation around the death penalty is dominated by death penalty opponents. Those who oppose the death penalty do so with a zeal that is uncommon among death penalty proponents. Intensity also explains to some extent why the NRA has had so much success over the years. Polls consistently show that gun control supporters outnumber gun control opponents in the United States by a wide margin. Yet the NRA has thousands more members than virtually all nationally active antigun groups combined. The reason is that gun control opponents oppose gun control with almost revolutionary zeal.

Studies of individual political participation suggest that those who feel intensely about political issues—those who follow politics, care about what happens, and care deeply about who wins and who loses—are more politically active than the less intense.[30] The same studies show that people who most strongly identify with a political party participate more in politics than those who do not.[31] Furthermore, not surprisingly, studies of individual membership organized interests—especially citizen groups and other types of organizations open to all citizens—show that group members generally feel very strongly about the issues on which they are politically active.[32]

The intensity advantage has several implications. First, it means that constituencies, no matter how large, which consist wholly or almost wholly of individuals who share an interest but do not feel very intensely about it are likely to be poorly represented by organized interests. A second and closely related implication is that the interests of the intense—even if these interests are decidedly unpopular with the majority of Americans—are seldom ignored by policymakers. In any policy battle, policymakers are likely to hear far more from

The golden rule: he who has the money makes the rules There is some truth to the widespread notion that the wealthy are better represented before government than the not so wealthy. This does not necessarily mean, however, that the government responds only to the interests of affluent Americans. *Library of Congress, LC-USZ6-787.*

the intense than they are from the rest. Again, none of this means that the most intense Americans always get their way on policy issues they care about. It does mean, however, that policymakers take into serious consideration the views of the intense.

Hope for the Rest of Us

The importance of both affluence and intensity begs the following question: What explains the formation and survival of organized interests representing people who are neither affluent nor intense? One answer is leadership. Studies have found that effective leadership is capable of overcoming the barriers to organized interest formation and survival, no matter how overwhelming these barriers seem.

Perhaps nothing else demonstrates the importance of leadership like the case of the United Farm Workers (UFW). Farmworkers are some of the lowest-paid and marginal participants in the American economy. They earn little money, for the most part they live and work amid squalor, many are uneducated, and many are immigrants.[33] In short, as a group, farmworkers seem unlikely candidates to overcome the barriers to organized interest formation and survival. In fact, few other constituencies in America seem less capable of overcoming the barriers to organized interest formation and survival. Yet in the late 1960s, the UFW managed to mobilize. By the early 1970s, the union had over 100,000 members and contracts with over 300 growers. Although its membership dropped in the conservative 1980s, it remains active to this day. The UFW not only mobilized but succeeded in reaching collective bargaining agreements with hundreds of California growers. It also succeeded in obtaining legislation that safeguarded the rights of farmworkers.

How did the UFW manage? Part of the answer is Cesar Chavez—the charismatic and gifted founder of the UFW. By all accounts, it was the late Chavez's sheer force of will that led to the creation of the UFW. By convincing farmworkers of the need to organize and enlisting powerful allies such as California governor Jerry Brown, Chavez was able to form an unlikely organized interest.

The lesson of the UFW is that virtually any constituency can overcome the barriers to organized interest formation and survival with effective leadership. Leaders can use skill and charisma to overcome the barriers to organized interest formation and survival. They may design attractive packages of benefits to attract members. They may successfully court patrons willing to subsidize their organizing efforts. Or they may convince individuals who share their interests that their participation is vital.

Leadership is not the only factor that explains the formation and survival of organized interests representing people who are neither affluent nor intense. Studies have found that social pressure can also help groups of poor, not-so-intense individuals overcome the barriers to organized interest formation and survival. In a ground-breaking study of the civil rights movement, political scientist Dennis Chong showed that many individuals who might otherwise have eschewed joining organized interests were persuaded to join civil rights groups by their friends and neighbors. Chong states: "Many people participate in causes out of a sense of obligation to their families, friends, and associates; they go along to get along, to repeat a trite but true aphorism."[34] On a similar note, Chong concludes that many people joined civil rights groups—groups in which their friends and neighbors and family members were active—because they feared that not doing so might result in damage to their "reputation, ostracism, or repudiation from the community."[35]

In short, Chong concludes that organized interests active in the civil rights movement were able to survive by relying on social pressure to get people to

Organized interest entrepreneur Cesar Chavez in action Strong leadership can help groups of people who are not affluent overcome the substantial barriers to organized interest formation and survival. Here, the late Cesar Chavez, the gifted founder of the United Farm Workers, leads fellow UFW members on a picket line in 1969. *AP/Wide World Photos.*

join up. This, of course, begs the question of how these groups got off the ground in the first place. In other words, Chong's ideas explain how civil rights groups were able to attract members once they got started, but they do not explain how these organizations got started in the first place. The key, according to Chong, was leadership. Thus, we have come full circle, back to leadership. In order to bring social pressure to bear, groups must get up and running, and leaders are the ones who do that. This begs yet another question: What motivates leaders to start groups? In many cases, according to Chong, the answer is altruism. That is, sometimes people start groups simply because they feel that it is the right thing to do.

The ability of leadership and social pressure to help groups of people overcome the substantial barriers to organized interest formation and survival means that virtually any group of people has some chance of successfully forming an organized interest, and thus being represented before government. This should not, however, cause you to lose sight of the larger message of this chapter: despite the fact that virtually any group of people can overcome the barriers to organized interest formation and survival, some groups of people are better suited to doing so than others.

Explaining Unequal Organized Interest Representation: A Summary

The major point of this section has been this: some interests are better represented by organized interests than others because there are substantial barriers to organized interest formation and survival, and not all constituencies are equally capable of overcoming these barriers. The interests in American society that are most likely to be well represented by organized interests are those of America's preeminent institutions. This is the case because institutions face far fewer barriers to organized interest formation and survival than do groups of individuals. Corporations in particular are in an excellent position to overcome these barriers. None of this means that the shared interests of groups of individuals go unrepresented by organized interests. As Chapters 1 and 2 attest, many groups of individuals are represented by organized interests. Not all groups of individuals with shared interests, however, are equally represented by organized interests. The reason is not simply that some constituencies are larger than others. Rather, which groups of individuals are best represented by organized interests is a function of which groups have the easiest time overcoming the barriers to organized interest formation and survival. We have learned that groups of affluent individuals and groups of intense individuals are better represented by organized interests than other groups of individuals. Taken together, all of this means that organized interest representation does not necessarily reflect objective societal conditions. In other words, you cannot determine the distribution of organized interests by looking at the distribution of interests.

THE EFFECT OF DISTURBANCES AND SOCIETAL CHANGE ON ORGANIZED INTEREST FORMATION AND SURVIVAL

This exploration of costs and benefits and leadership and barriers inevitably leads to one question: Do disturbances, events, or series of events that profoundly affect society or societal change play any role in organized interest formation and survival? A focus on costs and benefits and leadership, some argue, obscures the fact that societal change and disturbances play a large role in organized interest formation and survival. Consider the spread of AIDS and HIV. The HIV virus was not even identified until the mid-1980s. Thus, not surprisingly, before the mid-1980s, there were no organized interests concerned with AIDS. By the mid-1990s, however, *The Encyclopedia of Associations* listed hundreds of nationally active organized interests concerned with AIDS.[36] Clearly, these groups formed partially as a result of disturbances and societal change. Without AIDS, they would never have existed.

Societal change and disturbances often encourage the formation of organized interests by giving rise to new interests in society. Nonetheless, neither societal changes nor disturbances in and of themselves cause the formation of organized interests. In other words, although disturbances and societal changes may lead to the creation of new interests, they are not sufficient to create organized interests. Organized interests—actual organizations that engage in political activity—are like business firms in the sense that someone must start them, someone must run them, and someone must finance them. This takes time and money and effort. And no disturbance is capable of forcing an entrepreneur to form an organized interest or forcing a person or patron to support an organized interest. These decisions by individuals and institutions are made on the basis of costs and benefits, not just on the basis of objective societal conditions or shared interests.

CONCLUSION: EXPLAINING WHY SOME INTERESTS ARE BETTER REPRESENTED THAN OTHERS

This chapter began with the observation that despite the incredible size and enormous diversity of the universe of organized interests, some interests are better represented by organized interests than others. The reason is that there are substantial barriers to the formation and survival of organized interests and not all constituencies are equally capable of overcoming these barriers. In other words, some organized interests have an easier time forming and surviving than others. The most important barriers to organized interest formation and survival are cost, the free-rider problem, and the political efficacy problem.

Studies have shown that institutions have an easier time overcoming the barriers to formation and survival than groups of individuals. This is why the universe of organized interests is dominated by institutions, especially corporations. All is not lost, however, for groups of individuals who wish to form and maintain organized interests. These groups can overcome the barriers to organized interest formation and survival, but it is not easy. It requires the provision of selective incentives, coercion, the procurement of patronage, or some combination of the three.

Groups of affluent individuals seem to have an easier time forming and maintaining organized interests than groups of not-so-affluent individuals. Similarly, groups of intense individuals have an easier time forming and maintaining organized interests than groups of not-so-intense individuals. Nonetheless, it is possible for virtually any group of individuals to overcome the barriers to organized interest formation and survival. One key is leadership.

What's Next

Now that we have some idea of where organized interests come from and how they survive, we can turn to matters that are less recondite: what organized interests do. The following four chapters are devoted to this topic. We turn first to the nonlobbying activities of organized interests and then delve into lobbying—attempts by organized interests to influence public policy. Understanding how and why organized interests lobby is crucially important. For it is because organized interests lobby that political scientists (and media) pay them so much attention.

EXERCISES

1. Choose two citizen groups, and explore their web sites. Based on the information you find, compare and contrast the collective goods sought by each group. Describe how each group attempts to overcome the free-rider and political efficacy problems.
2. Using one of the organized interest directories listed in Chapter 1, choose a citizen group, professional association, think tank, or trade association that was founded before 1970. Learn all that you can about the circumstances surrounding the organization's founding. Can the organization's

formation be traced to one individual or small group of individuals? Where did the organization get the money it needed to get started? Were patrons involved? Find out what you can about how the organization obtains the resources it needs to survive. Does the organization obtain money from members? Approximately what percentage (if any) of the organization's money currently comes from members? What percentage comes from patrons?

3. Choose a think tank. Using the Internet or the directories listed in Chapter 1 (or both), determine whether the think tank is liberal, moderate, or conservative. What is its annual budget? Where does the organization get most of its money? Can you discern any link between the think tank's ideology and the sources of its financial support?

RESEARCH RESOURCES

Publications

Organized interest annual reports. Many organized interests publish yearly annual reports and financial statements, which generally contain detailed budgetary information. To obtain a copy of an organization's annual report or financial statement, contact the organization and ask for one.

Organized interest histories. Many organized interests publish brief histories of themselves that they send out to current and prospective members. The content of these histories depends on the organization in question. To obtain an organization's publications, contact the organization and ask for them.

Web Resources

Web directories. The following sites contain links to the web sites of hundreds of individual organized interests: *www.politicalindex.com, www.politicaljunkie .com, www.policy.com*. A comprehensive directory of citizen group web sites is located at *http://policy.com/community/advoc*. A comprehensive directory of think tanks is located at *http://policy.com/community/ttank*.

Notes

1. Dan Morgan, "Creditors' Money Talks Louder in Bankruptcy Debate; Consumer Groups Fight New Curbs on Insolvent Debtors," *Washington Post,* June 1, 1999, p. A04; Deirdre Shesgreen, "Credit Card Firms Demand Tough Bankruptcy Laws," *St. Louis Post-Dispatch,* May 23, 1999, p. A8.

2. Burdett A. Loomis and Allan J. Cigler, "Introduction: The Changing Nature of Interest Group Politics," in Allan J. Cigler and Burdett A. Loomis, eds., *Interest Group Politics* (5th ed.) (Washington, DC: Congressional Quarterly Press, 1998), p. 8.

3. *The American National Election Studies* (Ann Arbor, MI: Inter-University Consortium for Political and Social Research, 1992, 1996), accessed at *http://www.umich .edu/~nes/resources/data/nes94/94cbke-vars.html#1041,* November 8, 1998.

4. See *Encyclopedia of Associations* (33rd ed.) (Detroit: Gale Research, 1998), p. 1647.

5. Mancur Olson, *The Logic of Collective Action* (Cambridge, MA: Harvard University Press, 1965).

6. Loomis and Cigler, "Introduction: The Changing Nature of Interest Group Profiles," in Allan J. Cigler and Burdett A. Loomis, eds., *Interest Group Politics* (5th ed.) (Washington, DC: Congressional Quarterly Press, 1998), p. 8.

7. Peter B. Clark and James Q. Wilson, "Incentive Systems: A Theory of Organizations," *Administrative Studies Quarterly* 6 (September 1961): 129–166. The typology was refined in Robert H. Salisbury, "An Exchange Theory of Interest Groups," *Midwest Journal of Political Science* 13 (February 1969): 1–32.

8. James Q. Wilson, *Political Organizations* (Princeton, NJ: Princeton University Press, 1995), p. 45.

9. Paul Edward Johnson, "Organized Labor in an Era of Blue-Collar Decline," in Allan J. Cigler and Burdett A. Loomis, eds., *Interest Group Politics* (3rd ed.) (Washington, DC: Congressional Quarterly Press, 1991), p. 36.

10. Ibid., p. 35.

11. Pat Wechsler, "Coercion Charged at Pru Securities, Forced Political Contributions Alleged," *Newsday,* February 19, 1992, p. 35.

12. Bob Egelko, "Lawyers to Vote on Dumping State Bar," *San Diego Union-Tribune,* May 25, 1996, p. A3.

13. Jack L. Walker, *Mobilizing Interest Groups in America: Patrons, Professions, and Social Movements* (Ann Arbor: University of Michigan Press, 1991), p. 78.

14. Anthony J. Nownes and Allan Cigler, "Corporate Philanthropy in a Political Fishbowl: Perils and Possibilities," in Cigler and Loomis, eds., *Interest Group Politics,* (5th ed.) (Washington, DC: Congressional Quarterly Press, 1998), pp. 63–82.

15. See also E. E. Schattschneider, *The Semi-sovereign People* (New York: Holt, Rinehart, and Winston, 1960).

16. Robert Salisbury, "Interest Representation: The Dominance of Institutions," *American Political Science Review* 78 (March 1984): 74–75.

17. Ibid., p. 74.

18. Federal Election Commission, "Summary of PAC Financial Activity," June 8, 1999, accessed at *www.fec.gov/press/pacye98,* August 24, 1999.

19. See John T. Tierney and Kay Lehman Schlozman, "Congress and Organized Interests," in Christopher J. Deering, ed., *Congressional Politics* (Chicago: Dorsey Press), p. 198.

20. Alan Rosenthal, *The Third House: Lobbyists and Lobbying in the States* (Washington, DC: Congressional Quarterly Press, 1993), pp. 45–48.

21. Ronald J. Hrebenar, Matthew J. Burbank, and Robert C. Benedict, *Political Parties, Interest Groups, and Political Campaigns* (Boulder, CO: Westview Press, 1999), p. 105; Herbert Hyman and Charles Wright, "Trends in Voluntary Association Membership of American Adults," *American Sociological Review* 36 (April 1971): 191–206; Sidney Verba, Kay Lehman Schlozman, and Henry E. Brady, *Voice and Equality: Civic Voluntarism in American Politics* (Cambridge, MA: Harvard University Press, 1995), pp. 5, 18, 291–294, 346–347, 350; Raymond E. Wolfinger and Steven J. Rosenstone, *Who Votes?* (New Haven, CT: Yale University Press, 1980), p. 27.

22. Salisbury, "An Exchange Theory of Interest Groups," pp. 11–15.

23. Anthony J. Nownes and Grant Neeley, "Public Interest Group Entrepreneurship and Theories of Group Mobilization," *Political Research Quarterly* 49 (March 1996): 119–146.

24. Frank R. Baumgartner and Beth L. Leech, *Basic Interests: The Importance of Groups in Politics and in Political Science* (Princeton, NJ: Princeton University Press, 1998), p. 91; Frank R. Baumgartner and Jack L. Walker, Jr., "Survey Research and Membership in Voluntary Organizations," *American Journal of Political Science* 32 (1988): 908–928; Verba, Schlozman, and Brady, *Voice and Equality: Civic Voluntarism in American Politics* (Cambridge, MA: Harvard University Press, 1995), p. 190. See also Herbert Hyman and Charles Wright, "Trends in Voluntary Association Membership of American Adults," *American Sociological Review* 36 (April 1971): 191–206.

25. Hyman and Wright, "Trends in Voluntary Association Membership of American Adults."

26. Andrew McFarland, *Common Cause: Lobbying in the Public Interest* (Chatham, NJ: Chatham House, 1984), p. 48.

27. James Guth and John C. Green, "Political Activists and Civil Liberties: The Case of Party and PAC Contributions" (paper presented at the annual meeting of the Midwest Political Science Association, Chicago, April 1984).

28. R. Kenneth Godwin, "Money, Technology, and Political Interests: The Direct Marketing of Politics," in Mark P. Petracca, ed., *The Politics of Interests: Interest Groups Transformed* (Boulder, CO: Westview Press, 1992), pp. 308–325.

29. For details, see McFarland, *Common Cause: Lobbying in the Public Interest* (Chatham, NJ: Chatham House, 1984), pp. 46–52; Nownes and Neeley, "Public Interest Group Entrepreneurship and Theories of Group Formation," p. 136.

30. Lester W. Milbraith, *Political Participation* (Chicago: Rand McNally, 1965); Verba, Schlozman, and Brady, *Voice and Equality: Civic Voluntarism in American Politics* (Cambridge, MA: Harvard University Press, 1995), pp. 345–346.

31. Verba, Schlozman, and Brady, *Voice and Equality: Civic Voluntarism in American Politics* (Cambridge, MA: Harvard University Press, 1995), p. 349.

32. See McFarland, *Common Cause: Lobbying in the Public Interest* (Chatham, NJ: Chatham House, 1984), chaps. 2, 3; Lawrence Rothenberg, "Putting the Puzzle Together: Why People Join Interest Groups," *Public Choice* 60 (1989): 241–257; Paul

A. Sabatier, "Interest Group Membership and Organization: Multiple Theories," in Petracca, ed., *The Politics of Interests: Interest Groups Transformed* (Boulder, CO: Westview Press, 1992), pp. 99–129.

33. See J. Craig Jenkins, *The Politics of Insurgency: The Farm Worker Movement in the 1960s* (New York: Columbia University Press, 1985).

34. Dennis Chong, *Collective Action and the Civil Rights Movement* (Chicago: University of Chicago Press, 1991), p. 232.

35. Ibid.

36. *Encyclopedia of Associations,* pp. 2441–2442.

4 ▷ The Nonlobbying Activities of Organized Interests

Washington, D.C.
May 11, 1995

The National Rifle Association (NRA) is reeling after its most prestigious member, former president George Bush, resigns his membership in the group. Bush, a life member of the NRA, sends a terse letter to the group, arguing that it went too far in a recent fund-raising letter. The letter in question, which was sent to over 3 million NRA members, encouraged members to send money so that the group could continue its fight against gun control. The letter singled out for derision the Bureau of Alcohol, Tobacco, and Firearms (BATF), the federal bureau charged with implementing many federal gun laws, describing its agents as "jackbooted thugs" in "Nazi bucket helmets and black storm-trooper uniforms" who are intent on "attacking law abiding citizens." Federal agents, the letter continued, had to be reined in because they routinely "harass, intimidate, [and] even murder law-abiding citizens." In his resignation letter to the NRA, Bush writes: "Your broadside against federal agents deeply offends my own sense of decency and honor, and it offends my concept of service to country." Bush added that he knew one of the federal agents killed in the April 19, 1995, bombing of the Oklahoma City federal building and that the agent "was no Nazi." In the end, the NRA expresses little regret at Bush's resignation. The NRA's president, Thomas Washington, defends the letter, asserting that it contained "more truth than slander."[1]

The leaders of the NRA are no strangers to controversy. Because the organization so vehemently, actively, and effectively opposes almost all restrictions on gun ownership, it frequently draws the ire of gun control proponents, law enforcement officials, and left-leaning politicians. In short, the NRA's political activities are heavily scrutinized and often criticized. The NRA's fund-raising activities, however, are another story. Until the Bush brouhaha, neither the media, nor politicians, nor citizens paid much attention to any of the NRA's non-political activities.

To use a tired but true cliché, the case of George Bush versus the NRA is the exception that proves the rule. Most of us ignore the nonlobbying activities of organized interests because most of us consider lobbying the only important thing that organized interests do. Indeed, it is because organized interests lobby that political scientists study them in the first place. Nonetheless, the nonlobbying activities of organized interests are crucially important.

In this chapter, we take a brief look at three of the most important nonlobbying activities of organized interests—organizational maintenance, monitoring, and self-governance—because a full understanding of organized interests encompasses their nonlobbying activities as well as their lobbying activities.

ORGANIZATIONAL MAINTENANCE: THE OVERWHELMING IMPERATIVE

Political scientist James Q. Wilson has noted, "Whatever else organizations seek, they seek to survive."[2] Obviously if an organized interest ceases to exist, it cannot possibly achieve any of its political goals. Thus, surviving on a day-to-day basis is a priority for organized interests because they realize that survival is a necessary precondition of goal achievement.

Doing what it takes to stay alive is called *organizational maintenance*, and the cornerstone of organizational maintenance is obtaining money. Money is the key to organizational maintenance because it can be used to purchase or otherwise acquire the things that make an organized interest powerful. Money can be used, for example, to hire lobbyists, recruit members, attract competent staff personnel, rent office space, and pay the bills.

There are four basic ways that organized interests obtain money: perform a nonpolitical function, procure patron support, recruit members, and sell goods or services. These four ways are not mutually exclusive; many organized interests use a combination of these methods to obtain money.

Performing a Nonpolitical Function

Nonmembership organized interests that exist primarily for nonpolitical purposes, such as corporations, domestic governmental entities, foreign governmental entities, and colleges and universities, obtain almost all of their money by performing their primary functions. For example, corporations obtain money by selling goods and/or services, colleges and universities obtain money by charging students for educational services and acquiring grants for research and education, and domestic and foreign governmental entities obtain money primarily by collecting taxes.

Procuring Patron Support

Some organized interests obtain money by procuring patron support. Research has shown that two types of organized interests in particular rely heavily on patrons for financial support: citizen groups and think tanks.[3] The specific ways that organized interests go about procuring patron support vary, but in general, the process works something like this. First, an organized interest does research to determine which patrons might be willing to support it. For example, an environmental citizen group will seek information on patrons who support environmental causes. Second, the organized interest applies for patron support. The application process is straightforward: the organized interest fills out some forms, discusses its qualifications, and spells out how the granted funds will be used. In all, procuring patron support is analogous to applying for a scholarship. Just as a scholarship-seeking student does research to determine what group might be willing to give him or her college money, a patronage-seeking organized interest does research to determine who might be willing to give it money. Then, just as a scholarship-seeking student applies for the scholarships that he or she feels qualified for, an organized interest applies for the patronage that it feels it qualified for.

There is no guarantee that an organized interest that wants patronage will get it. Some organized interests cannot locate any patrons willing to support them. Others locate patrons willing to support them, but nonetheless have their applications for patron support rejected. Fortunately for patronage-hungry organized interests, over the past twenty-five years an extensive funding infrastructure has developed that helps organized interests locate potential patrons and procure patron support. The cornerstone of this infrastructure is the Foundation Center, a nonprofit educational institution funded by foundation and corporate patrons.

The Foundation Center acts as a clearinghouse for information on how and where organizations can obtain patron support. It has an annual budget of over $10 million and publishes a variety of indexes, directories, and guidebooks. For example, to help organized interests locate potential foundation patrons, the center publishes *The Foundation Directory,* an annual volume that contains information about thousands of private foundations and which types of organizations and causes each supports. It publishes several other annual volumes, including *The National Data Book,* a directory of foundation patrons in America; *Foundation Grants Quarterly,* a directory of recent foundation grants by state and subject; and *Corporate Foundation Profiles,* which contains comprehensive analyses of over 200 of the largest corporate patrons in America. It also publishes a number of books designed to help organizations procure money once they have located patrons willing to support them. For years, for example, the center has sold *Securing Your Organization's Future,* a book that contains help on how organizations can craft winning patronage applications.[4]

A number of other organizations publish volumes designed to help patronage-seeking groups as well. For example, the Taft Group publishes annual volumes including the *Corporate Giving Directory* and *The Foundation Reporter,* as well as two monthly newsletters, *Corporate Giving Watch* and *Foundation Giving Watch.*[5] All of these sources help organized interests identify and locate potential patrons. In addition, organized interests that wish to secure government support can consult government publications such as the *Catalog of Domestic Assistance, Federal Grants and Contracts Weekly,* and *The Federal Register,* which contain information on government grants and contracts.

The role of patrons in funding the activities of citizen groups and think tanks begs the following question: Why would a wealthy individual, corporation, or other patron donate large sums of money to an organized interest? Research suggests that the answer is twofold.[6] First, some patrons—especially wealthy individuals—provide patronage in return for purposive benefits. For example, wealthy individuals may provide patronage for a citizen group whose goals they share because it makes them feel as if they are "pitching in" and "doing their part" for the cause. Similarly, many labor unions provide money for liberal citizen groups because they support the groups' policy goals and wish to help advance them. Second, some patrons—corporations in particular—provide patronage because it provides them with material benefits. For example, many oil companies donate money to environmental citizen groups because they believe they will boost their public image, which is good for their bottom line. In short, oil companies believe that patronage eventually translates into material rewards: profits for the company.

Recruiting Members and Tapping Them for Donations

Many organized interests obtain money by recruiting members and tapping them for large donations. For example, most membership organized interests, including citizen groups, professional associations, trade associations, labor unions, churches, charities, coalitions, and political action committees, get most of their money from members. The primary means by which members provide money for organized interests is through the payment of membership dues. However, many members provide additional money by making donations above and beyond membership dues.

Few people go out of their way looking for organized interests to join. In other words, most people who join organized interests must be asked to do so. There are several methods by which membership organized interests recruit new members.

Direct Mail Advertising

The most common method is direct mail advertising—member recruitment through the mail. The direct mail advertising process starts with a *mailing list*—a list of names and addresses. Seldom do membership organized interests send direct mail blindly, that is, to a random bunch of people.[7] Instead, they start with *prospect lists*—lists of people who are likely to respond.[8] These prospect lists consist of people who have joined similar groups in the past. The prospect mailing list for an environmental citizen group, for example, will consist of people who have supported environmental causes in the past. Organized interests either rent prospect lists from list brokers specializing in putting together such lists or buy prospect lists from other organized interests with similar concerns.[9] The next step in the direct mail advertising process is to design a *direct mail package*—the parcel that contains the organization's direct mail advertisement. The typical direct mail package contains either a *front-end premium* or a *back-end premium* designed to make membership more attractive. A front-end premium is a free sample of something designed to captivate the direct mail recipient.[10] Common front-end premiums are personalized return address labels, stickers, and postcards. The idea behind a front-end premium is to show the potential member how beneficial joining up can be. A back-end premium is something that a new member will receive in addition to regular membership benefits, should he or she decide to join the organization.[11] Common back-end premiums are calendars, books, seals, and stamps.

To give you an idea of how an actual direct mail package looks, I will describe a mailing that I recently received from an environmental citizen group called the Natural Resources Defense Council (NRDC). The package consisted of four main items: an outside envelope, an appeal letter, a front-end premium, and a return envelope. The package came in a large (8 × 10) outside envelope, upon which the following words were printed in bold:

> "There is only one place left in North America where magnificent gray whales can give birth and raise their young without human interference. But maybe not for long . . . The Mitsubishi Corporation plans to build a massive industrial operation right next to the gray whale's last refuge."

Below this statement was another: "Inside: A personal letter from Robert F. Kennedy Jr." These statements are designed to set this letter apart from other "junk mail." Inside the package was an appeal letter. The letter, like most appeal letters, emphasizes a threat.[12] In this case, the threat is, in the words of the NRDC, the disappearance of "our continent's most spectacular wildlife nursery," which is threatened by "a massive industrial operation" planned by the Japanese company Mitsubishi. Interspersed throughout the rest of the letter are other words and phrases designed to appeal to the reader's emotions. For example, the letter warns that if the proposed industrial operation is not stopped, "toxic salt brine waste with deadly concentrations of magnesium, bromides, and other chemicals" will be pumped into the ocean. Such toxic waste, we are told, has "already killed 94 endangered sea turtles at a nearby Mitsubishi saltworks." Then the letter emphasizes how effective the group has been in the past and how effective it is likely to be in the future. The NRDC, we learn in the letter, "is a hard-hitting group with more than 150 attorneys, scientists, and environmental professionals who know how to get results." In addition, we are told that the NRDC has won many "important victories" and played a role in the "phase-out of lead in gasoline, the international treaty to protect the ozone layer, and the restriction of clearcutting in National Forests." Finally, the letters ask the reader to come aboard and offer a donation. "I am urging you to join forces with the Natural Resources Defense Council today," the letter reads, "to help us mobilize an all-out continent-wide protest on behalf of the whales."

The third item inside the direct mail package is a front-end premium—a picture postcard of a newborn gray whale. The fourth and final item inside the direct mail package is the return envelope—an envelope in which I can send the NRDC my money. The NRDC's direct mail package provides a great deal of insight into how organized interests use direct mail advertising to try to overcome the barriers to survival described in Chapter 3. The package, like most direct mail packages, tackles these barriers "head on." First, by its mere existence, the package attempts to deal with the cost barrier. Indeed, a major purpose of this direct mail package is to raise money for organizational maintenance. Second, the package attempts to overcome the political efficacy problem by trying to convince the recipient that a donation can "make a difference." The letter reads: "Your support will work to save the Gray whale. We can only defeat Mitsubishi if you make *your* voice heard—and *your* support felt." In essence, the letter says: "You are not a politically inefficacious person. Your contribution can make a difference. Your participation is important." Finally, the NRDC's direct mail package attempts to overcome the "free-rider" problem by providing a selective benefit and promising more such benefits in the future. The free postcard suggests that membership comes with certain privileges.

Membership organized interests use direct mail advertising primarily to recruit members. But they also use it to ask their members for money over and above membership dues. The process by which membership organized interests ask members for money is similar to that by which they recruit members. They start with a list—except in this case it is a list of their own members, so no prospect list is necessary. Then a direct mail package is sent in which a special appeal is made—one that tells the member that the organization needs "special help" at this time, usually because of some threat to the organization's goals. Direct mail expert R. Kenneth Godwin notes that most direct mail requests to members use fear to convince people that they must donate money "before it's too late."[13] Indeed, the mailing described in the opening vignette of this chapter is typical of the type of fear-mongering that is common in direct mail advertising.

Direct mail advertising to recruit members and tap members for donations is most common in charities, unaffiliated PACs, and citizen groups, but it is also common in professional associations, trade associations, and labor unions. The Chamber of Commerce of the United States, for example, often sends direct mail solicitations to potential members—people who have recently started businesses or businesspeople who are not currently members. Membership organizations spend a great deal of time and money designing their direct mail packages in order to get as much of a response as possible. Getting people to respond, however, is not easy. Studies show that even the most effective direct mail advertising campaign elicits a 2 to 3 percent response rate.[14]

On-line Computer Solicitation

There are two basic ways that organized interests use the Internet to recruit members and raise money. First, they use their web sites to tout their goals, accomplishments, and membership benefits.[15] Virtually every web site of an organized interest contains information on group membership—typically detailed information on precisely how an individual can join and what members get in return for membership dues. Second, membership organized interests recruit members and tap them for donations by sending out bulk e-mail. Bulk e-mail is much like regular direct mail, except that it arrives in a person's electronic mailbox. On-line solicitation remains in its embryonic stage. However, experts on fund raising predict that it is the wave of the future because it is easy and relatively inexpensive.[16]

Direct Telephone Marketing

Direct telephone marketing is like direct mail advertising, except that it uses the telephone rather than the mail. Studies have shown that direct telephone marketing is not very effective at recruiting new members, but *is* very effective in raising additional money from members.[17] Direct telephone marketing by organized interests is virtually identical to direct telephone marketing by telemarketing firms.

Personal Solicitation

Finally, some organized interests recruit members and raise money by means of personal solicitation—that is, by making direct contact with individuals. For example, some organized interests—the environmental citizen group Greenpeace and the civil rights group NAACP are prominent examples—raise money and recruit members in door-to-door campaigns.[18] Other organized interests recruit members and raise money at public events such as parades, festivals, and fairs. For example, a number of liberal citizen groups, including the antigun citizen group Handgun Control Inc. and the prochoice citizen group the National Abortion Rights Action League, have sent recruiters to large rock music festivals.[19] Finally, many organized interests recruit members and raise money by holding fund-raising events such as dinners and conferences. Most citizen groups, for example, have annual banquets at which they ask members to donate.

Sales of Goods and Services

Many organized interests obtain money from the sale of goods and services. Of course, corporations rely almost exclusively on the sales of goods and services to obtain money. But many noncorporate organized interests, including certain citizen groups, professional associations, trade associations, labor unions, churches, charities, think tanks, and colleges and universities, obtain some of their money in this way. Citizen groups are particularly noteworthy in the extent to which they obtain money from sales. The Sierra Club, for example, sells books, calendars, T-shirts, topographical maps, and greeting cards to members and nonmembers alike. In fact, sales are so important to the Sierra Club that it has its own bookstore (in Oakland, California), as well as an on-line store with a huge variety of items.[20] Another influential citizen group that relies heavily on sales is Consumers Union, the consumer advocacy group that gets almost all of its money from the sale of its magazine, *Consumer Reports*.

In all, hundreds of citizen groups earn some income from sales. But citizen groups are hardly alone in this regard. Almost all think tanks, for example, receive some money from the sale of books, research reports, and monographs.

Ralph Nader, government watchdog Monitoring—keeping track of what government is up to—is important for organized interests of all kinds. In fact, many organized interests are founded primarily to act as government "watchdogs." Ralph Nader (pictured here), the Green Party candidate for president in 2000, came to prominence in the 1960s when he founded the government "watchdog" group Public Citizen. *AP/Wide World Photos.*

For example, the Heritage Foundation, a high-profile conservative think tank, has its own on-line bookstore that sells hundreds of books published by the foundation's own press.[21] Even trade associations and labor unions sometimes use this avenue. Recently, for example, the United Farm Workers (UFW) labor union began selling a number of items, including prints of a famous Octavio Ocampo portrait of UFW founder Cesar Chavez, T-shirts with the UFW logo, and UFW mouse pads.[22] Similarly, the Chamber of Commerce of the United States sells a number of business-related publications, as well as a retirement program for small business owners.

Thus far, we have focused exclusively on the sales of goods, but some organized interests sell services as well. For example, the Chamber of Commerce of the United States has a number of consultants and staff people for hire. Through its Statistics and Research Center, it offers buyers "research, statistical information, and survey services that can enhance the operations and profitability of [a] business or organization."[23] Similarly, the American Federation of Government Employees, a labor union, sells legal services, mortgage and real estate financing, personal loans, dental insurance, and accidental death and dismemberment insurance.[24]

The Enduring Importance of Organizational Maintenance

In the end, it is impossible to overestimate the importance of organizational maintenance. Without resources, organized interests have no chance to achieve their political goals. The overriding imperative to raise funds means that many organized interests spend more time and energy on seeking and obtaining resources than they do on attempting to influence public policy.

MONITORING

Another nonlobbying activity is crucially important to organized interests of all kinds: *monitoring,* that is, keeping track of what government is up to. Monitoring is important for four reasons. First, it helps organized interests determine what their true interests are. The preeminent scholar of monitoring, Robert Salisbury, has noted that "the great expansion in the scope of [government] programs since World War II . . . has meant that many more elements of society are far more extensively affected by what the government does" than ever before.[25] As such, keeping track of what government does is very important. Continuing, Salisbury notes that

> in today's world of complex, interdependent interests and policies, it is often unclear what the "true interests" of [an organized interest] may be. The policy that will be maximally advantageous to an association often cannot even be framed without pro-

longed and searching analysis involving extensive discussion among those who are knowledgeable about both the technical substance of the issue and the feasibilities of the relevant political situation.[26]

Another way to put it is like this: monitoring helps organized interests determine where they stand on specific policy issues. Before organized interests can advocate a particular policy, they must find out what policy will best serve their interests.[27] A hypothetical example here is illustrative. Assume that Congress is considering federal legislation ostensibly designed to combat global warming. Now assume that you work for the National Association of Manufacturers, a massive trade association consisting of manufacturing companies. Before you do anything else—that is, before you take a stand on the legislation or begin lobbying—you must learn more about the legislation. What are its provisions? Will the law hurt or help your member companies? Are there alternative pieces of legislation being considered? How are they different? All of these questions must be answered before an organized interest undertakes political activity.

Monitoring can also provide important information about which lobbying strategies and tactics might be most effective. For example, if an organized interest is thinking about approaching a particular policymaker about an issue, it may like to know where that policymaker stands on the issue. If an organized interest finds, for example, that Republican members of Congress are completely unreceptive to its message, it may concentrate its effort on Democrats. Similarly, if an organized interest learns that a certain policy proposal has no chance at the federal level, it may shift its focus to the states. We will have much more to explore about lobbying strategies in the chapters that follow. For now, it must suffice to say that one of the reasons that organized interests monitor government is to gather information about what types of lobbying strategies are most likely to be effective.

Some organized interests monitor government to keep themselves and/or their members out of trouble. Political scientist Richard Harris notes that corporations, for example, spend a great deal of time and effort monitoring because government regulations and rules proscribe many aspects of their behavior.[28] There are literally hundreds of laws, rules, and regulations on the books that prohibit these companies from engaging in certain types of behavior such as polluting, hiring undocumented workers, and requiring people to work overtime for no pay. The costs of ignoring these laws, rules, and regulations are potentially high: fines can be imposed, executives can be punished, and profits can be threatened. Thus, it behooves the manufacturing companies to monitor government closely in order to keep up to date on new rules and regulations. Other types of organized interests that monitor to keep themselves out of trouble include domestic governmental entities and universities and colleges, which must keep abreast of government mandates.

Finally, many membership organized interests monitor government to gather information that they can pass on to their members. Environmental citizen groups, for example, keep abreast of governmental developments regarding the environment. They then pass this information on to their members, whom they know are keenly interested in environmental issues. Similarly, the AARP keeps a close watch on changes in social security and Medicare so that it can provide information to its elderly members who rely on these programs. Political scientist Paul Johnson has noted that many organized interests use the information that they obtain from monitoring government as a selective incentive to attract and keep members.[29] The types of organized interests that monitor to gather information for their members include citizen groups, professional associations, charities, churches, labor unions, professional associations, and PACs.

Most organized interests have several staff people whose job is to monitor government. In addition, most lobbyists spend a great deal of their own time monitoring.[30] Essentially, monitoring entails doing research—digging up reliable information on what government is up to. Where does this information come from? First, there are newspapers, magazines, and television and radio news broadcasts. Like the rest of us, organized interests rely to some extent on popular news publications and broadcasts. In fact, most studies of individual lobbyists suggest that most lobbyists start their days by reading the *New York Times* or the *Washington Post* or, if they operate in a state or a city, the local paper of record.[31] Second, organized interests obtain information from government itself. As you will see in the chapters that follow, governmental bodies at all levels of government often have meetings, proceedings, and hearings that are open to the public. City councils, for example, hold periodic public meetings, as do state and federal legislative committees and executive agencies. Public hearings and meetings offer a great deal of information about what government is doing.

While most ordinary citizens ignore such public proceedings, lobbyists and other organized interest personnel do not. Particularly when something pertinent to their organized interest is at stake, organized interest personnel attend public proceedings and pay attention to what happens there. In fact, it is no exaggeration to say that in the vast majority of governmental public proceedings, organized interest personnel outnumber ordinary citizens by a wide margin.

Organized interests also obtain information about what government is up to from specialized government publications. Governmental bodies at all levels of government issue publications that provide information about what they do. On the federal level, for example, the *Federal Register* lists new and pending government regulations. Most state governments publish similar volumes. Similarly, Congress and most state legislatures publish the legislative transcripts of hearings, as well as copies of new and pending laws. And at the local level, many cities and counties publish the minutes of public meetings. Finally, organized interests often obtain information from government policymakers themselves. As you will see in the next few chapters, many lobbyists spend a great deal of time with government policymakers and their staffs. Part of the reason they do so is to gather important information about what government is doing or planning to do.

In sum, monitoring helps organized interests determine their true interests and plan their lobbying strategies. In addition, some organized interests monitor to keep themselves and their members out of trouble, and others monitor to keep their members abreast of government activities.

SELF-GOVERNANCE

The final nonlobbying activity that we consider is self-governance: making decisions about how the organization goes about its business. All organized interests must make decisions about matters such as whom to hire and fire; how to raise money; how, whom, and where to lobby; and what issues to focus on. Making these decisions is not easy. Even in small and simple organizations, there are many conflicting points of view to consider and many options available.

The vast majority of organized interests organize themselves hierarchically to make self-governance easier and more efficient. Organizing hierarchically simply means giving some personnel more power and authority over decisions than others. The hierarchical structure that an organized interest chooses provides a basic framework in which organizational decisions are made. Although there is truly an infinite variety of ways whereby organized interests organize themselves, political scientists have studied self-governance in some detail and have reached a number of general conclusions about how organized interests organize themselves for self-governance.

First, most organized interests have a leader, variously called president, executive director, chairperson, chief operating officer, or chief executive. For organized interests that exist primarily for a political purpose—such as citizen groups, PACs, coalitions, and think tanks—the leader is unquestionably the most important person in the organization. This person oversees the day-to-day operations of the organization and, perhaps with a small cadre of other executives, sets the organization's political priorities and makes final decisions about whom, where, and on what issues to lobby; whom to hire and whom to fire; how to spend the organization's money; and how to raise money and recruit members. For organized interests that exist primarily or partially for a nonpolitical purpose, the leader is extremely important, but less so when it comes to making decisions about organizational involvement in politics. For these types of organized interests, the leader generally delegates the responsibility for political decisions to others within the organization. In most corporations, trade associations, professional associations, labor unions, colleges and universities, governmental entities, churches, and charities, for example, the leader spends most of his or her time on nonpolitical matters and delegates responsibility for decisions about political activities to the leader of a separate public affairs or governmental relations division. This is especially true in large organized interests. For example, in the typical corporation, the CEO spends most of his or her time on nonpolitical matters and delegates responsibility for decisions about political activities to the leader of a separate public affairs division.

Second, most organized interests have a board of directors—a small group of people who are the ultimate source of formal authority for the organization. Boards of directors of organized interests vary greatly. Highly paid corporate boards, for example, have very little in common with volunteer citizen group or charity boards. Nonetheless, there are some commonalities. First, most boards act more or less as oversight bodies—assemblies that meet periodically to evaluate how the organization is doing and to consider major changes. Second, most boards of directors have little say in the day-to-day activities of the organizations they oversee. Rather than micromanaging the organization, they tend to set basic rules, policies, and priorities and leave day-to-day decisions to leaders and staff people. Third, most boards have a large voice in choosing their organization's leader. Because the leader of an organized interest is usually highly influential, choosing a leader is an important responsibility.

Third, most organized interests have staff—people who perform day-to-day organizational activities such as monitoring, organizational maintenance, and lobbying and are answerable to the organization's leader. In essence, an organized interest's staff comprises the people who do the work of the organization. Most organized interests have two tiers of staff. On the top tier are executives and other managers who work closely with the leader and have some independent authority to make decisions. Many organized interests have executives who report directly to the leader and have some control over important decisions. Below this top tier is a lower tier of staff who does the organization's filing, answering telephones, and sending out mail. Staff size varies greatly by organization. Some of the country's best-known organized interests have thousands of staff members, and others are run and staffed entirely by one or two people.

Most organized interests have a leader, a board, and a staff. Beyond this, it is difficult to make any definitive statements about the ways that organized interests structure themselves for self-governance. There is, however, one other thing that political scientists have discovered about organized interest self-governance: in the vast majority of cases—no matter what organizational structure is adopted—decision making within organized interests tends not to be very democratic. Virtually everyone who studies organized interests agrees that true internal democracy is rare.[32] It is not hard to see why. First, many types of organizations are inherently undemocratic. Institutional organized interests such as corporations, governmental entities, and colleges and universities, for example, cannot very well be democratic because they do not represent the interests of people. Second, even organizations that do have members find it difficult, inefficient, and bothersome to include members in the decision-making process. Early in this century, political scientist Robert Michels formulated what is known as the *iron law of oligarchy*, which holds that within all organizations, a relatively small group of professionals dominate decision making.[33] Oligarchy is inevitable in most organizations, Michels argues, because running an organization, especially a large and complex one, takes special expertise and skills that are not commonly held by rank-and-file organization members. In addition, allowing rank-and-file members to have input over decisions is incredibly inefficient.

None of this is to say, however, that members have no voice over the decisions of the organized interests to which they belong. Some types of organized interests—especially citizen groups, labor unions, and trade associations—make special efforts to include members in the decision-making process. Most labor unions, for example, allow union members to choose their leaders in periodic elections. Similarly, many citizen groups allow rank-and-file members to elect some or all of their board members. In addition, many organized interests allow rank-and-file members mechanisms to communicate their desires to group leaders. The citizen group Common Cause, for example, polls its members periodically and asks them what issues they think are most important.[34] Similarly, many trade associations have advisory committees that consist of the heads of member firms. Second, members in any voluntary organization always have the option of exiting the organization if they are unhappy with its direction.[35] This provides a powerful incentive for an organization's leaders to be at least somewhat responsive to members' needs and desires.

In sum, self-governance is an important task for organized interests of all kinds. Most organized interests organize themselves hierarchically. This means that they have a leader, a board of directors, and staff. In most organized interests, important decisions are left to a handful of people, and members have limited input.

CONCLUSION: THE IMPORTANCE OF NONLOBBYING ACTIVITIES

It is easy to lose sight of the fact that in addition to lobbying, organized interests do several other things. This chapter has highlighted three of them: organizational maintenance, monitoring, and self-governance. Without question, the most important nonlobbying activity in which organized interests engage is organizational maintenance. Organizational maintenance is crucially important because if an organized interest does not survive, it will not be able to influence public policy. In short, survival must be the preeminent goal of any organized interest.

The key to organizational maintenance is obtaining money. Organized interests go about acquiring money in several different ways. Some acquire money in the course of performing their primary functions. Corporations, for example, acquire money by selling goods and services. Most other types of organized interests obtain money from some combination of patrons, members, and sales. To give you an idea of how important organizational maintenance is, consider this: the typical organized interest spends less than half of its revenues on political activity.[36] Institutions, in fact, typically spend less than 10 percent of their revenues on political activity.[37]

Monitoring is also extremely important for organized interests of all kinds. Keeping track of what government is doing helps organized interests obtain the information they need to be effective advocates. It also allows them to keep themselves and their members "out of trouble" and to keep their members abreast of what government is up to. In the end, monitoring is more important than it is glamorous.

Finally, all organized interests must engage in self-governance. The variety of organizational forms from which organizations can choose is virtually infinite. Therefore, it is hard to reach definitive conclusions about how organized interests organize themselves for self-governance. We can, however, make a few broad generalizations. First, most organized interests have a leader who is invested with great power. Second, most have a board of directors that oversees organizational activities. Third, most have staff who perform the day-to-day tasks that keep the organization running smoothly. And finally, most are undemocratic in their decision-making processes. Even organized interests that presume to represent the public tend to be dominated by a small group of individuals.

No one has ever done a thorough study of how much time, energy, and money organized interests spend on nonlobbying activities. It is safe to say, however, that many, if not most, spend more time on nonlobbying activities than they do on lobbying activities. This is surely the case with organized interests such as corporations, universities and colleges, governmental entities, labor unions, charities, and churches, which exist primarily for nonpolitical purposes. Similarly, many types of organized interests that exist for a multitude of purposes—trade associations and professional associations come to mind— surely spend a great deal of time, money, and energy on nonpolitical activities. And even explicitly political organized interests such as citizen groups and think tanks must be preoccupied with survival, which forces them to spend vital resources on obtaining money rather than on engaging in political activity. In the end, it is important to remember that organized interests of all kinds are multifaceted organizations that perform multiple functions. No organized interest lives by politics alone.

What's Next

The primary reason to study organized interests is that they lobby—that is, they try to influence public policy. Thus, as important as nonlobbying activities are to a full understanding of organized interest politics in the United States, lobbying is even more important. It is so important, in fact, that it is the subject of the next four chapters of this book. We begin our exploration of lobbying with two simple questions: What exactly is lobbying? And why do organized interests do it?

EXERCISES

1. Choose a citizen group. Find out what proportion of its budget it spends on fund raising.
2. Check your mail every day for two weeks for a direct mail advertisement from an organized interest. (If you cannot find one in your own mail, ask your friends and family to be on the lookout for one.) Once you have located a direct mail advertisement, answer the following questions: What is the name of the organized interest? What does it want from you? Does the direct mail package contain a front-end premium? If so, what is it? Does the direct mail package promise a back-end premium? If so, what is it? Does the direct mail appeal letter use fear and anxiety as a motivator? If so, what words and phrases are designed to elicit fear or anxiety? Does the appeal letter emphasize a threat? If so, what is that threat? How does the advertisement use persuasive language and/or images?
3. Pick one of the following oil companies: ARCO (Atlantic Richfield), BP (British Petroleum), Conoco, Exxon, Mobil, Shell, or Texaco. Does the company provide monetary support for any other organized interests? If so, find out which ones. Now imagine that you are the CEO of the company you chose. If your company did provide support for one or more organized interests, provide a justification for doing so. If your company did not provide support, provide justification for not doing so.

RESEARCH RESOURCES

Publications

Corporate foundation annual reports. Many corporations support organized interests through corporate foundations—separate organizations set up to provide support for nonprofit organizations. Corporate foundations are required by law to publish annual reports detailing their activities. The best way to obtain a corporate foundation's annual report is to contact the foundation directly.

Web Resources

Citizen group web sites. A particularly useful on-line directory of citizen group web sites is located at *http://policy.com/community/advoc*.

Oil industry web sites. To learn more about the political interests of the oil industry, go to *http://oil.com,* an on-line news service and directory for the oil and gas industry. Another useful site is *www.oillink.com.* To locate the sites of specific oil companies, use an Internet search engine.

Notes

1. Jonathan Freedland, "Right in Disarray as Bush Quits Gun Lobby," *Guardian,* May 12, 1999, p. 16; Sam How Verhovek, "Bush Resigns from the NRA: Ex-president Enraged over Fund-Raising Letter," *Denver Post,* May 11, 1999, p. A8.
2. James Q. Wilson, *Political Organizations* (Princeton, NJ: Princeton University Press, 1995), p. 10.
3. Jack L. Walker, "The Organization and Maintenance of Interest Groups in America," *American Political Science Review* 77 (June 1983): 390–406.
4. Foundation Center, "Publications and Electronic Resources," accessed at *http://fdncenter.org/marketplace/catalog/index,* September 23, 1999.
5. Taft Group, "Taft Catalog Online," accessed at *http://taftgroup.com,* September 23, 1999.
6. Anthony J. Nownes, "The Other Exchange: Public Interest Groups, Patrons, and Benefits," *Social Science Quarterly* 76 (June 1995): 381–401.
7. R. Kenneth Godwin, "Money, Technology, and Political Interests: The Direct Marketing of Politics," in Mark P. Petracca, ed., *The Politics of Interests: Interest Groups Transformed* (Boulder, CO: Westview Press, 1992), chap. 14; Paul E. Johnson, "Interest Group Recruiting: Finding Members and Keeping Them," in Allan J. Cigler and Burdett A. Loomis, eds., *Interest Group Politics* (5th ed.) (Washington, DC: Congressional Quarterly Press, 1998), chap. 2.
8. Godwin, "Money, Technology, and Political Interests: The Direct Marketing of Politics," in Mark P. Petracca, ed., *The Politics of Interests: Interest Groups Transformed* (Boulder, CO: Westview Press, 1992), p. 310.
9. Johnson, "Interest Group Recruiting: Finding Members and Keeping Them," in Allan J. Cigler and Burdett A. Loomis, eds., *Interest Group Politics* (5th ed.) (Washington, DC: Congressional Quarterly Press, 1998), p. 50.
10. Ibid., p. 48.
11. Ibid.
12. Godwin, "Money, Technology, and Political Interests: The Direct Marketing of Politics," in Mark P. Petracca, ed., *The Politics of Interests: Interest Groups Transformed* (Boulder, CO: Westview Press, 1992), p. 310.
13. Ibid.
14. Johnson, "Interest Group Recruiting: Finding Members and Keeping Them," in Allan J. Cigler and Burdett A. Loomis, eds., *Interest Group Politics* (5th ed.) (Washington, DC: Congressional Quarterly Press, 1998), pp. 48–51.
15. Luis Cabrera, "Extremist Groups Using Internet to Recruit, Guide Members," *Associated Press Newswires,* February 26, 2000.

16. Ibid.

17. Johnson, "Interest Group Recruiting: Finding Members and Keeping Them," in Allan J. Cigler and Burdett A. Loomis, eds., *Interest Group Politics* (5th ed.) (Washington, DC: Congressional Quarterly Press, 1998), Godwin, "Money, Technology, and Political Interests: The Direct Marketing of Politics," in Mark P. Petracca, ed., *The Politics of Interests: Interest Groups Transformed* (Boulder, CO: Westview Press, 1992), p. 312.

18. Erin Texeira, "Civil Rights Group Launches Recruitment Bid—NAACP Members to Go Door to Door," *Seattle Times,* August 15, 1999, p. A3.

19. Jim DeRogatis, "Some Food for Thought: Sideshows Make Political Issues Easy to Digest," *Chicago Sun-Times,* June 27, 1993, p. 5; David Klinghoffer, "Fair Lilith," *National Review,* September 14, 1998, p. 70; Jennifer Pinkerton, "RFK Will Shake, Rattle, and Roll," *Washington Times,* May 12, 1994, p. M18.

20. Sierra Club, "Sierra Club Books," accessed at *http://www.sierraclub.org/books,* November 30, 1999.

21. Heritage Foundation, accessed at *http://www.heritage.org/bookstore,* September 29, 1999.

22. United Farm Workers, accessed at *http://www.ufw.org/ufw/etgst,* September 29, 1999.

23. U.S. Chamber of Commerce, "Programs and Services," accessed at *http://uschamber .com/programs/research,* September 29, 1999.

24. American Federation of Government Employees, "It Pays to Be an AFGE Member," accessed at *http://www.afge.org/splash,* December 6, 1999.

25. Robert H. Salisbury, "The Paradox of Interest Groups in Washington—More Groups, Less Clout," in Anthony King, ed., *The New American Political System,* Second Version (Washington, DC: American Enterprise Institute, 1991), p. 225.

26. Ibid.

27. Ibid., pp. 225–226.

28. Richard A. Harris, *Coal Firms Under the New Social Regulation* (Durham, NC: Duke University Press, 1985).

29. Johnson, "Interest Group Recruiting: Finding Members and Keeping Them," in Allan J. Cigler and Burdett A. Loomis, eds., *Interest Group Politics* (5th ed.) (Washington, DC: Congressional Quarterly Press, 1998), pp. 43–45.

30. Salisbury, "The Paradox of Interest Groups in Washington—More Groups, Less Clout," in Anthony King, ed., *The New American Political System,* Second Version (Washington, DC: American Enterprise Institute, 1991), pp. 225–226.

31. Bruce Wolpe and Bertram J. Levine, *Lobbying Congress: How the System Works* (2nd ed.) (Washington, DC: Congressional Quarterly Press, 1996), pp. 20–33.

32. Jeffrey M. Berry, *The New Liberalism: The Rising Power of Citizen Groups* (Washington, DC: Brookings Institution, 1999), pp. 164–167; Jeffrey Berry, *Lobbying for the People* (Princeton, NJ: Princeton University Press, 1977), pp. 186–212; Kelly Patterson, "The Political Firepower of the National Rifle Association," in Cigler and Loomis, eds., *Interest Group Politics,* chap. 6; David Truman, *The Governmental Process: Political Interests and Public Opinion* (2nd ed.) (New York: Knopf, 1971), chap. 5.

33. Robert Michels, *Political Parties* (New York: Free Press, 1958 [1915]).

34. Common Cause, "About Common Cause," accessed at *http://www.commoncause.org/about/faq,* March 25, 2000; Andrew S. McFarland, *Common Cause: Lobbying in the Public Interest* (Chatham, NJ: Chatham House Publishers, 1984).

35. Albert O. Hirschman, *Exit, Voice, and Loyalty* (Cambridge, MA: Harvard University Press, 1970).

36. Anthony J. Nownes, "Where Does the Money Go?" Unpublished manuscript (1997), p. 3.

37. Ibid., p. 2.

Direct Lobbying, Part I—
Formal Lobbying

Phoenix, Arizona
April 30, 1990

> A little after 6:00 P.M., Representative Don Kenney, the chairman of Arizona's House Judiciary Committee, arrives at the office of Joseph Stedino, whom he thought was a shady businessman with underworld ties who is intent on legalizing casino gambling in Arizona. Kenney does not know that Stedino is actually a police informant working with the Phoenix district attorney's office in a major sting operation. After a bit of small talk, Stedino gets down to business. He hands Kenney a wad of bills totaling $55,000 and remarks, "You can call this anything . . . call it a gift, call it legal fees, the bottom line is that I want you to leave here today with your $55,000 understanding that it's really, in reality, it's for your vote." Kenney, eyeing the $55,000 covetously before stuffing it into an empty gym bag he brought to the illicit rendezvous, replies, "I understand that exactly."[1]

Is this what lobbying is all about: bagmen, bribery, shady underworld chicanery, and mendacious policymakers? Are media portrayals of unethical lawmakers and greedy and unctuous lobbyists overblown? Or do they accurately reflect the world of professional lobbyists? Chapters 5 through 8 speak to these questions. Specifically, they ask: What do organized interests and their lobbyists do? Chapters 5 and 6 examine *direct lobbying*—lobbying that entails face-to-face contact with public officials. Chapter 5 looks at *formal direct lobbying*—lobbying that entails contact with public officials in their offices or at formal governmental proceedings. And Chapter 6 examines *informal direct lobbying*—lobbying that entails contact with policymakers outside formal governmental processes. Chapter 7 examines the most controversial form of lobbying: *lobbying with campaign money*. Finally, Chapter 8 deals with *indirect lobbying*—lobbying that is aimed at citizens rather than public officials. If there is one central message of the following four chapters, it is this: lobbying takes a huge variety of forms. And contrary to the received wisdom, seldom is lobbying either dirty or sleazy. Most lobbyists go about their work in a routine, lawful, and businesslike manner.

This chapter begins our examination of lobbying with a look at the most common general form of lobbying: formal direct lobbying. We start with the question: Why do organized interests lobby? From here, we explore how lobbyists interact formally with policymakers in an attempt to influence what they do.

WHY LOBBY GOVERNMENT?

Why do so many organizations lobby government? After all, no organization *has* to lobby. Corporations, for example, can simply go about their business of trying to make money. Many companies, in fact, choose not to lobby at all. Similarly, colleges and universities, think tanks, governments, foreign countries, and other institutions can eschew lobbying and perform solely their primary functions. Membership organizations too can eschew lobbying if they wish. Professional associations, citizen groups, labor unions, and trade associations, for example, can provide information to their members, hold meetings, and do other things, while ignoring politics altogether.

In sum, lobbying is a choice, not an inevitability. The answer to the question of why so many organizations in America feel the need to lobby government is intuitive and straightforward: organizations lobby government because they want to affect what government does. This, of course, begs the following question: Why do so many organizations feel the need to affect what government does? The answer is, Because what government does affects them. It is virtually impossible to think of a government policy that does not affect some organization or interest. In fact, most government policies affect numerous organizations and interests. Several years ago, this point was driven home to me as I conducted a study of a relatively unknown but far-reaching piece of legislation called the Federal Insecticide, Fungicide, and Rodenticide Act (FIFRA).

FIFRA, originally adopted in the late 1940s and amended several times since, empowers the federal government to ban pesticides it deems unsafe. As Table 5.1 shows, during a series of congressional hearings on FIFRA in 1987, a startling number and variety of organized interests showed up in Washington to have their voices heard. On one side, environmental, labor, citizen, and governmental organized interests lobbied for tougher regulations. Environmental organized interests and many governmental entities worried about the environmental dangers of pesticide use, consumer organized interests worried about a tainted food supply, and labor unions worried about the health hazards of working with dangerous chemicals. On the other side, corporations, professional associations, and trade associations tried to thwart tougher regulations. Agricultural trade associations argued that pesticides protected crops from

TABLE 5.1 Organized Interests Represented at FIFRA 1987 House Committee Hearings

Citizen Groups
    Center for Science in the Public Interest
    Chesapeake Bay Foundation
    Consumers Union
    Friends of the Earth
    Human Ecology Action League
    Humane Society of the United States
    National Audubon Society
    National Wildlife Federation
    Pesticide Public Policy Foundation
    Public Citizen's Congress Watch
    Public Voice for Food and Health Policy
    Sierra Club
    U.S. Public Interest Research Group
Coalitions
    Maryland Alliance for the Responsible Regulation of Pesticides
    National Coalition against the Misuse of Pesticides
Corporations
    ConAgra Inc.
    FMC Corp.
    Griffin Corp.
    Prentiss Drug and Chemical Corp.
Governmental Entities
    Department of Environmental Conservation, State of New York
    Montgomery County Council
    Prince Georges County Government
Governmental Entities
    State of California
    State of Iowa
    State of Maryland
    State of Montana
    U.S. Department of Agriculture
    U.S. Environmental Protection Agency
Labor Unions
    AFL-CIO
Professional Associations
    Golf Course Superintendents Association
Trade Associations
    American Association of Nurserymen
    American Farm Bureau Federation
    American Sod Producers Association
    American Wood Preservers Institute
    Chemical Producers and Distributors Association
    Chemical Specialties Manufacturing Association
    Cotton and Grain Producers of the Lower Rio Grande Valley
    Florida Fruit and Vegetable Association
    Grocery Manufacturers of America, Inc.

Continued on next page

TABLE 5.1 (Continued)

Trade Associations (*continued*)

National Agricultural Aviation Association
National Arborist Association
National Cattleman's Association
National Council of Agricultural Employees
National Food Processors Association
National Forest Products Association
National Pest Control Association
Ohio Pesticide Applicators for Responsible Regulation
Professional Lawn Care Association of America
United Fresh Fruit and Vegetable Association

Source: U.S. House of Representatives, House Committee on Agriculture, *Federal Insecticide, Fungicide, and Rodenticide Act Amendments of 1987, Hearings,* April 7, June 10, 16, 17, 1987 (Washington, D.C.: Government Printing Office, 1987), Y4.Ag8/1, pp. 100–113.

dangerous pests, and chemical companies and their trade associations argued that pesticides were safe if used properly and that strict government regulations would cost them millions of dollars.

In the end, Congress passed and the president signed a bill that contained something for both sides. On the one hand, the legislation allowed the federal government to ban pesticides that it deemed unsafe. This provision satisfied organized interests worried about the health and safety aspects of pesticide use. On the other hand, the legislation streamlined the process by which chemical companies could prove to the government that their products were safe. This provision satisfied the producers and users of pesticides who had long argued that bureaucratic red tape inherent in pesticide regulation hamstrung their ability to do business.[2] The main point of this story is not that both sides in the battle over FIFRA got some of what they wanted. Rather, it is that virtually every government decision—large or small; federal, state, or local—is like FIFRA in that it affects some organizations and interests. This is why organized interests lobby government: they know that what government does affects them.

LOBBYING = THE PROVISION OF INFORMATION

In Chapter 1, we defined the term *lobbying* as attempting to influence government decisions. This definition is broad by design. As you will see, lobbying is an exceedingly variegated activity. Nonetheless, all lobbying techniques (except for one, lobbying with campaign money, discussed in Chapter 7) have something in common: they entail the provision of information through policy analysis, political analysis, and/or legal analysis.

Policy Analysis

Policy analysis is the term political scientists use to describe detailed and often technical information about the economic and/or social effects of a proposed or existing policy or program.[3] Lobbyists use policy analysis to make their cases for or against certain policies or programs.

Consider, for example, the type of information that lobbyists for tobacco companies provided Washington lawmakers when they debated antitobacco legislation in 1997 and 1998. The cornerstone of the proposed legislation was a large increase in federal taxes on cigarettes to pay for smoking-prevention programs. Tobacco companies, which opposed the new taxes, provided lawmakers with policy analysis showing that the taxes would be detrimental to the economy. They consulted numerous economists and found that some believed increased cigarette taxes would lead to a black market in cigarettes, much like the black market that existed for alcohol during prohibition. This black market, they said, would defeat the purpose of new taxes. It would actually decrease the price of cigarettes, because by procuring cigarettes through illegal channels, buyers and sellers could avoid taxes altogether. Tobacco lobbyists also argued that higher taxes might decrease government revenues, thus endangering prevention programs. In sum, tobacco lobbyists presented policy analysis—technical and detailed information about the potential effects of new cigarette taxes—to make their case against proposed taxes. This policy analysis was designed to show members of Congress that the taxes they were considering were a bad idea.

This discussion begs the following question: Isn't the policy analysis provided by tobacco (or any other) lobbyists likely to be biased? Of course it is. Lobbyists virtually always present policy analysis that makes their side look good and the other side look bad. This, however, is not the same as lying. In fact, as you will see in the next chapter, lobbyists cannot afford to lie because credibility is an important asset for them. Because policy analysts often come to differing conclusions about the same policy, however, lobbyists can usually find some policy analysis that supports their point of view.

Policy analysis is valuable to policymakers because most government officials truly are interested in making good policy—policy that produces positive results and serves the purposes for which it is designed. Policy analysis gives policymakers access to expert opinions and advice and helps them sort out competing claims.

Political Analysis

Another type of information a lobbyist may provide policymakers is *political analysis*—information about the political effects of a policy decision. Most policymakers certainly care about making good public policy, but they care even more about keeping their jobs and remaining popular with their constituents.

In other words, they care about their political futures. For legislators, chief executives, and other elected officials, political analysis entails information about how a policy proposal or program will affect their reelection chances. For bureaucrats and other appointed officials, political analysis may entail information about how a given policy proposal will affect an agency's budget or workload. Finally, for all types of government officials, political analysis often entails information about what is feasible—that is, what policies have a chance of being adopted. For a governor, for example, political analysis may entail information about the chances a proposal has of being approved by the state legislature.

To understand how a lobbyist might use political information, consider the hypothetical example of a lobbyist for a citizen group that supports the death penalty. Let us say that the governor of Texas has proposed a number of new crimes for which those convicted are eligible for the death penalty. One of the things that the pro–death penalty lobbyist might want to provide state legislators who will vote on the governor's plan is political analysis that shows how popular the death penalty is in Texas. The message inherent in this information is obvious: "You should support the governor's proposal because your constituents support it. If you don't, your constituents may vote for someone else in the next election." Often political analysis consists of poll or survey results. The pro–death penalty lobbyist might, for example, poll 2,000 people in a legislator's district, and if the results show that the legislator's constituents support the death penalty, he or she will show the survey results to the legislator and say, "See, your constituents agree with me!"

Unfortunately, political analysis often conflicts with policy analysis. Policy analysis may show, for example, that the death penalty does not actually affect crime rates, while political analysis shows that the death penalty is massively popular. This paradox can make a policymaker's job somewhat difficult.

Legal Analysis

Finally, lobbyists often provide policymakers with *legal analysis*—information about the legal ramifications of a proposed or existing policy or program. Laws, regulations, rules, and court rulings often raise difficult and complex legal questions. For example, every time a legislature considers passing a law, it must consider whether the law is constitutional, how it may affect other existing laws, and how difficult it will be to enforce. Thus, policymakers often look to lobbyists for legal analysis.

To understand how a lobbyist might use legal analysis, consider the hypothetical example of a lobbyist for a veterans' group that supports a federal law banning flag burning. Members of Congress who support the law know that it raises difficult legal questions. Some people, they realize, believe that banning flag burning may violate people's First Amendment rights to free speech. Supportive members ask themselves: Will any law we pass get declared unconstitutional by the Supreme Court? Is there some way we can craft a law that does not violate the First Amendment? Should we draft a constitutional amendment instead of a law? All of these are legal questions that influence the decisions of lawmakers. Realizing this, the veterans' group lobbyists may wish to give lawmakers legal advice on how to proceed with their flag-burning proposal.

Lobbying = Information Provision: A Summary

In summary, most policymakers face a daunting number of tasks each day and appreciate the fact that lobbyists provide them with information that may help them make decisions. Thus, although the conventional wisdom is that lobbyists often harass policymakers and buttonhole them to say their piece, the reality is that policymakers often value the information that lobbyists provide. In fact, recent research on lobbying shows that policymakers regularly solicit advice from lobbyists.[4] In its rawest form, lobbying amounts to a lobbyist's telling a policymaker, "Please do what I want you to do." Lobbyists know that the best way to get policymakers to heed their advice is to provide them with information that shows that doing so is a good idea.

LOBBYING THE LEGISLATURE

We begin the examination of lobbying techniques by exploring how organized interests and their lobbyists lobby the legislature. Why the legislature? Because at both the federal and state levels, the legislature attracts far more attention from lobbyists than the other branches of government. Recent surveys suggest that over 99 percent of state and federal lobbyists spend at least some of their time lobbying the legislature.[5]

The legislature attracts so much attention from lobbyists for two major reasons. First, in most policy areas, the legislature has the most power. For example, at the federal level, the Constitution gives far more power to Congress than to either the president or the judiciary. To be sure, the other branches of the federal government are far from impotent, but Congress is where most of the action is. As Article 1 of the Constitution states, Congress alone has the power to pass laws, tax, spend, declare war, and approve presidential appointments to the judiciary and the highest levels of the bureaucracy. Similarly, in most states, in most policy areas, the legislature is the most powerful component of government.

Second, the legislature is accessible to lobbyists. Legislatures provide a multitude of access points for lobbyists. Legislatures have lots of members. Congress has 535 members, and most state legislatures have hundreds of them. In contrast, there is only one president, and every state has only one governor.

Legislatures also have lots of staff. Members of Congress, for example, have personal staffs that help members do their jobs. Currently over 11,000 personal staffers are working for members of Congress. House members average between 15 and 20 staffers each, and senators average over 40.[6] State legislators generally have much smaller staffs, but even in sparsely populated states like South Dakota and Vermont, legislators have several personal staff members to assist them. Finally, legislatures are broken up into committees, providing organized interests and their lobbyists yet more points of access to policymakers. Congress, for example, does almost all of its work in standing committees—semipermanent subject matter committees in which bills are written. Currently there are eighteen standing committees in the House and sixteen in the Senate. State legislatures too use standing committees. And beneath each standing committee are numerous subcommittees—smaller units within committees that are first to consider proposed legislation. These provide yet more points of access, as do committee staff—the people who help committee members write laws. Currently there are 3,000 committee and subcommittee staffers in Congress.[7] Legislatures in all states also have hundreds of committee staffers.

Lobbyists who lobby the legislature use two basic techniques: they testify at legislative hearings, and they meet personally with legislators and their staffs.

Testifying at Legislative Hearings

Most of the work done in legislatures is accomplished in committees. And thus, most lobbying of the legislature is done in committees. Although most Americans think of floor action—debates and votes that take place on the floor of legislative bodies—when they think of legislatures, most important legislative decisions are made in committees and subcommittees. Before a bill is *marked up*—that is, written down in its final form—it generally receives a committee hearing at which witnesses are called to speak for and against it. Legislative committee hearings are somewhat like judicial hearings: members of the committee sit at a big table and listen to people testify for and against a particular proposal, often interjecting with questions and comments. Legislators use committee hearings primarily to educate themselves about pending legislation.[8] Thus, committee hearings are an ideal place for lobbyists to provide all three forms of information to legislators. As political scientist John Wright puts it, "Hearings help legislators determine which options are most likely to achieve the desired policy objectives, which options are politically feasible, and which can be effectively implemented."[9]

Organized interests can testify at legislative hearings in person or in absentia by submitting a written statement. Committee hearings are ideal places for organized interests to lobby. Hearings allow them to present their views on pending policy proposals directly to policymakers and, because they are often attended by members of the media, can bring publicity to an organized inter-

Legislative testimony: the most common lobbying technique One of the most common techniques of direct formal lobbying is testifying before legislative committees. Here, the heads of the nation's largest tobacco companies prepare to testify before a House Energy subcommittee on April 14, 1994. *AP/Wide World Photos.*

est's issue position. Moreover, testifying is not as costly as some other forms of lobbying. To be sure, it may require dozens of hours of a lobbyist's time, but because most lobbyists are stationed in the capital—be it Washington, Albany, Nashville, or wherever else—testimony requires little travel and is thus often cheaper and easier than other forms of lobbying.

How common is testifying at legislative hearings? Table 5.2, which contains information on the use of thirteen direct lobbying techniques, shows that 99 percent of all Washington lobbyists and 98 percent of all state lobbyists regularly testify at congressional hearings. No other lobbying technique is used more.

Meeting with Legislators and Legislative Staff

Another way that lobbyists try to influence legislators is by meeting personally with legislators and legislative staff. These meetings allow lobbyists to make their cases personally. Like legislative hearings, they are ideal for lobbyists to present both policy analysis and, especially, political analysis.

Lobbyists consistently cite personal meetings as the most effective way to influence legislation.[10] The purpose of personal meetings is much the same as that of congressional testimony: to convince policymakers that the lobbyist's

TABLE 5.2 Proportion of Respondents Reporting That They Engage in Each Lobbying Technique

Technique	States (N = 595)	Washington (N = 175)
1. Testifying at legislative hearings	98	99
2. Contacting government officials directly to present point of view	98	98
3. Helping to draft legislation	96	85
4. Alerting state legislators to the effects of a bill on their districts	96	75
5. Consulting with government officials to plan legislative strategy	88	85
6. Attempting to shape implementation of policies	88	89
7. Helping to draft regulations, rules, or guidelines	84	78
8. Engaging in informal contacts with officials	83	95
9. Serving on advisory commissions and boards	58	76
10. Attempting to influence appointment to public office	44	53
11. Filing suit or otherwise engaging in litigation	36	72
12. Doing favors for officials who need assistance	41	56

Note: Each respondent was given a list of advocacy techniques and asked to indicate which he or she had used in the past year.

Sources: The state data come from Anthony J. Nownes and Patricia K. Freeman, "Interest Group Activity in the States," *Journal of Politics* 60:1 (February 1998): 92. Nownes and Freeman surveyed 595 lobbyists in California, South Carolina, and Wisconsin. The Washington data come from Kay Lehman Schlozman and John T. Tierney, *Organized Interests and American Democracy* (New York: Harper and Row, 1986), p. 150.

side is the right one. Most lobbyists realize that time is precious to legislators and their staffs, so they are careful to make their cases as forcefully as possible. This entails not only having their facts straight but also appearing to be intelligent, honest, decent, and diligent.[11] Getting personal meetings with legislators or their staff members is not easy. Legislators, of course, are very busy (this is why they have so many staff people in the first place). But even staff members tend to be overworked and harried. Thus, lobbyists consistently report that developing a relationship with a legislator and his or her staff is the key to getting a personal meeting. The ability to get meetings is often called "having access." Because face-to-face encounters are such an important and effective lobbying tool, lobbyists value access above all else. (We examine how lobbyists gain access in Chapter 7.)

As Table 5.2 shows, almost all lobbyists, over 95 percent, have some face-to-face contact with legislators and their aides. In fact, face-to-face meetings with legislators are so common that huge numbers of lobbyists help legislators draft legislation. The table shows that 96 percent of state organized interests and 85 percent of Washington lobbyists help legislators and their aides draft legislation.

LOBBYING THE CHIEF EXECUTIVE

In the American system of separated powers, few policies are determined solely by the legislature. One actor who has a great deal of power over policy outcomes is the chief executive. The president, for example, has the power to veto bills passed by Congress and is arguably more powerful than Congress in policy areas such as trade and foreign affairs. State governors have veto power as well, and many also have line-item veto power. Chief executives also have a variety of other powers, including the power to appoint judges and many high-level bureaucrats, formulate legislation, and prepare the budget.

Lobbyists who lobby the chief executive use two basic techniques: they meet with the chief executive or staff (or both), and they interact with special liaison offices.

Meeting with the Chief Executive and Staff

The ultimate accomplishment for any lobbyist is to meet personally with the chief executive. This, of course, is quite uncommon because chief executives are busy people. The president of the United States, for example, seldom meets personally with any lobbyists for any length of time. Typically personal meetings with the president are little more than photo opportunities in which someone is ushered in and out of the Oval Office and a photograph is snapped. Governors are more accessible to lobbyists than the president, but they too eschew personal meetings with lobbyists for the most part.

Aides and advisers, however, are a different story. Like legislators, chief executives typically have dozens, if not hundreds, of staff people. The president, for example, has a whole slew of advisers. First, there is what presidential scholar Paul Light has called the "inner circle"—the dozen or so advisers closest to the president. The inner circle generally consists of a handful of White House staffers in whom the president has the most trust, the vice president, a few particularly loyal or important department heads, the first lady, and even a few personal friends with special White House passes. Each of these people is a tad more accessible than the president, and many, including the vice president and the first lady, have their own staffs. Second, there are the sixty or so members of the White House staff—political advisers who help the president with the day-to-day details of his job. White House staffers often have titles like "counsel," "special assistant," "assistant to the president," and so on. These staffers also have their own staffs. Most governors do not have staffs as large as the president's but have extensive staffs nonetheless. Governors of large states like California, Texas, and New York, for example, typically have over one hundred advisers and staff people, while the governors of smaller states have several dozen.

Interacting with Special Liaison Offices

Chief executives, like legislators, realize that organized interests and their lobbyists can be important sources of information. In fact, most recent presidents have viewed lobbyists and the organized interests they represent as important allies that can help them achieve their goals. This is why the White House now has the Office of Public Liaison (OPL), an official entity that maintains contact with organized interests. The OPL was created in 1970 by Richard Nixon, who designed it to reach out to constituencies he felt were important to his reelection.[12]

The OPL has become a permanent feature in the White House. The idea behind it is to provide organized interests a place to go if they wish to lobby the White House. The OPL is staffed by people who maintain constant contact with friendly organized interests. For Democratic presidents, this generally means labor unions, civil rights groups, environmental groups, and women's rights groups. For Republican presidents, it generally means business groups, religious conservative groups, and conservative think tanks. The OPL also provides a place where unfriendly organized interests can communicate their desires to the president. However, unfriendly organized interests generally receive far less attention from OPL staffers than friendly groups. Many state governors have some formal body akin to the OPL.

The OPL is not the only special liaison between the White House and lobbyists. The Intergovernmental Affairs Office (IAO) keeps in contact with state and local governments, so it is an important place for government lobbyists to communicate with the White House. Not many governors have offices akin to the IAO, but there is evidence that the number has increased recently. Furthermore, many chief executives form short-term specialized liaison entities to interact with organized interests. When George Bush was president, for example, he formed the Quayle Council on Competitiveness, which served as a special liaison between the White House and certain hand-picked business organized interests. The council held periodic meetings at which Vice President Dan Quayle and other White House aides listened to the demands of business organizations.[13] The organized interests invited to these meetings were grateful for the opportunity to interact personally with the vice president and other executive branch heavyweights. Similarly, while formulating his ill-fated health care reform package in 1993 and 1994, President Clinton formed a special task force headed by Hillary Rodham Clinton. In a series of private meetings, the task force solicited advice from a number of organized interests, including labor unions, corporations, and health care providers. Specialized entities like the Quayle Council on Competitiveness and Clinton's health care task force are not very common on the state level, but they do exist.

The surveys used to construct Table 5.2 did not contain any questions on the frequency with which lobbyists either meet personally with chief executives and their aides or interact with special liaison offices. One recent study suggests, however, that 76 percent of state lobbyists consider the chief executive a highly important target of lobbying attention.[14] Moreover, anecdotal and qualitative evidence suggests that a similar proportion of Washington lobbyists have some contact with the president or his aides, or both.[15]

LOBBYING THE BUREAUCRACY

The chief executive is only one part of the executive branch. The other part is the executive bureaucracy, broadly defined as the set of agencies and bureaus that implements public policy. The federal government and all states have large bureaucracies. The federal bureaucracy alone consists of over 2,000 separate agencies. It currently employs close to 3 million people and costs approximately $1.5 trillion per year.[16] There are several thousand more agencies at the state and local levels. Together, state and local governments employ about 18 million people, approximately one-tenth of the American workforce.

The primary job of the bureaucracy is to implement policies made by other branches. For example, the Internal Revenue Service enforces and implements tax laws made by Congress and the president. Over the years, however, bureaucratic agencies have become important policymaking bodies in their own right because elected officials often delegate some of their policymaking responsibilities to these agencies.[17] For example, Congress has granted the Federal Communications Commission (FCC) broad powers to issue regulations regarding radio and television broadcasts and the Food and Drug Administration (FDA) leeway to issue new regulations regarding food and drug safety. In short, because bureaucratic agencies often have the power to adopt regulations and rules—policy mandates that have the force of law—they are important players in the policy process.

Lobbyists who lobby the bureaucracy use five basic techniques: they testify before agencies, meet personally with bureaucrats, serve on advisory committees, take part in adjudication, and attempt to influence bureaucratic appointments.

Testifying Before Agencies
and Meeting with Bureaucrats

Bureaucratic agencies write and adopt regulations and rules through a process known as *rule making*. Rule making comprises three stages: (1) regulations are drafted, (2) regulations are published (in Washington, in the *Federal Register*; in states, in similar periodic registers), and (3) agencies decide whether to adopt them. Lobbyists can participate in both of the first two stages. In Stage 1, they can help bureaucrats craft rules and regulations. In Stage 2, they may submit comments for or against a proposed rule or regulation. In fact, this is the whole idea behind this stage—to give affected parties a chance to comment about proposed rules and regulations. Sometimes agencies hold administrative hearings between Stages 2 and 3, at which lobbyists can make their views known.

As Table 5.2 shows, lobbying the bureaucracy is very common. Surveys show that 84 percent of state lobbyists and 78 percent of Washington lobbyists help agencies draft rules and regulations. Furthermore, 88 percent of state lobbyists and 89 percent of Washington lobbyists report meeting with bureaucrats to shape implementation of policies.

Serving on Advisory Committees

Many federal and state agencies periodically establish special committees that advise agency personnel who write rules and regulations.[18] These advisory committees generally serve two purposes. First, they provide technical information to regulators. Because rules and regulations are often arcane, technical, and complex, many agencies feel the need to call on experts for technical information. Second, advisory committees "serve as sounding boards for testing agency proposals."[19] In other words, regulators use advisory committees to discuss their plans with lobbyists and other interested parties. Lobbyists are often invited to serve on these committees. Advisory committees allow lobbyists unprecedented access to the people who write rules and regulations, which gives them yet more opportunities to help draft regulations.

Studies have shown that lobbyists highly prize access to executive agency personnel. Here, as is so often the case in lobbying, the key to getting on one of these committees is access. As Table 5.2 shows, membership on advisory boards and commissions is not uncommon: 58 percent of state lobbyists and 76 percent of Washington lobbyists report having some presence on such boards.

Participating in Adjudication

Agency regulations generally have the force of law. As political scientist John Wright puts it, "Once an agency regulation is established, alleged violations are brought before the agency in the form of formal complaints, which are then dismissed as frivolous or sent before an administrative law judge for adjudication."[20] Lobbyists participate in these proceedings much like they participate in agency hearings and congressional hearings. They may file briefs, initiate complaints, or provide legal or policy expertise to other participants. The surveys used to construct Table 5.2 did not contain questions on adjudication. Thus, we do not know how often organized interests are involved in agency adjudication.

Attempting to Influence Bureaucratic Appointments

Organized interests lobby the bureaucracy by attempting to influence bureaucratic appointments. The vast majority of bureaucrats get their jobs through the civil service system. That is, they are hired based on merit or expertise just like employees in the private sector. At both the federal and state levels, however, many high-level bureaucrats obtain their jobs through appointment. For example, the heads of all fourteen federal cabinet departments are appointed to their positions. Moreover, approximately 3,400 other federal bureaucrats obtain their jobs by appointment.[21] The heads of many state agencies are also appointed. Because they control the general direction of the bureaucratic agencies they lead, high-level bureaucrats can have a profound impact on public policy. This is why organized interests are active in the bureaucratic appointment process.

Virtually all bureaucrats who obtain their jobs through appointment are appointed by chief executives. Some appointees can assume their positions as soon as the chief executive appoints them. For example, in most states and in Washington, a chief executive's personal staffers can begin work as soon as they are appointed. However, a large number of bureaucratic appointees, including virtually all of those who hold high-level positions in executive agencies, must be confirmed before they can assume their positions. At the federal level, the Senate must confirm presidential bureaucratic appointments. And in most states, the upper chamber of the state legislature confirms bureaucratic appointees.

Organized interests are active at both stages of the appointment process. During the first stage, an organized interest may try to convince the chief executive not to appoint a certain person to a certain position. In cases for which confirmation is not required, this stage is obviously vital. But even when confirmation is required, the initial appointment stage is extremely important. This is the case because well over 90 percent of bureaucratic appointees who require confirmation are eventually confirmed.[22] Organized interests get involved in this stage of the appointment process by making suggestions to chief executives and their staffs about whom they would like to have appointed to various bureaucratic positions. During the Reagan and Bush administrations, for example, conservative organized interests such as the Christian Coalition and the Heritage Foundation pushed their preferred candidates for high-level bureaucratic positions by meeting with the president and his staff. They also engaged in the tried-and-true method of sending résumés to the president. During the early years of the Bush administration, the Heritage Foundation sent 2,500 résumés to the president. All told, Bush received over 70,000 résumés from conservative organized interests.[23] These résumés, of course, were not so subtle suggestions about whom the president should appoint to various positions. Presidents are inevitably bombarded with résumés shortly after taking office.

Some organized interests are active at the second stage of the appointment process. At this stage, they may try to convince the legislators who will vote on an appointee's confirmation that the appointee should or should not be confirmed. Most bureaucratic appointees sail through the confirmation process easily, as legislators defer to the chief executive's wishes. Nevertheless, some bureaucratic appointees are quite controversial and thus are not ensured of being confirmed. Organized interests that wish to lobby for or against a particular bureaucratic appointee have a number of options. First, they can lobby legislators and their staffs personally. Second, they can go public by sending letters to voters, appearing on television or radio, or buying advertising in an attempt to turn public opinion toward or against a nominee. Third, they can testify at legislative confirmation hearings, at which legislators gather information about bureaucratic appointees before they vote on them.

Technically, when organized interests attempt to influence bureaucratic appointments, they aim their efforts at the executive branch, the legislature, or the public. But because the ultimate goal of such efforts is to affect the makeup of the bureaucracy, we consider them forms of bureaucratic lobbying.

The surveys used to construct Table 5.2 did not contain questions on attempting to affect bureaucratic appointments. Both surveys did, however, contain an item on how often lobbyists "attempted to influence appointment to public office." In all, 44 percent of state lobbyists and 53 percent of Washington lobbyists reported that they attempted to influence appointments to public office. However, this question applies to both lobbyists who attempt to influence appointments to the judiciary and lobbyists who attempt to influence appointments to the bureaucracy. Thus, we have no clear picture of precisely what proportion of organized interests attempt to influence bureaucratic appointments.

LOBBYING THE COURTS

There are fifty-one court systems in the United States—one federal court system and fifty state court systems. These courts exist primarily to resolve civil and criminal disputes, but they also have broad powers to make public policy. Courts have the power, for example, to interpret laws. Many legislative scholars have noted that seldom do laws cover each eventuality that may occur during implementation. Thus, courts are often called on to determine precisely what the laws passed by the legislature really mean. Courts also have the power to declare laws and acts of the executive branch unconstitutional. The Supreme Court of the United States, for example, can review state and federal laws and declare them invalid if they violate the Constitution. Similarly, many state supreme courts can declare state and local laws unconstitutional. Courts have similar powers to declare the actions of executive branch personnel unconstitutional. Obviously, if an individual in the executive branch is determined to have acted unconstitutionally, he or she must stop this unconstitutional behavior.

Lobbyists who lobby the judiciary use three basic techniques: they litigate, they file amicus curiae briefs, and they attempt to influence judicial appointments.

Litigating

The most direct way for organized interests to lobby the courts is to *litigate*—to bring a suit or a series of suits before the courts to obtain court rulings that favor the litigating group. The purpose of litigation is to force some sort of policy change. This may mean either stopping an impending or existing policy or getting a new policy adopted. No organized interest in history has used litigation more effectively than the National Association for the Advancement of Colored People (NAACP). A brief summary of its litigation activities illustrates how organized interests use litigation.

The Fourteenth Amendment to the Constitution, passed in 1868, guarantees "equal protection of the law." From 1868 to 1964, however, many state and local governments actively circumvented the Fourteenth Amendment by mandating "separate-but-equal" policies designed to keep blacks from achieving true equality. In one of the most famous cases in all of American law, the NAACP sponsored litigation challenging the separate-but-equal doctrine. The case they chose to litigate involved a girl in Topeka, Kansas, named Linda Brown. Brown lived less than a block from a white public school but was nonetheless forced to attend a black school far from her home. This, according to the NAACP, was an unconstitutional violation of her Fourteenth Amendment rights to equal protection of the law. The idea behind the lawsuit was simple: the NAACP wanted separate-but-equal policies declared unconstitutional by the federal judiciary. If this took place, state and local governments would have no choice but to scrap such policies.

In 1952, the group filed suit on behalf of Brown, alleging that her rights were violated by separate-but-equal policies. The case went all the way to the U.S. Supreme Court, which ruled unanimously in *Brown v. Board of Education* that Brown's rights had indeed been violated. The Court also declared that policies such as the one that mandated Brown's attendance at an all-black school were unconstitutional and must be scrapped.[24]

The NAACP's litigation resulted in a court ruling, which essentially had the force of law, that served the policy goals of the group. Of course, *Brown* did not occur in a vacuum. The NAACP and other civil rights groups had been lobbying Congress, the president, and state and local governments for decades before they filed the *Brown* case. In addition, the NAACP had filed numerous other court cases designed to challenge the constitutionality of the separate-but-equal doctrine and discriminatory Jim Crow laws.

Most cases of organized interest litigation are similar in a broad sense to this case: organized interests essentially sue some level or branch of government to get it to start or stop acting in a certain way. Since the *Brown* decision, organized interest litigation has become more common. Not just any organized interest, however, can litigate. Federal and state laws strictly proscribe who can and cannot bring lawsuits. For the courts to consider a case for review, the party bringing the suit must have something called *standing*—a direct interest or stake in the litigation in question. For example, the Sierra Club probably would not have standing in a case that involves the drinking age or the rights of homosexuals. It may have standing, however, in a case involving new emission standards for motor vehicles. Since the 1960s, the rules of standing (which are far too complex to discuss in any great detail here) have been relaxed in both state and federal courts. Today organized interests have wide latitude to participate in litigation if they can show that the individual or institutional interests they represent are affected by the law or policy in question.[25]

Filing Amicus Briefs

Another way that organized interests can lobby the courts is through the filing of *amicus curiae briefs*. The term *amicus curiae* means "friend of the court" in Latin. Amicus curiae briefs are short memos in which information is presented on behalf of one party or the other in a court case. The idea behind an amicus brief is to provide additional ammunition for one side or the other in a court case in hopes of influencing the court's final decision. Each time the Supreme Court considers the constitutionality of an abortion restriction adopted by a state government, for example, both pro- and antiabortion organized interests file amicus briefs that explain their positions on the pending law. In order for an organized interest to file an amicus brief, it must obtain the permission of either the litigants or the court itself. Generally such requests are granted.

Attempting to Influence Judicial Appointments

Organized interests lobby the judiciary by attempting to influence judicial appointments. Technically, when organized interests attempt to influence judicial appointments, they actually aim their efforts at the executive branch, the legislature, or the public. However, because the ultimate goal of such lobbying efforts is to affect the composition and direction of the judiciary, we will label all attempts to affect judicial appointments as judicial lobbying.

At the federal level, all judges are appointed by the president and must be confirmed by the Senate. At the state level, the appointment process varies considerably from state to state, but most states have a process similar to that operative in Washington: the chief executive appoints judges, and one house of the state legislature votes on confirmation. Organized interests that wish to affect judicial appointments generally lobby either the chief executive or the legislators who vote on confirmation, or both.

To illustrate how organized interests lobby to affect judicial appointments, let us consider the case of Clarence Thomas. In 1991, shortly after liberal Supreme Court justice Thurgood Marshall retired from the Court, President

Bush appointed Clarence Thomas to take his place. At the time, Thomas was a fairly obscure federal appellate court judge with strong conservative credentials. After Thomas was nominated, the Senate Judiciary Committee held a confirmation hearing at which they heard a great deal of testimony for and against Thomas. The hearings became a public spectacle due to the testimony of University of Oklahoma law professor Anita Hill, who testified that Thomas had sexually harassed her while she worked for him at the Equal Employment Opportunity Commission.[26] Hill's accusations began a titanic battle over Thomas's appointment. After several days of televised hearings, the Senate eventually voted 52–48 to confirm Thomas.

Organized interests were involved in the Thomas appointment every step of the way. Early in the process, a number of conservative citizen groups lobbied President Bush and his staff to appoint a conservative to fill Marshall's seat on the Court. In fact, conservative organizations had been pressuring Bush since his election to appoint conservatives to the bench.[27] After Bush named Thomas, organized interests stepped up their activities, aiming their lobbying efforts at two targets: senators and the public. Not surprisingly, organized interests on both sides of the struggle made entreaties to the senators who were to decide Thomas's fate. They met personally with senators and their staffers, and many provided testimony at Thomas's confirmation hearings. Organized interests also targeted the public. For example, the Christian Coalition spent more than $1 million on a public advertising campaign designed to convince Americans that Thomas would make a great Supreme Court justice and should be confirmed.[28] Similarly, the conservative Family Research Council spent $500,000 on television and print advertisements in support of Thomas's nomination. Thomas's opponents also lobbied the public. For example, a coalition of liberal organized interests that included the National Organization for Women, the Leadership Council on Civil Rights, and People for the American Way asked liberal activists to contact their senators and express opposition to Thomas's confirmation.[29]

As Table 5.2 shows, the judiciary attracts less attention than either the executive branch or the legislature. Surveys show that 72 percent of Washington lobbyists and only 36 percent of state organized interests engage in judicial lobbying. The reason that judicial lobbying is so uncommon in the states is that the rules of standing are considerably more relaxed in federal courts.

CONCLUSION: DIRECT LOBBYING AND THE PROVISION OF INFORMATION

Organized interests lobby because what the government does affects them, and often profoundly. Contrary to accounts like the one at the beginning of this chapter, lobbying is seldom sleazy. At its core, most lobbying consists of providing information to policymakers through policy analysis, political analysis, and legal analysis.

Lobbyists often provide information directly to policymakers through direct formal lobbying. Such lobbying takes place in the legislature, the executive, and the judiciary. Although the legislature attracts the most attention from lobbyists, the other two branches of government attract a great deal of lobbyist attention as well. Despite the delineated approach in this chapter to studying lobbying techniques, lobbying in practice is seldom an either-or type of activity. In other words, lobbying one branch of government does not preclude lobbying another. In fact, in a recent study of state lobbyists, I found that the typical lobbyist lobbies all three branches of government and uses a dozen different lobbying techniques.[30] Studies suggest that lobbyists diligently lobby whenever and wherever they can. This means deploying a wide variety of techniques, contacting policymakers in all branches of government, and developing relationships with as many public officials as possible. In short, lobbyists try hard to spread themselves thin. How thin often depends on the resources their organization has at its disposal.

What's Next

Direct formal lobbying is the most common general form of direct lobbying but by no means the only form. The next chapter looks at some of the informal ways that lobbyists present information to policymakers. As we shall see, it is the cozy and informal relationships between lobbyists and public officials that create cynicism about the role of organized interests in American democracy.

EXERCISES

1. Go to your college or university library, and find a recent issue of the *Federal Register*. Pick one of the proposed regulations in the issue you have chosen. List the types of organized interests that you think have a stake in it. Why do you think the types of organized interests you have identified have a stake in the regulation?
2. In the past ten to fifteen years, several high-profile presidential appointments have aroused organized interest attention and activity. Among the most controversial appointments have been (1) the appointment of Clarence Thomas to the Supreme Court (1991), (2) the appointment of Robert Bork to the Supreme Court (1987), (3) the appointment of John Tower as secretary of defense (1988–1989), (4) the appointment of Zoe Baird as attorney general of the United States (1992–1993), (5) the appointment of Lani Guinier as head of the civil rights division of the Department of Justice (1993), and (6) the appointment of Edwin Meese as

attorney general of the United States (1984–1985). Choose one of these cases (or pick one of your own), and answer the following questions. What organized interests were involved in the appointment process? What did the various organized interests do? What was the outcome of the appointment battle? What role do you think organized interests played in determining the outcome?

RESEARCH RESOURCES

Publications

Congressional hearing transcripts. The Government Printing Office publishes the transcripts of all congressional hearings. Many college and university libraries keep copies of some hearing transcripts in their government documents section.

Federal Register. The *Federal Register,* the official daily publication for rules, proposed rules, and notices of federal agencies and organizations, is a wonderful source of information. Many college and university libraries carry it.

Web Resources

Congressional web sites. Transcripts of congressional hearings, including those of hearings on presidential appointments, are available at *www.senate.gov.* In addition, *www.fednet.net* provides live audio feeds of congressional hearings.

Other federal government web sites. The *Federal Register* is available on-line at *www.access.gpo.gov/su_doc/aces/aces140.* A number of other federal government web sites may also prove useful for learning about presidential appointments or regulations. For an exhaustive directory of such sites, go to *http://lcweb.loc.gov/rr/news/extgovd.html.* A comprehensive listing of all federal regulations can be found in the on-line version of the *Code of Federal Regulation,* located at *www.access.gpo.gov/nara/cfr/index.*

Notes

1. This dialogue is taken verbatim from surveillance tapes recorded by the Phoenix police. This passage is drawn from Joseph Stedino with Dary Matera, *What's in It for Me?* (New York: HarperCollins, 1992), p. 35.

2. Anthony J. Nownes, "Interest Groups and the Regulation of Pesticides: Congress, Coalitions, and Closure," *Policy Sciences* 24:1 (January 1991): 1–18.

3. Paraphrased from B. Guy Peters, *American Public Policy: Promise and Performance* (3rd ed.) (Chatham, NJ: Chatham House, 1993), chap. 14.

4. See Anthony J. Nownes, "Solicited Advice and Lobbyist Power," *Legislative Studies Quarterly* 24 (February 1999): 113–123.

5. On state lobbyists, see Anthony J. Nownes and Patricia Freeman, "Interest Group Activity in the States," *Journal of Politics* 60:1 (February 1998): 86–112. On Washington lobbyists, see Kay Lehman Schlozman and John T. Tierney, *Organized Interests and American Democracy* (New York: Harper and Row, 1986), p. 150.

6. Norman J. Ornstein, Thomas E. Mann, and Michael J. Malbin, *Vital Statistics on Congress, 1997–1998* (Washington, DC: Congressional Quarterly Press, 1998), pp. 135, 139.

7. Roger H. Davidson and Walter J. Oleszek, *Congress and Its Members* (7th ed.) (Washington, DC: Congressional Quarterly Press, 2000), pp. 153–155, 219–221.

8. John R. Wright, *Interest Groups and Congress: Lobbying, Contributions, and Influence* (Boston, MA: Allyn and Bacon, 1996), pp. 41–42.

9. Ibid., p. 41.

10. Lester Milbraith, *The Washington Lobbyists* (Chicago: Rand McNally, 1963), pp. 209–235; Wright, *Interest Groups and Congress: Lobbying, Contributions, and Influence* (Boston, MA: Allyn and Bacon, 1996), pp. 39, 43.

11. Bruce C. Wolpe and Bertram J. Levine, *Lobbying Congress: How the System Works* (2nd ed.) (Washington, DC: Congressional Quarterly Press, 1996), pp. 13–20.

12. Joseph A. Pika, "Reaching Out to Organized Interests: Public Liaison in the Modern White House," in Richard W. Waterman, ed., *The Presidency Reconsidered* (Itasca, IL: F. E. Peacock Press, 1993), pp. 195–214.

13. See Jeffrey M. Berry and Kent E. Portney, "Centralizing Regulatory Control and Interest Group Access: The Quayle Council on Competitiveness," in Allan J. Cigler and Burdett A. Loomis, eds., *Interest Group Politics* (4th ed.) (Washington, DC: Congressional Quarterly Press, 1995), pp. 319–347.

14. Nownes and Freeman, "Interest Group Activity in the States," p. 97.

15. See Mark A. Peterson, "The Presidency and Organized Interest Groups: White House Patterns of Interest Group Liaison," *American Political Science Review* 86 (September 1992): 612–625.

16. *Budget of the United States, Fiscal Year 1998: Analytical Perspectives* (Washington, DC: Government Printing Office, 1997), p. 207.

17. For details, see James Fesler and Donald Kettl, *The Politics of the Administrative Process* (Chatham, NJ: Chatham House, 1991); Charles Goodsell, *The Case for Bureaucracy: A Public Administration Polemic* (2nd ed.) (Chatham, NJ: Chatham House, 1985).

18. See A. Lee Fritschler, *Smoking and Politics: Policymaking and the Federal Bureaucracy* (4th ed.) (Englewood Cliffs, NJ: Prentice Hall, 1989).

19. Wright, *Interest Groups and Congress: Lobbying, Contributions, and Influence* (Boston, MA: Allyn and Bacon, 1996), p. 52.

20. Ibid.

21. Twentieth Century Fund Task Force on the Presidential Appointment Process, *Obstacle Course* (New York: Twentieth Century Fund Press, 1996), p. 43.

22. Ibid., p. 63; Judith E. Michaels, *The President's Call: Executive Leadership from FDR to George Bush* (Pittsburgh, PA: University of Pittsburgh Press, 1997), p. 104.

23. Michaels, *The President's Call,* p. 105.

24. See Lee Epstein and C. K. Rowland, "Interest Groups in the Courts: Do Groups Fare Better?" in Allan J. Cigler and Burdett A. Loomis, eds., *Interest Group Politics* (2nd ed.) (Washington, DC: Congressional Quarterly Press, 1986), pp. 275–288.

25. For details on standing, see Karen Orren, "Standing to Sue: Interest Group Conflict in the Federal Courts," *American Political Science Review* 70 (September 1976): 723–741.

26. Jane Meyer and Jill Abramson, *Strange Justice* (Boston, MA: Houghton Mifflin, 1994), pp. 225–233.

27. Ibid., p. 13.

28. Twentieth Century Fund Task Force, *Obstacle Course,* p. 123.

29. Christine DeGregorio and Jack E. Rossotti, "Campaigning for the Court: Interest Group Confirmation in the Bork and Thomas Confirmation Process," in Cigler and Loomis, eds., *Interest Group Politics* (4th ed.), pp. 215–238.

30. Nownes and Freeman, "Interest Group Activity in the States," p. 104.

6 ▷ Direct Lobbying, Part II— Informal Lobbying

Arctic National Wildlife Refuge, Alaska
June 30–July 3, 1997

> Representative Diana DeGette (D, Colorado) and a top aide spend a week camping in the Arctic National Wildlife Refuge (ANWR). The cost of their excursion: $3,950. Was this wilderness experience worth $3,950? DeGette would not know, because she did not pay for it. Instead, the Alaska Wilderness League, an organization opposed to oil drilling in the ANWR, picked up the tab for transportation, accommodations, and meals. DeGette later tells a reporter that she generally does not believe in "junkets." In fact, she says, she regularly declines such trips. The trip to Alaska, however, is different. "I only travel when it's an issue I'm involved with," DeGette says. "This [trip] illustrated the conflicting land values in the West."[1]

For many years, the conventional wisdom held that lobbying was all about giving policymakers free stuff and, to put it bluntly, "sucking up" to them. Today the conventional wisdom is quite the opposite. Lobbying, most scholars agree, is all about providing accurate and timely information to policymakers. "Sucking up" does not get lobbyists anywhere if they do not know what they are talking about. Nevertheless, there is no question that wining and dining, doing favors, and just "hanging out"—techniques that comprise informal direct lobbying—are staples of the lobbying business. How common are such practices? What forms do they take? And how often do they mutate into unethical and illegal practices? These are the questions addressed in this chapter.

We begin with a look at some of the scandals and questionable practices that have earned lobbyists their unfavorable reputations. As you will see, most such scandals concern informal direct lobbying. From here, we examine how the informal lobbying practices of the past have evolved into contemporary practices such as junketing, doing favors, and schmoozing. Finally, we take a

Where would you expect to find a lobbyist? The term *lobbyist* evolved from the term *lobby agent,* which was first used in the early 1800s to describe association representatives active in New York state politics. Popular mythology has it that lobby agents were so deemed because they waited in the corridors of power to buttonhole legislators. Here, lobbyists and reporters wait in the halls outside the New York State Assembly Chamber in 1999. *AP/Wide World Photos.*

closer look at the men and women who lobby for a living. Ultimately, this chapter is designed to reveal the often harmless but sometimes sordid informal underbelly of lobbying.

SCANDALOUS PRACTICES: LOBBYING AND CORRUPTION

Throughout our history, organized interests and their lobbyists have sometimes resorted to questionable practices to achieve their goals. As political scientists Larry J. Sabato and Glenn R. Simpson have pointed out, political corruption "is truly a staple of our Republic's existence."[2] Among the most common questionable practices in which lobbyists have engaged are bribery and the use of sex or alcohol to gain favorable treatment from policymakers.

Bribing public officials is not a common lobbying technique. Nonetheless, it does happen. Perhaps the most outrageous example of lobbyist bribery in our history took place in the early 1920s, in an incident known as the Teapot Dome affair. Shortly after his election in 1920, Republican president Warren G. Harding began to make a name for himself as one the nation's worst presidents. He was particularly notorious for his disastrous political appointments. His worst appointment was Interior Secretary Albert B. Fall of New Mexico. Fall, who left the Senate to join Harding's cabinet, was financially destitute when he took over at the Interior Department. In short order, however, he began buying huge and expensive pieces of land around his modest ranch in New Mexico. Fall's purchases seemed odd in the light of his $12,000 annual salary. The money, it turns out, came from oil companies that wanted favors from him. Fall turned out to be big oil's dutiful servant. In late 1921, he asked President Harding to transfer control of some naval petroleum reserves from the Department of the Navy to the Department of the Interior. Fall then turned around and sold the drilling rights to millionaire oilmen Edward Doheny and Harry Sinclair. The oilmen received immensely valuable land at a fraction of its actual value, and Fall received over $400,000 for his work on their behalf. Eventually Fall was tried and convicted of graft. He was the first cabinet officer in history to go to prison.[3]

This is not the only incident of bribery in our history. Fifty years before Teapot Dome, a company called Crédit Mobilier, which was hired to construct America's first transcontinental railroad, staved off congressional inquiries into its corrupt billing practices by illegally distributing stock and cash to members of Congress.[4] Ultimately a congressional investigation uncovered evidence that Vice President Schuyler Colfax, Speaker of the House James G. Blaine, and others had received payoffs from Crédit Mobilier. More recently, in the midst of his Watergate troubles, Richard Nixon extorted massive and illegal cash campaign contributions from lobbyists. In the 1990s, state legislators in Arizona, California, Kentucky, and South Carolina were convicted of receiving bribes from lobbyists.

Sex and alcohol have also featured prominently in lobbying scandals. Although lobbyists understandably often decline to discuss in public the role of either, periodic scandals show that both can be used as lobbying tools. For example, lobbyist Paula Parkinson reported that she regularly traded sex for votes on Capitol Hill in the late 1970s and early 1980s. Parkinson, a for-hire lobbyist and political consultant, admitted to wining, dining, and servicing a number of Republican members of Congress in exchange for their votes on important legislation. Parkinson claims to have had sex with half a dozen Republican members of Congress and even claims that one member paid for her 1980 abortion.[5] No legislator has ever acknowledged having sex with Parkinson.

As for alcohol, it has always been in ample supply in cities where public policy is made. The relationship between alcohol and lobbying was particularly apparent in a 1986 episode in Tallahassee, Florida, where, after an evening of carousing and drinking, a state legislator and a lobbyist were involved in a hit-and-run accident. When the police caught up with them, the lobbyist quickly confessed that he was driving the car when the accident occurred. The legislator later admitted that *he* had been driving the car. When asked about the incident, the lobbyist replied: "You know, I am a lobbyist, and you have to take the fall when you work for a legislator."[6]

Despite these examples, interest group scholars agree that bribery, sexual and substance-related misconduct, and illegal lobbying activities are not very common. The public perception that lobbyists are sleazy, disreputable characters who regularly violate the law is simply mistaken. Like all other professions, the lobbying profession has its "bad apples" who have occasionally engaged in behavior that has brought the worst aspects of the lobbying business to the light. But virtually every scholarly study of lobbying has concluded that most lobbyists abide by the law and conduct themselves in a thoroughly professional manner. Why, then, does the lobbying profession have such a bad reputation? There are two answers to this question.

First, the media tend to focus attention on the bad apples rather than the "good eggs." Most of the time, the news media ignore lobbying. Covering lobbying extensively would be difficult and also somewhat silly; there is nothing particularly newsworthy about professional lobbyists' testifying before congressional subcommittees, filing lawsuits, or commenting on proposed federal regulations. Lobbying becomes newsworthy when illegal behavior is involved. Bribery, sexual peccadilloes, and other unsavory practices, even if they occur infrequently, make the news. Thus, when the public at large does hear about lobbying, it tends to hear things that make lobbying seem much dirtier than it is.

Another reason that lobbying has a bad reputation is that lobbyists often operate behind the scenes in American politics. In other words, lobbyists often meet with policymakers in informal settings outside the halls of government. Many Americans seem to think that this illustrates a disregard for the law and the democratic process. As we shall see, however, most informal contacts between lobbyists and policymakers are quite harmless. In fact, they generally entail an exchange of information and little more. Nevertheless, the widespread existence of informal lobbying does raise legitimate questions about democracy, representative government, and the role of lobbyists in politics. In the remainder of this chapter, we begin to explore these questions by taking a closer look at how informal direct lobbying works.

THE TECHNIQUES OF INFORMAL LOBBYING

Occasional scandal is the inevitable result of a political system that allows lobbyists such high levels of access to policymakers. For better or worse, public officials in the United States generally develop close relationships with lobbyists as a result of extensive informal contacts between them. Both parties to the exchange of information benefit from this closeness. Public officials obtain valuable information. As for lobbyists, closeness allows them access to the people who make the policies that affect them and their clients. In what follows, we examine the most common forms of informal lobbying: wining, dining, and schmoozing; gift giving; and providing favors.

Wining, Dining, and Schmoozing

Drinking, schmoozing, dining out, playing golf, and otherwise hanging out with public officials is an undeniable part of lobbying. As Table 5.2 shows, 83 percent of state lobbyists and 95 percent of Washington lobbyists report engaging in informal contacts with policymakers. Informal contacts often take place in bars and restaurants. Most state capitals have well-known watering holes, pubs, and grills at which lobbyists and policymakers mingle.[7] In Washington, restaurants and bars along "the K Street corridor" serve as meeting places for public officials, lobbyists, journalists, and others involved in Washington politics.

At these informal meetings, lobbyists provide information to policymakers. In other words, informal get-togethers, meetings, and encounters are forums at which lobbyists pass on policy, political, or legal analysis to policymakers. Also, lobbyists receive information from policymakers. In their roles as monitors, lobbyists often use informal meetings to gather information about political happenings. A lobbyist may inquire, for example, about the status of a given bill in the legislature or ask when a certain piece of legislation is going to the floor for a vote. Finally, lobbyists and public officials use informal meetings to develop relationships. Alan Rosenthal, the preeminent scholar of lobbying, has noted that lobbying often "comes down to basic human relationships."[8] He concludes that "[W]hatever the political system or culture, the lobbyist's goal is to make connections and develop close relationships" with as many policymakers as possible.[9] In fact, Rosenthal says, many lobbyists "spend more time developing relationships than they do on direct lobbying."[10] According to Rosenthal, building relationships allows lobbyists to prove their credibility, honesty, and reliability. He concludes that lobbyists try to develop relationships "that allow them to demonstrate the worthy attributes they themselves possess, which is prerequisite for promoting their client's wares."[11] Developing relationships is also important because it leads to increased access to policymakers. For example, if a lobbyist strikes up a friendship with a legislator, this relationship may translate into more invitations to congressional hearings or greater input during the markup of a bill.

Gift Giving, Favors, and Junkets

Drinking and eating are not the only ways lobbyists informally lobby policymakers. Lobbyists also give gifts and do favors. As Table 5.2 shows, 41 percent of state lobbyists and 56 percent of Washington lobbyists report doing favors for policymakers who need assistance. Lobbyists provide everything from perishables like flowers, candy, cigars, and peanuts, to free babysitting, tickets to athletic events, and rides to work.[12] For many years, members of Congress received special gifts from lobbyists called honoraria. An *honorarium* is *a stipend given for a speech to an organized interest.* For a brief speech before breakfast or lunch, a member would receive a check for between $100 and $2,000. Congress outlawed honoraria for federal legislators in 1992. Several states, however, still allow these most coveted of all gifts.

Lobbyists agree that gifts and favors contribute to building relationships because they help policymakers see a lobbyist's clients in a favorable light. One of the most popular lobbyist gifts is the *junket,* which is a free trip. Junkets are generally provided only to legislators and their aides, because other policymakers are barred from accepting them. Junkets can take many forms. Until 1995, when Congress adopted a law that banned some types of junkets, the typical junket was an all-expense-paid trip to a "conference" or "forum." Expenses included airfare, luxury hotel accommodations, meals, drinks, and other incidentals. Organized interests that could afford to usually held these conferences and forums at well-equipped hotels and resorts in Hawaii, the Virgin Islands, Las Vegas, San Diego, and Florida. Members of Congress defended the junkets, saying that they were important opportunities to listen to their constituents. Although Congress banned some types of junkets in 1995, they survive in the form of all-expense paid trips for "fact-finding missions" and "conferences" at which federal legislators serve as panelists or speakers. Junkets are also common in most states, although some states have recently passed laws that strictly limit their use.

The value of junkets is demonstrated by the case of the Commonwealth of the Northern Mariana Islands (CNMI), a U.S. territory in the Pacific. Unlike all other U.S. territories, CNMI is exempt from American minimum wage laws and immigration laws. Local businesses and the government of CNMI like things this way. CNMI, they say, benefits economically from low wages and cheap foreign labor. In 1996, when Senator Daniel Akaka (D, Hawaii) tried to pass legislation that would force CNMI to abide by U.S. minimum wage and immigration laws, the territory began its junketeering in earnest. Between April 1996 and December 1997, CNMI paid for six House members to visit. Two of the members brought their wives, and another brought his fiancée.[13] During the same period, more than seventy congressional staffers and party officials flew to CNMI. The junketeers stayed at the Hyatt Regency in Saipan, which, its brochure points out, is surrounded by "14 acres of lush, tropical gardens, lagoons, and magnificent micro beach." Amenities included "rooms [with] balconies and an ocean view. . . . Complimentary use of the Club Elan Fitness Center, including the health club, steam room, sauna, and spa area is included in the room rate."[14]

In 1998, House and Senate leaders vowed never to let Senator Akaka's legislation see the light of day. CNMI, they said, was thriving economically and would only suffer from the imposition of U.S. minimum wage and immigration laws. There is, of course, no way to prove that the CNMI junket affected the

Only the names have changed Lobbyists have been a part of American politics for two centuries. In this lithograph from 1866, lobbyists wait for legislators debating the passage of the Civil Rights Bill of 1866. *Library of Congress, LC-USZ62-33274.*

votes of House and Senate leaders, but at the very least, the junket made congressional leaders aware of the island government's point of view.

IS THERE ANYTHING WRONG WITH INFORMAL DIRECT LOBBYING?

Critics of informal lobbying call it corrupt, wrong, and unfair because it allows lobbyists to buy public officials. They may have a point. Close relationships between policymakers and lobbyists clearly raise the dismaying possibility that the former make decisions based not on what they or their constituents think is best but rather on what the most profligate lobbyists think is best. Moreover, informal contacts and munificent lobbyists may be bad for the political system in the end, because they may increase public cynicism by fostering the notion that everyone in public life is for sale. Finally, gifts may distort representation by privileging the views of the richest sectors of American society—those who can afford to pay for such things. In short, many critics believe that informal lobbying is likely to amplify the voices of the affluent and squelch the voices of the not so affluent.

Congress itself acknowledged some of the problems with informal lobbying when it passed the Lobbying Disclosure Act of 1995, the most comprehensive piece of federal lobbying legislation ever passed. Before we discuss lobbying laws, it is important to note that the most egregious types of corrupt and unethical lobbying activities, such as bribery, blackmail, and threatening with bodily harm, are forbidden under criminal statutes unrelated to lobbying. Thus, although heinous practices such as these are not explicitly banned in lobbying legislation, they are nonetheless against the law. It is also important to note that the federal government, as well as most state and local governments, have long banned the provision of gifts, meals, and travel to most policymakers in the judicial and executive branches. Gifts and junkets, it turns out, are reserved largely for legislators.

The Lobbying Disclosure Act of 1995, which replaced the loophole-ridden and ineffectual Lobbying Disclosure Act of 1946, contains two main provisions. The first requires lobbyists to register with the federal government and disclose their activities. The act defines a lobbyist as "anyone who spends more than 20 percent of his or her time lobbying, or who receives more than $5,000 from a single client to lobby."[15] The act defines the term *lobbying* quite broadly as virtually any direct attempt to influence the decisions of government officials including the president, the vice president, White House staff members and aides, members of Congress, congressional staffers, and high-ranking bureaucrats.[16] Registration, political scientist Ronald G. Shaiko has noted, "is a two-step process." First, "within 45 days of an initial lobbying contact, lobbyists are required to register with the clerk of the House and the secretary of the Senate." Initial registration entails "providing pertinent information regarding the lobbyist, his or her clients, the issues, the activities, and the governmental institutions associated with the lobbying efforts."[17] The second step in the registration process is the filing of semiannual reports of lobbying activities containing information on how much lobbyists spend, exactly what they do to influence policy, and how much they are paid by the organized interests that employ them. The idea behind the lobbyist registration provision is that as long as lobbyists are forced to make their activities public, they are less likely to engage in corrupt, unethical, or illegal practices.

The second set of provisions of the Lobbyist Disclosure Act of 1995 bans certain kinds of informal lobbying activities—specifically, the act bars lobbyists from providing expensive gifts, meals, and travel to members of Congress. The "gift ban" provisions, as they are called, contain slightly different rules for the House and the Senate. In the Senate, the law forbids legislators and their staffs from accepting gifts or meals valued at more than fifty dollars. It also bans legislators from accepting more than one hundred dollars per year in gifts from a single lobbyist. In the House, the law forbids members and their staffs from accepting any gifts or meals. Gifts of nominal value, such as T-shirts, coffee mugs, and caps, are exempted. As for travel, the gift ban provisions forbid all members of Congress and their staffs from accepting all-expense-paid trips from lobbyists.[18] The idea behind the gift ban provisions is that lobbyists should not be allowed to buy access to policymakers with expensive trips, meals, and gifts. The proponents of the provisions contend that gifts corrupt the integrity of the federal government and increase the probability that legislators will respond to lobbyists rather than their constituents.

Currently, all states and thousands of local governments have regulations that require lobbyists to register and report their activities.[19] Moreover, many states and localities have gift bans similar to the federal gift ban. Because each state and locality is different, it is extremely difficult to generalize about the nature and extent of state and local lobbying laws. Some have rather strict lobbying laws that require virtually all active lobbyists to register, while others have rather lax laws that force only the most active and well-heeled lobbyists to register. Similarly, many states and localities have lobbying laws that forbid all sorts of informal contacts and gifts, and others have lax laws that allow lobbyists to do almost anything short of bribery.

No matter where they operate, most lobbyists are subject to some regulations. Most federal lobbyists, as well as many state and local lobbyists, are required to register with the governments that they lobby so that policymakers and the public can keep abreast of what lobbyists are doing. In addition, virtually all lobbyists are barred from doing certain things. Bribery, blackmail, assault, and other heavy-handed tactics are, of course, unlawful for lobbyists just as they are for the rest of us. Furthermore, federal lobbyists and many state and local lobbyists are barred from providing public officials with expensive gifts, meals, and trips.

At this point, the obvious question is: How well do lobbying laws work? Scholars who have addressed this question have concluded that the evidence is mixed. Registration laws, designed primarily to publicize and expose the activities of lobbyists, appear to be quite successful. Evidence suggests that most federal lobbyists, as well as the most active state and local lobbyists, abide by registration laws and dutifully identify themselves, report whom they represent, and report what they do to the governments that they lobby. But the gift ban provisions appear to have had little effect on the behavior of lobbyists. For example, since Congress passed the Lobbying Disclosure Act of 1995, lobbyists have proven quite adept at sidestepping some of its major provisions. For example, though the act prohibits lobbyists from providing all-expenses-paid trips to members of Congress, lobbyists still manage to pay for expensive junkets. A loophole in the law allows lobbyists to finance trips for legislators and their immediate families as long as the trips are for "fact-finding" purposes or "for conferences in which Members or aides have significant roles on panels or as speakers."[20] As for the ban on expensive gifts and meals, the act has several gaping loopholes. For one thing, it specifically exempts books, tapes, awards, and prizes. Similarly, a meal is not a meal if it is provided at a "widely attended event." Thus, if a lobbyist wants to provide an expensive meal for a member of Congress, all he or she has to do is plan a convention or a conference and invite lots of other people in addition to the targeted legislator. State and local lobbying laws also have loopholes that lobbyists have freely exploited. In the end, although gift bans have had some effect on the way lobbyists do business, it is safe to say that they do not have a large impact on lobbying activities. Speaking of state and local lobbying laws, political scientist Thomas R. Dye has concluded that "these laws do not restrain lobbying."[21] The same can be said of federal lobbying laws.

In the end, nothing is likely to stop gift giving, junkets, and other forms of informal lobbying that many people find objectionable. Lobbying remains a people business; that is, it is generally about one person's supplying information to another. As long as this is the case, lobbyists and policymakers are bound to grow close in some instances, lobbyists are bound to try to exploit or use personal relationships to their clients' advantage, and policymakers are bound to trust and like some lobbyists more than others.

For lobbyists, the value of informal lobbying is obvious. First, it allows close and often protracted opportunities to make their case. Second, doing favors for policymakers or giving them gifts may tip the scales in a lobbyist's favor. Finally, and perhaps most important, informal lobbying may allow him or her to build a close relationship with policymakers and thus may improve access to policymakers in formal settings. Many lobbyists, in fact, believe that building relationships with policymakers may increase the chances that their telephone calls will be returned, that they will be able to set up personal meetings with policymakers, that they will be invited to testify at legislative or executive hearings, or that they will be asked for their input during the drafting of a bill or regulation.

THE LOBBYISTS: WHO THEY ARE AND WHERE THEY COME FROM

Because people skills are so important in the lobbying business, this chapter closes with a look at the people who lobby.

Like the organized interests for which they work, lobbyists are ubiquitous in the United States. In fact, as Figure 6.1 attests, there are more lobbyists in the United States today than ever before. Over 25,000 professional lobbyists are located in Washington alone. No one knows for sure how many lobbyists there are elsewhere in the United States, but surely there are tens of thousands more operating in states and localities across the country.

The term *lobbyist* evolved from the term *lobby agent*, which was first used in the early 1800s to describe association representatives active in New York State politics. Popular mythology has it that lobby agents were so deemed because they waited in the corridors of power to buttonhole legislators. Political scientists generally distinguish between two basic types of lobbyists: *hired guns* and *association lobbyists*. An association lobbyist works for and is employed by a single organization. In contrast, a hired gun lobbyist has a number of clients and works for whomever hires him or her. Newspaper and magazine stories on lobbyists tend to focus on powerful hired gun lobbyists like Clark

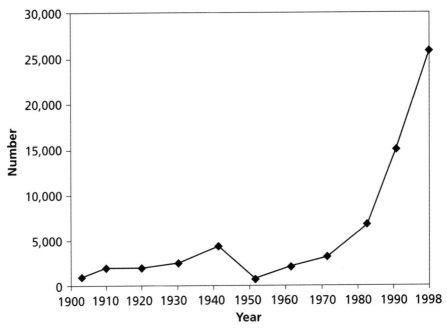

FIGURE 6.1 Trends in the Number of Washington Lobbyists, 1900–1998

Sources: *Washington Representatives* (Washington, D.C.: Columbia Books, various years); Robert Salisbury, "The Paradox of Interest Groups in Washington—More Groups, Less Clout," in Anthony King, ed., *The New American Political System* (Washington, D.C.: American Enterprise Institute, 1991), pp. 204–206; Mark Petracca, "The Rediscovery of Interest Group Politics," in Petracca, ed., *The Politics of Interests* (Boulder, CO: Westview Press, 1992), pp. 14–21.

Clifford, who reportedly received over $1 million for some advice he gave to the DuPont family several years ago, and former Reagan administration official Michael Deaver, who in one year in the 1980s received a retainer of $250,000 from just one of his many clients. These "super-lobbyists" make for fascinating copy, but they are the exceptions rather than the rule in national, state, and local politics. Studies show that between 75 and 80 percent of all lobbyists are association lobbyists.[22] It is important to note, however, that many organized interests both have their own lobbyists *and* hire out for special lobbying services. Thus, although association lobbyists outnumber hired guns by a large margin, hired guns are used at one time or another by most organized interests.

One reason the media focus on hired guns is that their numbers have increased in recent years. This recent proliferation has produced a new player in organized interest politics: the *lobbying law firm*, which is a law firm that employs a number of hired guns. The number of lobbying law firms is on the rise in both Washington and state capitals. A lobbying law firm provides a wide variety of services, including public relations, indirect lobbying (which we discuss in Chapter 8), media services, political consulting, fund raising, and direct lob-

TABLE 6.1 Selected Characteristics of Lobbyists in Three States and Washington, D.C.

	States (N = 595)	Washington (N = 776)
Female (%)	27	12
College degree (%)	94	91
Attended graduate or professional school (%)	65	74
Nonwhite (%)	N.A.	3
Contract lobbyist (%)	29	16
Government experience (%)	57	54
Part-time (%)	43	N.A.
Mean age	N.A.	49
Mean salary	$86,215 (in 1996 dollars)	$90,489 (in 1982 dollars)

Sources: The state data come from Anthony J. Nownes and Patricia K. Freeman, "The People Who Lobby State Governments: Who They Are and What They Do" (unpublished manuscript, 1998), p. 5. Nownes and Freeman surveyed 595 lobbyists in California, South Carolina, and Wisconsin. The figures here are overall percentages and means from all three states combined. The Washington data come from Robert Salisbury, "Washington Lobbyists: A Collective Portrait," in Allan J. Cigler and Burdett A. Loomis, ed., *Interest Group Politics* (2nd ed.) (Washington, D.C.: Congressional Quarterly Press, 1986), pp. 152–156.

bying. The trend toward all-purpose lobbying shops has seemingly accelerated as lobbying has become increasingly technological. Lobbyists now rely heavily on computers for everything from data analysis to email. Thus, lobbying firms with technological expertise are in huge demand.

Table 6.1 summarizes the basic characteristics of state and federal lobbyists. Over thirty years ago, political scientist Lester Milbraith found that the typical lobbyist was a well-educated, upper- or upper-middle-class, white male between forty and sixty years old.[23] Virtually every subsequent study of lobbyists has painted a similar picture.[24] There is some evidence, however, that the lobbying community is becoming more diverse, as women and ethnic and racial minorities invade previously inaccessible "good ole boy" lobbying networks.[25]

Lobbyists make a good living.[26] Some of Washington's "super-lobbyists," for example, make well over $1 million a year.[27] And lesser Washington insiders such as former senators and House members may take home $500,000 annually.[28] State lobbyists are also well paid. Some of Texas's and California's top lobbyists, for example, make over $1 million annually.[29] Moreover, even in smaller states such as Arkansas and Wisconsin, a number of lobbyists make close to $100,000 per year, while the average lobbyist brings home approximately $50,000.[30]

Although lobbyists make a great deal of money and exert substantial power over policy outcomes, few children grow up aspiring to lobby for a living.

Most people who become lobbyists do so because of previous jobs they held. Government is the primary training ground for Washington, state, and local lobbyists. In fact, as Table 6.1 shows, over half of all Washington lobbyists and a similar proportion of state lobbyists have some sort of government experience.[31] Among the most common government positions previously held by lobbyists are legislator, legislative aide, chief executive aide, and executive agency official. Not all lobbyists come to lobbying from government. Many association lobbyists, for example, serve their employers for many years in other capacities before they become lobbyists.[32] Excluding public service, law and business are the two occupations that produce the most lobbyists.

All told, lobbying is an elite profession. Its practitioners are well educated, well off, well paid, and well traveled. There is a reason for this: lobbying requires a great deal of expertise. Policy analysis, for example, often requires substantive knowledge about a specific policy area. Similarly, most political analysis requires an intimate understanding of the powers, roles, and motives of policymakers, as well as the intricacies of the policymaking process. Finally, legal analysis requires legal expertise—familiarity with the law and the legal process. Where do lobbyists get expertise? The career paths of lobbyists tell the story. Both policy and political expertise come from a combination of education and government experience. Not surprisingly, legal expertise comes from going to law school and subsequently practicing law.

Expertise is essential if a lobbyist is to make his or her case. But as valuable as expertise is, it may be less valuable in direct lobbying than *access*—having the opportunity to present one's case to policymakers. Access is the ability to put one's expertise to work. Virtually all forms of direct lobbying require some level of access. And, of course, access is critical if a lobbyist wishes to have personal contact with any policymaker. The importance of access explains why most lobbyists have government experience. As I pointed out in the previous section, having a close relationship with policymakers is important to lobbyists, and building a relationship with policymakers is not necessary for someone who already has a relationship with them.

Organized interests, realizing the importance of access and closeness, often make every effort to hire former government officials.[33] In fact, all manner of high-profile erstwhile government officials and employees are the subject of bidding wars by lobbying firms and organized interests wishing to cash in on their connections. For example, when Senator Bob Dole decided to retire from public life after his defeat in the 1996 presidential election, a number of high-powered Washington lobbying firms tried to lure him on board. Eventually he accepted a job with the Washington law firm Verner, Liipfert, Bernhard, McPherson, and Hand, reportedly for an annual salary of approximately $600,000. He also received a fourteen-office suite and was able to bring a number of old staff members with him. Dole's official title is special counsel, but make no mistake about it: Dole is now a lobbyist.[34]

Dole is not the first high-powered politico landed by Verner, Liipfert, Bernhard, McPherson, and Hand, which in many ways exemplifies the new breed of lobbying law firms. Dole's colleagues at the firm include former Senate majority leader George Mitchell, former Texas senator and failed vice-presidential candidate and secretary of the treasury Lloyd Bentsen, former Texas governor Ann Richards, and former Hawaii governor John D. Waihee III. The firm's roster is also laden with high-profile ex-staffers for everyone from President Lyndon Johnson to Senator Edmund Muskie. Dole's firm is not the only one in Washington with such an impressive roster of talent. All over town lobbying firms and organized interests of all kinds pay large salaries to land ex-government officials because they think these people have connections that make them more effective (and, not coincidentally, more expensive) lobbyists.

The prevalence of *"in and outers"*—government officials who become lobbyists after they quit or are removed from government—has raised eyebrows among many who fear that the "revolving door" may harm the integrity of government. The revolving door raises a number of ethical dilemmas. First, like informal lobbying, junkets, and gifts, it may bias organized interest representation in favor of the few. Because ex-government officials are very expensive, the richest people and institutions in America are generally the only ones that can afford to hire them. Second, many critics feel that the revolving door may make government officials still in office more responsive to their future potential employers than to their constituents. For example, a member of Congress who plans on retiring before the next election may make decisions while in office that are designed to make him or her attractive to certain organized interests that may hire this person after leaving office. Similarly, a bureaucrat at the Department of Defense may do what he or she can while employed by the agency to curry the favor of weapons manufacturers, in hopes of receiving a lucrative job later.[35]

Finally, the revolving door raises questions about the propriety of selfishly parlaying a government job into a lucrative lobbying career. Political analyst Pat Choate imagines the following disturbing scenario.[36] An individual is working for the Department of Commerce on trade issues, at taxpayers' expense. While working for the government, this person receives invaluable experience and expertise in matters of international trade. After a few years on the job, the government employee quits and is quickly hired by a foreign corporation at a salary several times higher than that he or she received at the Department of Commerce. As the head lobbyist for this company, the erstwhile government employee works hard to help the company compete more effectively against American companies. This scenario and others like it, says Choate, are played out on a daily basis in Washington. Choate asks: Why should taxpayers in effect subsidize organized interests by training their future employees, especially when these employees often work against the interests of vast numbers of Americans?

Over the years, a number of office holders have paid lip-service to ending the revolving door and its attendant problems. When he first took office, for example, President Clinton issued new rules that forbade former presidential appointees from lobbying their former employers for five years after they left their government positions. These rules, like most others designed to thwart the revolving door, proved ineffective. One of Clinton's first presidential appointees, deputy chief of staff Roy Neel, left the White House in late 1993 to take a job with the United States Telephone Association (USTA), a trade group that represents local telephone companies. Technically, Neel was not a lobbyist and did not directly contact the White House. He did, however, begin immediately to supervise lobbyists who regularly contacted the White House.

Stories like this one demonstrate how hard it is to stop the revolving door. The real reason the revolving door continues to operate unabated is that policymakers like it that way. Many believe that they should be able to do what they want with their lives after they quit government service. Moreover, many ex-government officials enjoy politics and become lobbyists to remain involved and active.

WHAT MAKES A SUCCESSFUL LOBBYIST?

There is no easy answer to what separates the successful lobbyist from the unsuccessful lobbyist. In any policy battle, several factors determine the outcome, and most of these are beyond a lobbyist's control. For example, in the battle over President Clinton's health care reform package, the legislators deciding on various aspects of the plan were influenced by ideology, political party affiliation, public opinion, their opinion of the president, the opinions of their constituents, and several other factors. In short, lobbyists were simply one small element in a huge variety of factors that influenced the outcome of the policy battle. Because many factors affect policy outcomes and many are beyond a lobbyist's control, lobbying is seldom determinative. Thus, it is impossible to identify the factor or factors sufficient to ensure lobbying success. The best we can do is identify factors that—all other things being equal—maximize a lobbyist's chances of being successful. Lobbyists themselves agree that a number of factors increase their chances of success. In a recent book on lobbying, lobbyist-turned-teacher Bruce Wolpe and his colleague Bertram Levine, argue that adherence to five commandments is necessary if a lobbyist is to be successful.[37]

Commandment #1: Tell the truth. For the lobbyist, lying may seem like a good idea. It is not. Telling the truth is important for several reasons. First, if a lobbyist is caught lying to a policymaker, chances are that that policymaker, as well as his or her friends and colleagues, will never listen to that lobbyist again. This is a problem because very few lobbyists lobby only once and then quit. Moreover, lying damages the reputation and credibility of the organized interest on whose behalf the liar is lobbying.

Commandment #2: Never promise more than you can deliver. Lobbyists are sometimes tempted to exaggerate, especially when it comes to political analysis. A lobbyist may, for example, tell a legislator that the group he or she represents has more allies than it actually does or that he or she has received commitments from other legislators or the chief executive to "vote his [or her] way" on a pending piece of legislation. Exaggerating, however, is unwise. "If an assurance is made," Wolpe argues, "that labor support is in hand," for example, or that grass-roots pressure is mounting, these things "must be forthcoming."[38] Like lying, exaggerating undermines a lobbyist's credibility, threatens his or her reputation, and may limit his or her access to policymakers in the future.

Commandment #3: Know how to listen so that you accurately understand what you are hearing. Listening and understanding are important for several reasons. First, monitoring—keeping track of what government is up to—is a big part of lobbying. The key to effective monitoring is listening carefully and accurately interpreting the information. Second, the language of politics, according to Wolpe, is "baroque and pregnant with meaning and shades of meaning."[39] (In other words, sometimes it is hard to figure out what politicians really mean when they talk.) Thus, it is vital for a lobbyist to listen "with careful attention and applied discipline."[40] Lobbying experience is especially helpful in listening. Over time, lobbyists get used to political language, which is often laden with jargon and awkward "legalese," and get better at reading what policymakers really mean when they say certain things. Finally, listening carefully is important for tactical reasons. It is especially important when it comes to garnering commitments from policymakers. "There is too often the temptation," Wolpe argues, to believe that a policymaker "is on your side . . . before, in fact, a commitment of support has been given."[41] This is a nice way of saying that most policymakers play their cards close to the vest when it comes to committing themselves. That is, policymakers often wait until the last minute to make iron-clad commitments. Not listening carefully may cause a lobbyist to believe that a policymaker is on his or her side when in reality the policymaker is not. This is problematic because it may lead a lobbyist to stop lobbying a policymaker when he or she should continue. Even worse, it may lead a lobbyist to tell other policymakers erroneously that "such and such policymaker is 'in the bag.'" This obviously violates Commandment #2.

Commandment #4: Staff are there to be worked with and not circumvented. The most obvious reason to work with staff is that these people often do more work than their bosses. In legislatures, for example, the work of drafting pieces of legislation is often left to staff people. Another reason to work with staff is that they can be a valuable source of advice and guidance for a lobbyist. Wolpe points out that for a lobbyist, a member of Congress's staff, for example, is an invaluable source of "guidance on how to most effectively approach the member on your behalf."[42]

Commandment #5: Spring no surprises. The final commandment reflects the common belief among lobbyists that public officials "hate the unexpected."[43] Policymakers, Wolpe argues, like to have information in a timely manner so that they may act instead of react. Thus, if a lobbyist "knows something"—for example, that opposition to his or her position is mounting, or that a policymaker is about to be the subject of a negative story on television—he or she should pass it along to the policymaker as soon as possible, which allows the policymaker more time to plan for all contingencies.

Beyond adherence to these five commandments, studies of lobbying have shown that three other factors are particularly important if a lobbyist is to be successful. First is experience. In perhaps the most extensive study of Washington lobbying and lobbyists ever conducted, political scientist Robert Salisbury and his colleagues concluded that experience produces increased knowledge about policy issues, as well as contacts and familiarity with the policy process,[44] all three of which increase a lobbyist's effectiveness. Second, people skills are important to a lobbyist's success. Lobbyists themselves feel that good social skills and a good attitude are crucial to their success. Finally, because lobbying can be hard, arduous, and unrewarding work, patience is important. People who desire immediate results from their work have no business in the lobbying profession. Many policy battles last months, years, or even decades.

CONCLUSION: INFORMAL LOBBYING AND THE PROVISION OF INFORMATION

At many points in our history, lobbyists have resorted to questionable practices to achieve their goals. However, bribery and other forms of unethical lobbyist conduct are quite uncommon. Nonetheless, a number of controversial and questionable lobbying practices remain in use today. Specifically, many lobbyists wine, dine, and do favors for policymakers, and some pay for expensive junkets.

Critics of gift giving, favor providing, junkets, and schmoozing believe that such practices may compromise the ability of policymakers to make good and fair decisions. Policymakers and lobbyists alike, of course, deny that gifts and junkets and favors and dinners influence policy decisions. Ultimately, however, to determine the impact of informal lobbying, we will have to take a closer look at the overall impact of organized interests on policy decisions, the task of Chapter 9. For now, it must suffice to say that informal contact, close personal relationships, and after-hours carousing are part of the territory when it comes to lobbying. And as with direct formal lobbying, much of informal lobbying is harmless—it entails the provision of information.

Lobbying is an elite profession populated by mostly well-educated, well-paid white men. Success as a lobbyist appears to depend most on honesty, experience, and access. Some lobbyists must earn access, but others have built-in access by dint of their prior government service.

What's Next

The next chapter looks at the one form of lobbying that does not entail the provision of information: lobbying with campaign money. Although few public officials bear a strong resemblance to Albert Fall, who engineered his own fall by taking bribes from wealthy oilmen, many are recipients of large amounts of cash from lobbyists nonetheless. Most of this cash, however, is legal. The U.S. campaign finance system allows organized interests to contribute large sums of money to policymakers. Lobbying with campaign money is a common, important, and extremely controversial form of lobbying.

EXERCISES

1. For the state or community in which you live, describe the laws and regulations that govern what lobbyists can and cannot do. How do these regulations compare to those in surrounding states and communities? What do you think accounts for the differences and similarities?
2. In the past ten years, have any lobbyists or policymakers in your state been accused and/or convicted of bribery? If the answer is yes, describe the circumstances surrounding the scandal. What organized interests were involved? What did they want? What means other than bribery did the organized interest use to try to affect policy?

RESEARCH RESOURCES

Publications

Your local and/or state government statutes. Many states and localities have statutes that govern lobbying. These statutes are often published and available to the public.

Web Resources

Good government group web sites. A number of good government citizen groups act as watchdogs for lobbyist corruption. For example, both Common Cause and the Center for Public Integrity offer on-line information on lobbyist corruption. Their web sites are located, respectively, at *www.commoncause.org* and *www.publicintegrity.org.*

Legislation. To find out about lobbying regulations in your state, go to *http://findlaw.com* and read the actual legislation. This site allows you to search for laws by state and by topic. Another site that contains the full text of statutes and legislation by state is located at *www.prarienet.org/~scruffy/f.*

Searchable databases. Stories of lobbyist corruption and perfidy are always good grist for the journalistic mill. Your college or university library probably has one or more databases that allow you to search for articles in magazines, newspapers, and scholarly journals. Among the most useful databases are: *Dow Jones Interactive* (*http://nrstg1p.djnr.com*), *Lexis-Nexis Academic Universe* (*http://web.lexis-nexis.com*), *Pro-Quest Research Library* (*http://proquest.umi.com*), and *JSTOR* (*www.jstor.org*).

State government web sites. Many state governments have web sites that provide on-line access to state laws and regulations. State government web sites are indexed at *www.commoncause.org/states/stategovs*. You can also find state government sites using an Internet search engine.

Notes

1. Adriel Bettleheim, "Lawmakers at Work or Play?" *Denver Post,* November 24, 1997, p. B01.

2. Larry J. Sabato and Glenn R. Simpson, *Dirty Little Secrets* (New York: Times Books, 1996), p. 10.

3. Ibid., pp. 12–13.

4. For more information about the Crédit Mobilier scandal, see Ronald G. Athearn, *Union Pacific Country* (Lincoln: University of Nebraska Press, 1976).

5. Rudy Maxa, "The Paula Parkinson Story," *Washington Post,* March 29, 1981, p. F1.

6. Alan Rosenthal, *The Third House: Lobbyists and Lobbying in the States* (Washington, DC: Congressional Quarterly Press, 1993), p. 105.

7. Ibid., pp. 94–109.

8. Ibid., p. 112.

9. Ibid.

10. Ibid.

11. Ibid., p. 113.

12. Ibid., pp. 116–117.

13. Kenneth Silverstein, *Washington on $10 Million a Day: How Lobbyists Plunder the Nation* (Monroe, ME: Common Courage Press, 1998), pp. 148–149.

14. Ibid., p. 149.

15. Gannett News Service, "New Rules on Lobbying Are Signed," *Des Moines Register,* December 20, 1995, p. 5.

16. Kenneth A. Gross, "Lobbying Reform: The Ins and Outs of the New Federal Lobbying Registration and Reporting Law," *The Hill,* January 31, 1996, p. 27.

17. Ronald G. Shaiko, "Lobbying in Washington: A Contemporary Perspective," in Paul S. Herrnsen, Ronald G. Shaiko, and Clyde Wilcox, eds., *The Interest Group Connection* (Chatham, NJ: Chatham House, 1998), p. 14.

18. Peter Stone, "Lobbyists on a Leash?" *National Journal,* February 3, 1996, p. 242.

19. Thomas R. Dye, *Politics in States and Communities* (9th ed.) (Englewood Cliffs, NJ: Prentice Hall, 1997), p. 109.

20. Stone, "Lobbyists on a Leash?" p. 242.

21. Thomas R. Dye, *Politics in States and Communities* (9th ed.) (Upper Saddle River, NJ: Prentice Hall, 1997), p. 109.

22. Robert Salisbury, "Washington Lobbyists: A Collective Portrait," in Allan J. Cigler and Burdett A. Loomis, eds., *Interest Group Politics* (2nd ed.) (Washington, DC: Congressional Quarterly Press, 1986), pp. 146–161; Anthony J. Nownes and Patricia Freeman, "The People Who Lobby State Governments: Who They Are and What They Do," unpublished manuscript, 1998.

23. Lester Milbraith, *The Washington Lobbyists* (Chicago: Rand McNally, 1963), pp. 89–114.

24. See, for example, Salisbury, "Washington Lobbyists," pp. 151–153.

25. See Allan J. Cigler and Dwight C. Kiel, *The Changing Nature of Interest Group Politics in Kansas* (Topeka: Capitol Complex Center, University of Kansas, 1988).

26. Jonathan Rauch, *Government's End: Why Washington Stopped Working* (New York: Public Affairs, 1999), p. 92.

27. Lloyd Grove, "Lobbyists and Their Lucre," *Washington Post,* January 13, 2000, p. C3; Richard Whittle, "Lobbyists' Increasing Use of 'Revolving Door' Raises Concerns," *Dallas Morning News,* August 29, 1999, p. 1A.

28. Greg Hitt, "Former Speaker Re-Emerges as Lobbyist," *Wall Street Journal,* January 21, 2000, p. A20; Whittle, "Lobbyists' Increasing Use of 'Revolving Door' Raises Concerns."

29. Rosenthal, *The Third House: Lobbyists and Lobbying in the States* (Washington, DC: Congressional Quarterly Press, 1993), p. 32.

30. Ibid.; Steven Walters, "Lobbying's Top 40 Dominate Capitol Business," *Milwaukee Journal Sentinel,* March 26, 2000, p. 15A.

31. Salisbury, "Washington Lobbyists," pp. 152–153; Robert H. Salisbury and Paul E. Johnson, with John P. Heinz and Edward O. Laumann, "Who You Know Versus What You Know: The Uses of Governmental Experience for Washington Lobbyists," *American Journal of Political Science* 81 (February 1989): 1217–1234.

32. See Robert L. Nelson, John P. Heinz, Edward O. Laumann, and Robert Salisbury, "Private Representation in Washington: Surveying the Structure of Influence," *American Bar Foundation Research Journal* (Winter 1987): 141–200; and Salisbury, "Washington Lobbyists."

33. Lee Leonard, "Can 'Consultant' Bend the Rules?" *Columbus Dispatch,* February 7, 2000, p. 41; G. Galvin MacKenzie, *The In and Outers: Presidential Appointees and Transient Government in Washington* (Baltimore, MD: Johns Hopkins University Press, 1987); Lori Montgomery, "Former Legislators Enjoy Lobbying Afterlife," *Washington Post,* March 23, 2000, p. M1; Stephen Power, "Some Government Officials Turned Pipeline Lobbyists," Gannett News Service, October 27, 1999.

34. Peter H. Stone, "Starstruck," *National Journal,* June 21, 1997, pp. 1262–1265.

35. Paul J. Quirk, *Industry Influence in Federal Regulatory Agencies* (Princeton, NJ: Princeton University Press, 1987); Gordon Adams, *The Iron Triangle* (New York: Council on Economic Priorities, 1981).

36. Pat Choate, *Agents of Influence* (New York: Knopf, 1990).

37. Bruce C. Wolpe and Bertram J. Levine, *Lobbying Congress: How the System Works* (2nd ed.) (Washington, DC: Congressional Quarterly Press, 1996), pp. 13–19.

38. Ibid., p. 14.

39. Ibid.

40. Ibid.

41. Ibid., p. 15.

42. Ibid., p. 17.

43. Ibid., p. 18.

44. John P. Heinz, Edward O. Laumann, Robert L. Nelson, and Robert H. Salisbury, *The Hollow Core: Private Interests in National Policy-Making* (Cambridge, MA: Harvard University Press, 1993), chap. 11.

7 ▷ Lobbying with Campaign Money

Washington, D.C.
April 2, 1987

Senators Alan Cranston (D, California), John Glenn (D, Ohio), and John McCain (R, Arizona) arrive at the office of Senator Dennis DeConcini (D, Arizona). They are here to confront Edwin Gray, the head of the Federal Home Loan Bank Board, the regulatory body that oversees the nation's savings and loans. When Gray arrives, the senators ask him why he is pursuing his investigation of Charles Keating, Jr., so resolutely. Keating, a California businessman with a questionable past and an even more questionable business record, is the head of California's Lincoln Savings and Loan. Gray, taken aback by the senators' meddling, responds that he believes Keating may be violating a number of state and federal laws. Gray knows of what he speaks. On the basis of evidence he and other regulators gather, Keating is eventually convicted of looting Lincoln Savings and Loan of $2 billion. On this day, however, Keating is portrayed by the senators as an upright businessman who is being unfairly persecuted by overzealous regulators. This is not the only instance in which Keating's friends in high places have intervened on his behalf. Between 1987 and 1989, the four senators contact regulators at least a dozen times. Why do four U.S. senators[1] work so hard to help Charles Keating? Apparently the answer is money. Between 1980 and 1989, Keating gave the five senators $1.3 million in campaign contributions. Keating later acknowledges that he contributed the money in hopes that the senators would help him deal with federal and state regulators.[2]

As Charles Keating can attest, money is an important weapon in a lobbyist's arsenal. In this chapter, we explore how and why organized interests lobby with campaign money. We begin with a look at campaign finance in the United States and then examine precisely how organized interests lobby with campaign money. We pay special attention to political action committees—organized interests that exist solely to collect and spend money on electoral campaigns. Next we ask: What does organized interest money buy? As you will see, this question is difficult to answer. Finally, we examine the ethical implications of lobbying with campaign money. As you might expect, lobbying with campaign money is quite controversial with the American public.

CAMPAIGNS IN AMERICA

Political campaigns in America are expensive. In all, candidates and their parties spent over $2 billion on the 1996 presidential and congressional elections.[3] In the presidential election alone, major party candidates spent $387 million.[4] Political parties and PACs spent additional hundreds of thousands of dollars on behalf of presidential candidates.[5] In 1996 House races, candidates spent $477 million, and Senate candidates spent $287 million.[6] The corresponding numbers for 1998 were $452.5 million for House candidates and $287.8 million for Senate candidates.[7] To put these numbers in perspective, consider this: in 1998, the mean spending by House candidates was approximately $600,000, while the mean Senate candidate spent $4.8 million.[8] These figures, huge as they are, actually understate the cost of campaigns in America. Every year, political parties spend millions of dollars more that do not show up in these campaign cost estimates.

No one knows precisely how much state and local candidates spent in 1998. There is no central source for information on the thousands of subnational elections that take place each year. The evidence suggests, however, that like those at the federal level, state and local campaigns are quite costly. A number of recent races indicate just how costly. In the 1997 New York City mayoral race, for example, incumbent candidate Rudolph Giuliani spent approximately $10 million.[9] He won easily. Upstate, Giuliani's analogue in Albany, New York, spent $330,000 to win reelection.[10] In California, the average successful state legislative candidate typically spends well over $250,000 per election cycle, and many candidates spend over $1 million.[11] Candidates in less populous states also spend copiously. Candidates for the Indiana State General Assembly, for example, spent a combined $8 million in 1996.[12] Similarly, two candidates for a seat on the Wisconsin Supreme Court (many states have retention elections for state high court judges) combined to spend $1.4 million in 1999.[13] In all, political scientists estimate that candidates for state and local offices spend from $2 billion to $3 billion in a typical election year.[14]

In short, winning elective office in the United States is expensive. This does not mean, of course, that money ensures victory. No one knows this better than failed presidential candidate Ross Perot, who spent $70 million—over $63 million of his own money—in his failed 1992 presidential campaign. He spent another $40 million in 1996.[15] Other high-profile, free-spending losers include California Senate candidate Michael Huffington, who spent $27.9 million of his own money in a failed 1994 attempt to unseat Senator Dianne Feinstein, and Steve Forbes, Jr., who spent $42 million in the 1996 Republican presidential primaries.[16]

Although money does not guarantee success, virtually every candidate for elective office knows that to win an election requires spending serious money. What do candidates buy with all this money? The answer is fourfold. First, they buy advertising. Candidates advertise everywhere they can afford to, including on television and radio and in newspapers and magazines. Many also distribute yard signs, pass out bumper stickers, and knock on doors. One of the reasons that campaigns are so expensive is that television, the most common medium for campaign advertising, is also the most expensive. Second, candidates buy goods and services associated with advertising. The most obvious costs associated with advertising are copying and mailing costs. Third, candidates buy campaign help. Most candidates for statewide and national positions employ highly paid assistants who have titles like campaign manager, media consultant, and pollster, as well as clerical staff. Finally, candidates spend money on travel. Most candidates for public office travel a great deal while campaigning, especially to meet and greet voters. No matter what form of transportation a candidate uses to get around, travel is costly.

WHERE DOES THE MONEY COME FROM?

There are five main sources of campaign money: individuals, organized interests, political parties, the government, and candidates themselves.[17] To understand how organized interests lobby with campaign money, we must examine the part of the campaign finance system that pertains to organized interests.

Organized interests are important sources of money for electoral campaigns, although this has not always been the case. For most of the twentieth century, political parties accounted for virtually all campaign spending.[18] Of course, campaigns were much cheaper before 1960, because television was not a big factor in politics, and parties relied heavily on volunteer labor to do campaign legwork. In a system known as the patronage system, parties rewarded loyal party workers with favors, jobs, gifts, and improved public services. As for the money that parties did spend, they got it from two sources: the candidates themselves, who were chosen partially on the basis of how much money they were willing to spend on their own campaigns, and *fat cats,* wealthy individuals willing to underwrite party activities.[19]

The party-dominated system of campaign finance was relatively simple: parties nominated candidates and bankrolled their campaigns. Beginning in the late 1950s and early 1960s, as Americans increasingly turned to television for news and entertainment, candidates came to rely more and more on televised advertisements to get their messages out, producing an explosion in campaign spending. As Figure 7.1 indicates, spending in all American electoral campaigns

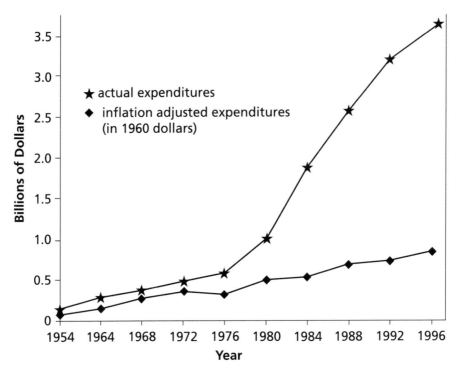

FIGURE 7.1 Estimated Campaign Costs, 1954–1996

Note: Figures are total expenditures for the nomination and election of public officials at all levels of government. Sources: William J. Keefe, *Parties, Politics, and Public Policy in America* (7th ed.) (Washington, D.C.: Congressional Quarterly Press, 1994), p. 152; Frank J. Sorauf, *Inside Campaign Finance: Myths and Realities* (New Haven, Conn.: Yale University Press, 1992), chap. 1, 2; Paul Allen Beck, *Party Politics in America* (8th ed.) (New York: Longman, 1997), p. 273.

rose from approximately $140 million in 1954 to $200 million in 1964, and from $200 million in 1964 to $425 million in 1972.[20] Spiraling campaign costs forced candidates to locate new sources of support. One place they looked was ordinary people. For example, a number of presidential candidates, including Barry Goldwater in 1964, George Wallace in 1968, and George McGovern in 1972, looked to individual contributors to bolster their chances. Candidates also came to rely more and more on their own fat cats, circumventing parties in the process. Richard Nixon, for example, found a really fat cat in 1968 when he received a campaign gift of $2.8 million from insurance tycoon W. Clement Stone. This still stands as the single largest individual contribution to a political candidate in American history.

As candidates scoured the landscape for new sources of money, they came to rely less and less on party money and on other forms of party support. Increasingly, they began to hire their own staffs, raise their own money, and call

Farewell When the extent of President Richard Nixon's misdeeds became known, he resigned the presidency. In the end, the Watergate scandal convinced Congress and the public that further campaign finance reforms were needed. *AP/Wide World Photos.*

their own shots. As campaign expert Frank Sorauf has written, "Whereas the people and events of the old campaigning had pivoted around the political party, the new configuration centered on the candidate."[21] By the late 1960s, national electoral campaigns had become free-for-alls in which candidates desperately sought ever-increasing sums of money needed to win office.

Responding to public concern about the deleterious effects of big money on elections, Congress passed the Federal Election Campaign Act of 1971 (FECA 1971). Just as FECA 1971 took effect, the Watergate scandal convinced Congress and the public that still more reforms were needed. On the heals of Richard Nixon's resignation from the presidency, Congress passed the Federal Election Campaign Act Amendments of 1974 (FECA 1974). FECA 1974, which essentially elaborated on FECA 1971, was amended twice more in the 1970s—once in 1976 and once in 1979. (Henceforth we will refer to FECA 1971 and all of its amendments simply as FECA.)

FECA mandated six major changes in federal campaign finance law. First, it established contribution limits. For example, individuals were limited to giving $1,000 per candidate per election (a primary and a general election count as two separate elections), up to a total of $25,000 per calendar year to all candidates and political action committees. In addition, PACs were limited to giving $5,000 per candidate per election, with no aggregate limit. Second, FECA instituted a disclosure regime. Specifically, it required all candidates for federal office to file itemized reports of all contributions and expenditures over $100. Third, FECA mandated the creation of the Federal Election Commission (FEC), the federal agency charged with keeping track of disclosure reports and punishing wrongdoers. Fourth, FECA created a system of public financing for presidential election campaigns. This system is extremely complex, but its basic contours are as follows. During the presidential primaries, the federal government provides matching funds for small donations to viable presidential candidates. During the general election, presidential candidates receive full public financing for their campaigns. The money used for matching funds and public financing comes from the $3 voluntary check-off on citizens' annual tax return. In return for public money, presidential candidates in both the primaries and the general election agree to limit their spending. In the general election, the recipients of federal funds agree not to raise or spend money from other sources. Fifth, FECA instituted spending limits for congressional candidates. These limits, however, were subsequently ruled unconstitutional by the Supreme Court in *Buckley v. Valeo*.[22] Finally, FECA clarified the role of organized interests in campaign finance: it banned direct contributions to candidates from all organized interests other than PACs.

Although FECA does not apply to state and local elections, in the 1970s many states and localities passed rules akin to it, although it is difficult to generalize about these rules because they differ from place to place. For now, it must suffice to say that most states and localities have some rules that govern campaign finance, and many have rules similar to those found in FECA.

LOBBYING WITH CAMPAIGN MONEY: THE USE OF POLITICAL ACTION COMMITTEES

The people who wrote FECA were concerned about the role of organized interests in federal election campaigns. They worried that candidates for public office would increasingly look to organized interests for the large sums of money they needed to be competitive. The reformers knew that there were rules on the books, but these rules were antiquated and ineffective. They noted, for example, that the outright ban on direct corporate contributions, which had been in place since 1907, did not stop President Nixon from tapping corporations and their executives for big money in 1972. They also acknowledged that a similar ban on direct labor union contributions, which had been on the books since 1943, did not stop unions from forming special PACs to collect voluntary contributions from members, to be passed along to candidates for federal office.

In short, the authors of FECA were concerned that the rules governing organized interest involvement in federal election campaigns were neither clear nor effective, and so one of their goals was to clarify and strengthen these rules. To this end, Congress included a provision in FECA that outlawed all direct contributions from organized interests other than PACs to candidates for federal office. Nonetheless, thousands of organized interests other than PACs are active in election campaigns. How is this possible? This is the question we address in this section. Specifically, we examine the five traditional techniques by which organized interests lobby with campaign money: making PAC contributions to federal candidates, making PAC contributions to state and local candidates, spending independently on behalf of or in opposition to candidates, making in-kind contributions, and bundling.

Making PAC Contributions to Federal Candidates

One way that organized interests lobby with campaign money despite FECA's ban on most direct contributions to federal candidates is by making PAC contributions. To understand how organized interests lobby with campaign money by making PAC contributions, we must delve more deeply into what PACs are and how they operate.

Before we do this, however, it is important to note that giving money directly to public officials to influence their decisions is against the law. This is bribery. However, as you will see subsequently, contributing money to policymakers' electoral campaigns is not against the law. The fact that direct contributions to policymakers are illegal while contributions to electoral campaigns are not has two important implications. First, it means that when a PAC contributes money to a policymaker, it does not actually contribute money to the policymaker as an individual. Rather, it contributes money to the policymaker's electoral campaign. Let us say that a PAC wishes to give $1,000 to Senator Trent Lott (R, Mississippi). It cannot simply hand Lott a check for $1,000. Rather, it must write a check to Lott's campaign committee, a separate organizational entity that exists solely to help Lott win elections. This committee, however, is not allowed to pass any money along to Lott himself; it can only spend money on Lott's behalf in electoral campaigns. The fact that direct contributions to policymakers are illegal while contributions to electoral campaigns are not has one other important implication: the vast majority (over 99 percent) of policymakers at all levels of government are ineligible to receive monetary contributions of any kind. Because most government policymakers, including legislative staff, bureaucrats of all stripes, federal judges, and chief executive aides, do not run for office, they are ineligible to receive monetary contributions. In sum, when organized interests contribute money to policymakers, they are not contributing money to policymakers themselves; they are contributing money to policymakers' campaign committees.

Now let us return to precisely how organized interests lobby with campaign money. Although FECA does not allow organized interests other than PACs to contribute money to candidates for federal office, it does allow corporations, trade associations, labor unions, professional associations, citizen groups, and coalitions to create affiliated PACs to do so. Specifically, FECA states that these types of organized interests may make monetary contributions to federal candidates by setting up separate segregated funds called PACs. A *separate segregated fund* is defined by FECA as one that does not contain "membership dues or other money as a condition of employment or membership or any money obtained through a commercial transaction."[23] This language in the law exposes an important catch for organized interests that wish to set up PACs: the money that flows to an organized interest's PAC cannot come from the treasury of that organized interest, but rather must come from individuals affiliated with that organization. This is an important point and thus bears repeating: FECA states that all PAC money must come from individuals. Further, FECA states that an *affiliated PAC*—a PAC connected to another organized interest—can obtain money only from individuals associated with its parent organization. A corporate PAC, for example, can receive money only from its parent company's executives, employees, and stockholders.

The rules that govern organized interests and their PACs are complicated. To illustrate how these rules work in practice, consider the hypothetical case of an oil company called EXOFF that wishes to make a contribution to an oil-friendly senator from Texas. FECA does not allow EXOFF to take money from its treasury—money it obtains from selling petroleum products—and contribute it to the senator. However, FECA does allow EXOFF to set up a separate affiliated organization called EXOFF PAC to contribute money to the oil-friendly Texan. EXOFF PAC can collect money from EXOFF employees, executives, and shareholders but not from anyone else. In line with FECA's contribution limits, EXOFF PAC can contribute up to $5,000 per election to the senator.

Our hypothetical scenario begs the following question: Can't EXOFF simply create a PAC, transfer money from its corporate treasury to the PAC, and have the PAC pass money on to the senator? No. FECA forbids organized interests from funding their affiliated PACs in this matter. Nonetheless, the relationship between a parent organization and its PAC is generally a close one. In 1975, the Sun Oil Company went to the FEC and asked if it was allowed to pay for the administrative and fund-raising costs of operating its affiliated PAC. The FEC, which Congress empowered to interpret FECA, answered yes.[24] Thus, although organized interests are not allowed to contribute money directly to their affiliated PACs, they are allowed to pay the expenses incurred by their affiliated PACs. This administration loophole blurs the line between a PAC and its parent organization. Nonetheless, the line still exists and is drawn most obviously at the point at which a PAC can contribute money to candidates while a parent organization cannot.

Thus far, we have discussed only *affiliated PACs*—PACs that are affiliated with other organized interests. FECA also allows the creation of *nonaffiliated PACs*—PACs that have no parent organizations. A nonaffiliated PAC is essentially a citizen group that does nothing but collect money from individuals and spend it on election campaigns. As is the case for affiliated PACs, nonaffiliated PACs may raise money only from individuals. However, virtually any individual may give money to a nonaffiliated PAC. Nonaffiliated PACs constitute only about 25 percent of all PACs.

FECA opened the door to far-reaching organized interest involvement in federal election campaigns. As Figure 7.2 attests, the number of PACs active in federal elections increased almost exponentially between 1970 and 1984. In 1972, there were only 113 PACs registered with the FEC. By the end of 1974, there were five times that many (608).[25] By the end of 1984, there were 4,009, an increase of 3,500 percent in twelve years. Since 1984 the number of nationally active PACs has leveled off and actually fallen a bit.[26] As of late 1999, there were 3,778 PACs registered with the FEC.[27]

As the number of PACs has grown, so has the level of PAC involvement in federal electoral campaigns. During the 1995–1996 election cycle, PACs contributed $217.8 million to candidates for federal office, up $28.5 million, or 13 percent, from the 1993–1994 election cycle, and up $77.9 million, or 36 percent, from 1985–1986.[28] PAC spending remained flat two years later, as PACs contributed $219.9 million to candidates for federal office during the 1997–1998 election cycle.[29]

Although PACs are important sources of campaign money for candidates, they are by no means dominant. Of all the money raised during the 1996 presidential primary campaign, for example, 52 percent came from individuals, 23 percent came from the federal government, and 19 percent came from the candidates themselves. Only 1 percent came from PACs.[30] During the general

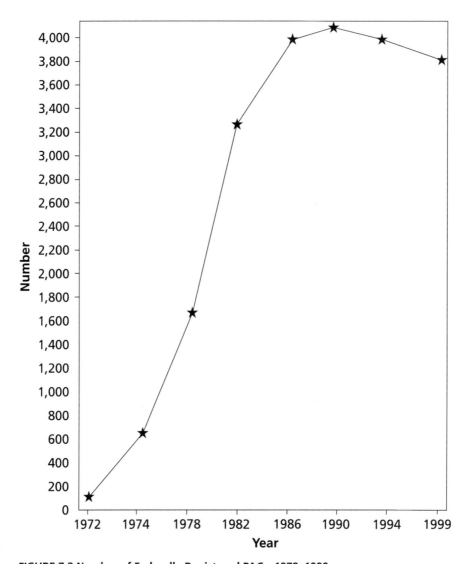

FIGURE 7.2 Number of Federally Registered PACs, 1972–1999

Sources: Federal Election Commission, "PAC Count, 1974–Present," accessed at *http://www.fec.gov/press/paccount*; Federal Election Commission, "FEC Issues Semi-Annual Federal PAC Count," accessed at *http://www.fec.gov /press/pcnt799*, November 16, 1999.

election, neither Bob Dole, the Republican presidential candidate, nor Bill Clinton, the Democratic candidate, received any PAC money.

PACs are much more active in congressional elections, but they are still far from the most important sources of campaign money. In the 1995–1996 congressional elections, for example, contributions from individuals accounted for 56 percent of total receipts by congressional candidates, while PACs accounted for only 25 percent—16 percent of receipts in Senate races and 31 percent in House races.[31] Similarly, in the 1997–1998 congressional elections, individuals accounted for 54 percent of total receipts by congressional candidates, while PACs accounted for only 26 percent—17 percent of receipts in Senate races and 32 percent in House races.[32]

Making Contributions to State and Local Candidates

Another way that organized interests lobby with campaign money despite FECA's ban on most direct contributions to federal candidates is by making contributions to state and local candidates. Although campaign finance laws vary from place to place, virtually all states and localities allow organized interests, either directly or indirectly through PACs, to support candidates. In states and localities that allow direct contributions to candidates, organized interests simply donate money from their treasuries to candidates they support.[33] In states and localities with regulations like FECA, organized interests establish PACs that behave much like nationally active PACs.

Definitive data on the number of organized interests active in state and local campaigns are not available. Nevertheless, it is clear that the number of subnational PACs has increased dramatically since the early 1970s. One study found that in most states, PAC numbers had risen between 200 and 800 percent between the mid-1970s and mid-1980s.[34] Another study estimates that there are well over 12,000 active subnational PACs.[35] We do not know precisely how much organized interests and their PACs spend in state and local elections, but evidence from many quarters suggests that the total is in the tens of millions of dollars. In Iowa, for example, the seven largest PACs in the state combined to spend almost $700,000 from 1993 to 1996.[36] Similarly, in Minnesota, PAC spending topped $3 million in 1996.[37] And between 1994 and 1996, just three Alabama PACs combined to contribute more than $11 million to candidates for statewide office.[38] In all, the evidence suggests that PACs are fast becoming major sources of campaign money in subnational elections. In some states, PACs regularly account for over 30 percent of contributions to legislative candidates. And in several states, PACs regularly account for over half of all contributions to incumbent legislators.[39]

Independent Spending

Another way that organized interests lobby with campaign money despite FECA's ban on direct contributions to federal candidates is by using their PACs to spend money independently on behalf of or in opposition to candidates. FECA stipulates that organized interests, through their PACs, may conduct independent spending campaigns on behalf of or in opposition to candidates for federal office. Most states and localities allow independent PAC spending as well.

In general, PACs that spend independently do so on pro- or anticandidate advertisements on television or radio, in newspapers or magazines, or through mailings and brochures. The appeal of independent spending at the federal level is that a PAC may spend as much as it wants for or against a candidate. There is no $5,000 limit as there is with contributions. FECA stipulates, however, that independent spending must be truly independent. That is, a PAC that spends independently on a candidate's behalf must refrain from coordinating its efforts with that candidate. States and localities have different rules on precisely how independent spending must be.

Independent spending was perhaps most noticeable in the 1980 congressional elections, during which the National Conservative Political Action Committee (NCPAC) spent over $3 million.[40] NCPAC targeted six liberal Democratic senators, four of whom lost. Despite NCPAC's apparent success, independent expenditures typically account for under 5 percent of all PAC spending in both federal and subnational campaigns in a typical election year.[41] In the 1995–1996 election cycle, for example, independent spending accounted for only 4.8 percent of PAC spending in federal elections.[42] Independent spending accounted for approximately the same proportion of federal PAC spending in 1997–1998.[43]

There are two reasons that independent spending is so uncommon. First, most organized interests are loath to alienate candidates with whom they may have to deal subsequently. If a PAC takes a strong, public, and expensive stand in favor of one candidate over another in a particular election, it runs the risk of supporting the loser and alienating the person with whom it will eventually have to deal. Most organized interests like to have good relationships with all legislators, not just those who share their views. Second, independent spending is expensive. Television advertisements in particular are very costly.

Bundling

Some organized interests lobby with campaign money by *bundling*: collecting checks from individual contributors and then turning them over to a candidate or candidates. On the federal level, only PACs may bundle. Thus, when an organized interest that is not a PAC wishes to bundle, it must form a PAC to do so. Some states and localities also allow all types of organized interests to bundle. Even so, today virtually all bundling is done by PACs.

Here is how bundling works. A PAC collects a large number of checks. Each individual check, however, is addressed not to the PAC but rather to the candidate who will eventually receive the money. The PAC then bundles each candidate's checks together and passes them along to him or her. Thus, when a PAC bundles, it is not technically the source of the money, but rather acts as a conduit or middle man. Bundling allows PACs to circumvent the limits on PAC contributions. Thus, instead of giving a one-time-only PAC contribution of $5,000 to a candidate for federal office, a PAC may bundle a bunch of individual checks together and contribute much more than $5,000.

An example will illustrate how bundling works in practice. The most prolific and successful PAC bundler in history is a feminist organization, EMILY's List. EMILY is an acronym for "early money is like yeast." It is like yeast, the founder of EMILY's List likes to say, because "it makes the dough rise." EMILY's list was founded in 1986 by political veteran Ellen Malcolm, who designed it as a vehicle to support prochoice, Democratic, female congressional candidates.[44] EMILY's List relies almost solely on bundling to support candidates. To join EMILY's List, a contributor must make a $100 contribution to the PAC itself and must also pledge to contribute at least $100 to a minimum of two candidates endorsed by EMILY's List. The $100 direct contribution goes to cover the PAC's fund-raising and administrative costs. The contributions to the candidates are sent not to the candidates themselves but rather to EMILY's List, to be bundled with other contributions and then passed on to candidates.[45] Individuals are still subject to the $1,000 contribution limit spelled out in FECA. However, EMILY's List is not limited in how much bundled money it can give to any specific candidate.

EMILY's List, which is widely recognized as one of the pioneers of bundling, has demonstrated to other PACs that bundling can work. EMILY's List first flexed its muscle in 1986, when it contributed $150,000 to successful upstart Senate candidate Barbara Mikulski, a prochoice Democrat from Maryland. EMILY's List continued its winning streak in 1990 when it bundled $400,000 for Ann Richards, the successful prochoice Democratic governor of Texas. Today EMILY's List is the most generous PAC in the nation. It boasts over 45,000 members and spent $13,619,906 during the 1995–1996 election cycle and $10,295,325 during the 1997–1998 election cycle. Most of this money was bundled and contributed to congressional candidates.

Bundling is not as common as direct PAC giving, but its popularity is growing. Recently a group of Republicans set up a Republican version of EMILY's List called WISH List (*WISH* stands for "Women in the Senate and House").[46] In addition, a number of state and local PACs have begun bundling in recent years.[47] Nonetheless, despite the success of EMILY's list, bundling remains the purview of a few nonaffiliated, ideologically driven PACs. For reasons we discuss later, most PACs would rather contribute money directly to candidates than bundle.

Making In-Kind Campaign Contributions

Finally, organized interests lobby with campaign money by using their PACs to make *in-kind campaign contributions*—a gift other than money that a PAC gives to a candidate. The most common types of in-kind gifts are services with monetary value.

One of the most prolific users of in-kind contributions is a PAC called the National Committee for an Effective Congress (NCEC), and it nicely illustrates how PACs make in-kind campaign contributions. The NCEC, the oldest PAC in the United States, was founded by Eleanor Roosevelt in 1948 to support "progressive" candidates for Congress.[48] Although it contributes money to candidates, it spends most of its money on in-kind campaign contributions. Specifically, NCEC provides services designed to help candidates get elected. For example, it provides candidates with expert advice on how to mobilize liberal voters. In addition, it provides polling services and advertising advice.[49] EMILY's List also provides in-kind contributions to candidates. In addition to money, a candidate backed by EMILY's can expect campaign consulting services, voter mobilization help, and fund-raising assistance.[50] In-kind contributions are not nearly as common as monetary contributions. But there is some evidence that they are becoming more common.

Using PACs to Lobby with Campaign Money: A Summary

Studies show that approximately half of all organized interests active at the state level and 60 percent of organized interests active in Washington engage in some form of lobbying with campaign money.[51] Although we have no way of knowing how often each of these five techniques is used by political action committees, we do know that making PAC contributions is the most common form of PAC activity, with independent spending, bundling, and in-kind giving lagging behind. Evidence from recent elections suggests, however, that all of these activities are becoming more common.

THE NEW WAYS TO LOBBY WITH CAMPAIGN MONEY: ELECTION ISSUE ADVOCACY AND SOFT MONEY

Ostensibly, FECA requires organized interests that are not PACs to form PACs before they can make monetary or in-kind contributions to candidates for federal office, spend money on behalf of or in opposition to candidates for federal office, or engage in bundling. Similarly, most states and localities have laws that require organized interests other than PACs to form PACs before they can engage in any of the five monetary lobbying techniques. One of the ideas behind FECA and similar state and local laws was to eliminate most direct organized interest involvement in electoral campaigns. Another was to control the amount an organized interest could spend on electoral activity. All told, the authors of FECA and similar state and local statutes intended to constrain the activities of organized interests in electoral campaigns.

It has become clear that these laws did not work.[52] Larger numbers of organized interests than ever before have PACs and are thus involved in election campaigns, and bundling and independent spending have allowed organized interests and their PACs to circumvent contribution limits. Nothing, however, better demonstrates the failure of campaign finance laws to limit organized interest activity and influence in electoral campaigns like the prevalence of two relatively new ways that organized interests lobby with campaign money: engaging in issue advocacy campaigns and making soft money contributions to political parties.

Engaging in Election Issue Advocacy

Many organized interests lobby with campaign money by engaging in *election issue advocacy,* defined as spending that advocates a particular position on an issue rather than the election or defeat of a particular candidate, but is nonetheless intended to affect the outcome of an election.[53] We use the term *election issue advocacy* rather than simply *issue advocacy* to distinguish organized interest spending that advocates a particular issue position but is *not* intended to affect the outcome of an election from organized interest spending that advocates a particular issue position but *is* intended to affect the outcome of an election. The former activity is a type of indirect lobbying (which we call *lobbying to affect public opinion*) that we discuss in some detail in the next chapter.

Election issue advocacy is much like spending independently but is different in two important respects. First, election issue advocacy does not explicitly urge the election or defeat of a candidate. It does, however, implicitly urge the election or defeat of a candidate. Second, election issue advocacy is not subject to FECA regulations. This means that in addition to PACs, other types of organized interests, including labor unions, citizen groups, corporations, trade associations, and professional associations, may engage in election issue advocacy. It also means that there is no limit on the amount an organized interest can spend on election issue advocacy and that organized interests that engage in election issue advocacy do not have to disclose their activities to the government or the public.

Election issue advocacy was virtually unheard of in the 1970s and early 1980s. Since then, however, it has evolved into a relatively common lobbying technique. Beginning in the mid-1980s, a number of organized interests began experimenting with election issue advocacy as a way to get around the provisions of FECA. If you recall, FECA's provisions ostensibly limit the extent of organized interest involvement in federal campaigns. But many organized interests were not happy with these limits. They felt hamstrung and wished to do more, spend more, and disclose less. The result was election issue advocacy.

Organized interests engage in election issue advocacy in two basic ways: they air election issue advertisements on television and radio, and they distribute voter guides. First, we will look at advertising. Two examples illustrate how organized interests use this technique. The first example comes from the 1992 presidential election campaign, during which a citizen group called the Christian Action Network (CAN) funded a television advertisement that set the standard for election issue advocacy advertising. CAN's advertisement opened up with a color picture of Bill Clinton's face superimposed on a billowing American flag. As the narrator somberly reports that Bill Clinton supports "radical homosexual causes," the color picture of Clinton morphs into a black-and-white negative. Next, the advertisement shows a series of pictures of gay rights advocates. The pictures come from a gay rights parade, and many of the activists pictured are wearing rather provocative (often leather) clothing and aggressively yelling slogans and chants. As the images of radical gay rights advocates stream across the screen, the narrator asks, "Is this your vision for a better America?" In closing, the narrator states, "For more information on traditional family values, contact the Christian Action Network."[54] This election issue advocacy advertisement was an ingenious way for the organization to work against the election of Bill Clinton without having to abide by FECA's rules. Because the advertisement did not *explicitly* advocate the defeat of Bill Clinton, CAN was not required to abide by FECA. That is, it was not required to form a PAC, disclose its activities to the FEC, or limit its spending. In sum, CAN was free to do whatever it pleased.

The second example of election issue advocacy advertising comes from the 1996 congressional campaign. During that campaign, the AFL-CIO ran a series of advertisements designed to help Democratic challengers unseat Republican House incumbents. One of the organization's advertisements was aired in Republican House member George Nethercutt's (Washington) district and featured the following voice-over:

> Congressman George Nethercutt voted to cut our Medicare benefits. George Nethercutt knows it. And so do we. Fact: on November 17, 1995, Nethercutt voted with Newt Gingrich to cut $270 billion from Medicare funding, while voting for tax breaks for the wealthy. Now he's trying to deny it. Tell George Nethercutt we know the truth about his vote to cut our Medicare benefits. Another vote is coming. This time, we'll be watching.[55]

Note that this advertisement, like CAN's, does not explicitly advocate the defeat of a candidate. It does, however, implicitly do so.

Advertisements like these are becoming increasingly common. In all, there was more election issue advocacy advertising during the 1996 presidential election campaign than in any previous presidential election campaign in history.

Similarly, there was more such election issue advocacy advertising during the 1996 and 1998 congressional election campaigns than ever before. In fact, the AFL-CIO advertisement was part of the largest election issue advocacy campaign in American history. The purpose of the campaign was to defeat 105 House Republicans whom the AFL-CIO viewed as hostile to working Americans. All told, the AFL-CIO spent $35 million on television and radio advertisements designed to hurt Republican candidates.[56] The advertisements did not explicitly urge the defeat of Republican candidates, but were clearly intended to mobilize opposition to Republicans.

The AFL-CIO's campaign set off a chain reaction of sorts. In response to the campaign, the National Federation of Independent Business (NFIB), the U.S. Chamber of Commerce, the National Association of Manufacturers, the National Restaurant Association, and the National Association of Wholesaler-Distributors formed The Coalition—Americans Working for Real Change, which launched a multimillion-dollar issue advocacy counterattack. The coalition spent nearly $5 million on 6,000 television commercials and 7,000 radio advertisements designed to help Republican candidates in thirty-seven House elections. Republican House candidates were also helped by the Christian Coalition and the National Rifle Association, which launched large-scale issue advocacy campaigns of their own.[57]

The second way that organized interests engage in election issue advocacy is by distributing *voter guides*, brief tracts that present candidates' positions on issues of concern to organized interests and their supporters.[58] David Magleby, an expert on issue advocacy in congressional elections, describes voter guides as follows: "These guides portray numerous issues on which the candidates have either voted or voiced their platform; the [organized interests] judge these responses with a thumbs up or down or a numerated scale."[59] Most organized interests say that their voter guides are objective. In reality, however, most voter guides obviously tilt in favor of one candidate over the other.

An example illustrates how voter guides are used. In 1996, the Sierra Club spent $3.5 million to distribute over 150,000 voter guides in twenty-three states.[60] The guides, one observer noted:

> displayed candidate positions on the issues without explicitly advocating the election of any one candidate. Each guide presented voters with a chart showing candidate stands on environmental issues. By identifying voters with environmental sympathies and targeting races in which one of the candidates had a poor environmental record, the Club allowed voters to draw their own conclusions, knowing full well what they would be.[61]

The Sierra Club distributed its voter guides to people it believed were sympathetic to environmental causes. Some voter guides were mailed to voters, and others were delivered personally by volunteers. Voter guides, like election issue advocacy advertisements, are a way for organized interests to engage in campaign activity without having to abide by the provisions of FECA. As long as voter guides do not explicitly argue for or against a specific candidate, an organized interest is free to distribute them with impunity.

No other organized interest has used voter guides more than the Christian Coalition. In 1994 alone, the Christian Coalition spent $25 million on voter guides.[62] The voter guides were "distributed widely at churches, shopping malls, convenience stories, and even gas stations," and are credited by many observers with helping Republicans gain a majority in Congress.[63] The coalition continued its extensive use of voter guides in 1996 and 1998. During the 1998 campaign, for example, it distributed tens of millions of voter guides. In one race alone—the campaign for a Senate seat in Kentucky—the organization distributed over 500,000 voter guides.[64]

Because election issue advocacy is virtually unregulated, it is very controversial. Critics of election issue advocacy charge that it is antithetical to the spirit, if not the letter, of campaign finance law. For example, many observers note that unlimited spending makes a mockery of FECA and similar state and local campaign finance laws and regulations. The problems with unlimited spending, critics say, are threefold. First, it allows wealthy organized interests to have a louder voice than not-so-wealthy organized interests. In other words, unlimited spending introduces the kind of bias into the electoral system that FECA was designed to eliminate. Second, unlimited spending contributes to public cynicism. Clyde Wilcox and Wesley Joe, two experts who are critical of election issue advocacy, note that election issue advocacy campaigns contribute to the public perception that "the current election finance system privileges affluent organized interests."[65] Finally, election issue advocacy is problematic because it can remain secret and undisclosed. At the federal level and in most states and localities, organized interests that engage in election issue advocacy are not forced to report where their money comes from, how much they spend, or what they spend their money on. Critics maintain that this makes it impossible for voters to know which organized interests back which candidates. Without disclosure, critics say, democratic accountability suffers.

No one knows exactly how prevalent election issue advocacy is. The fact that organized interests that engage in federal election issue advocacy are not required to disclose their activities makes it exceptionally hard to determine exactly how much they spend on issue advocacy in federal elections. Moreover, no one has ever studied issue advocacy at the state or local level. Although we know that many organized interests at the state and local levels use election issue advocacy, we do not know to what extent. Despite a lack of data, however, it is clear that election issue advocacy is more common than ever before. One study estimates that thirty-one organized interests spent a combined $135 million to $150 million on election issue advocacy in federal election campaigns during the 1995–1996 election cycle.[66] This amount doubled in 1997–1998, as approximately fifty organized interests spent between $275 million and $340 million on election issue advocacy to influence federal elections.[67]

Contributing Money to Political Parties:
The Soft Money Controversy

Another relatively new way that organized interests lobby with campaign money is by contributing money to political parties. FECA and virtually all states and localities allow organized interests, including corporations, trade associations, labor unions, professional associations, citizen groups, PACs, and coalitions, to contribute money to political parties. This is the simple part. The difficult part is explaining how and for what purposes organized interests contribute money to political parties.

We start with the federal rules on organized interest contributions to national political party committees. The Democrats have three main national party committees—the Democratic National Committee, the Democratic Congressional Campaign Committee, and the Democratic Senatorial Campaign Committee—and the Republicans have four—the Republican National Committee, the National Republican Congressional Committee, the National Republican Senatorial Committee, and the Republican Senate-House Dinner Committee. These committees are set up to help candidates get elected. FECA stipulates that organized interests other than PACs may *not* make direct contributions to national party committees for the purpose of influencing elections. PACs, in contrast, are allowed to contribute up to $15,000 per year to any national party committee for the purpose of influencing elections. These rules seem straightforward, but they are not. In the late 1970s and early 1980s, the two major political parties' national committees began to accept large direct contributions from labor unions and corporations, seemingly in violation of FECA. They also began soliciting PAC contributions in excess of $15,000. The national Democratic and Republican political parties argued that because FECA applied only to federal elections, it did not bar their national committees from accepting contributions that defied FECA's guidelines as long as these contributions were *not* used to finance activities related to federal elections. These contributions, the parties argued, could be used for "party-building activities" such as voter registration drives, voter education, and get-out-the-vote drives and to influence state and local elections.

When both parties' national committees began to accept large donations directly from corporations, labor unions, and individuals in the early 1980s, some observers charged that they were breaking the law. Other observers—particularly fund raisers for the two major political parties—held that FECA, particularly through amendments added in 1979, explicitly allowed unrestricted donations to national party committees as long as donated funds were not used to influence federal elections. Although initially the FEC balked at the parties' arguments, eventually it agreed that money that is not spent to affect federal elections is not subject to FECA's rules. By sanctioning the parties' acceptance of huge individual, corporate, and labor contributions, the FEC essentially allowed national party committees to accept unlimited direct organized interest contributions "beyond the statutory limits as long as that money is not spent to promote federal candidates."[68] These extrastatutory contributions are called *soft money*, which is defined as money contributed outside the guidelines of FECA. A more accessible definition is "the unlimited amounts of money contributed to political party committees by individuals, corporations, labor unions, and other organized interests."

Soft money can be used to raise more soft money, support candidates for state and local office directly, support state and local parties for "party-building activities that do not promote federal candidates (e.g., slate cards, yard signs, bumper stickers, and sample ballots distributed by volunteers)," "promote the party or its candidates as a class without mentioning specific names," and pay for national committees' administrative and overhead costs.[69] Technically, soft money cannot be used in direct support of candidates running for federal office. But many soft money contributions indirectly support federal candidates nonetheless. Covering administrative and overhead costs for national party committees, for example, clearly benefits candidates for federal office by freeing up *hard money*—money donated to political parties that is given and spent within the confines of FECA—that can be funneled directly to candidates for federal office. Moreover, soft money is often used to fund party election issue advocacy advertisements much like those funded by organized interests.

Another form of soft money is money donated by organized interests to state and local party committees. Because these contributions are governed by state and local rules rather than FECA, they too are considered soft money. Some states and localities allow direct contributions from organized interests such as corporations, labor unions, trade associations, professional associations, citizen groups, and coalitions to political party committees, and virtually all states and localities allow PAC contributions to state and local political party committees. Soft money donated to state and local party committees, like soft money donated to national party committees, cannot be used to influence federal elections directly. However, it can be used for the same purposes for which national party committee soft money is used, and thus it often indirectly affects federal elections.

Critics of soft money argue that it completely undermines campaign finance laws. The nonpartisan good government group Common Cause, for example, argues that soft money "is precisely the kind of money which federal law and policy have sought to exclude from national campaigns."[70] What is wrong with soft money? First, critics contend that it makes a mockery of campaign contribution limits. They may have a point here. Table 7.1 contains a list of the top soft money donors to the two major parties in 1999. As you can see, organized interests use soft money to circumvent FECA's contribution limits. Second, critics argue that although soft money is not supposed to be used to affect federal elections, in practice it often is. Critics point out, for example, that during the 1996 presidential campaign, soft money was used by both political parties to fund party advertisements designed to influence the outcome of the presidential election. As political analyst Brooks Jackson has noted, Democratic issue

TABLE 7.1 Top Ten Soft Money Donors, 1999

Contributor	Amount	Recipient
American Federation of State, County, and Municipal Employees	$1,405,000	Democrats
Communications Workers of America	1,175,000	Democrats
Philip Morris and Cos. Inc	922,067	Republicans
Service Employees International Union	818,250	Democrats
AT&T	761,908	Republicans
United Parcel Service	608,559	Republicans
Aviation Product Management	561,000	Democrats
AT&T	553,350	Democrats
American Financial Group	550,000	Republicans
Dominion Resources	513,378	Republicans

Note: Amounts include contributions from subsidiaries and executives.
Source: Common Cause, "100 Percent Special-Interest Financing," accessed at *http://www.commoncause.org /soft_money/study99/top*, April 18, 2000.

ads funded by soft money attacked "Bob Dole relentlessly by name while praising President Clinton," while Republican issue ads funded by soft money praised "Dole as the protector of 'America's values.'"[71]

No one knows precisely how many organized interests make soft money contributions. Nonetheless, it is clear that more and more organized interests are contributing more and more soft money than ever before. The figures tell the story. During the 1997–1998 off-year election cycle, the national Republican party raised $131.6 million in soft money, while the Democrats raised $92.8 million.[72] During the 1995–1996 presidential election cycle, the national Republican party took in $141 million in soft money, while the Democrats collected $122 million.[73] During the 1991–1992 election cycle, the totals were $50 million for Republicans and $37 million for Democrats. Thus, the 1995–1996 numbers represent a threefold increase in soft money receipts. In all, soft money accounted for 30 percent of the total $881 million contributed to the two national parties in 1995–1996.[74] There is evidence that the 1999–2000 election cycle will set new records for soft money contributions.

For our purposes, the most important point to remember about soft money is this: it constitutes a way for organized interests to contribute huge sums of money to political parties and thus influence elections at all levels of government. Soft money remains controversial. To critics, it represents precisely the kind of unlimited and unregulated organized interests involvement in elections that FECA and similar state and local statutes were designed to eliminate. In the end, many observers view soft money as a simple way to circumvent campaign finance laws designed to dampen organized interest influence on electoral outcomes.

WHAT DOES CAMPAIGN MONEY BUY?

Few other things invite cynicism and suspicion like campaign contributions. The reason is simple: contributing money smacks of bribery. Many people feel that monetary contributions make elected officials beholden to organized interests. Veteran political reporter Brooks Jackson has concluded that campaign contributions "twist the behavior of ordinary" policymakers by rewarding "those who cater to well-funded interests" and punishing those who do not.[75] Is Jackson right? Does organized interest campaign money skew policy outcomes toward the interests of big money donors and away from those of ordinary citizens?

Overall the weight of the evidence seems to suggest that the answer is no.[76] Academic studies indicate that in most cases, lobbying with campaign money does not substantially influence policymakers' behavior, for two reasons. First, there are too many other factors that influence policymakers' decisions for money to have much of an impact. Factors such as political party, ideology, and constituent opinion, for example, are far more influential than money. Second, most organized interest contributions are not large. Although organized interests and their PACs give tens of millions of dollars to candidates and parties each year, most campaign contributions are very small. Political scientist Frank Sorauf has discovered, for example, that the average PAC contribution to a House candidate is about $1,000, and the average PAC contribution to a Senate candidate is just over $2,000.[77] Organized interest contributions to state and local policymakers are generally even smaller. Few elected officials are willing to sell out for a thousand dollars or so.

If money does not substantially alter the policy decisions of elected officials, why do so many organized interests give so much of it away? The answer lies in what money can buy: access, small favors, and a government more to one's liking.

Access

One of the most important things that campaign money can buy is access.[78] Table 7.2 contains a list of the twenty PACs that contributed the most to federal candidates during the 1997–1998 federal election cycle. What is most noticeable about the PACs listed is that all are affiliated with parent organizations. Eleven are affiliated with labor unions, five with trade associations, two with professional associations, one with a corporation, and the other with a citizen group. Similarly, virtually all of the organized interest soft money donors listed in

TABLE 7.2 Top Twenty Nationally Active PACs, 1997–1998

Name	Amount Contributed to Candidates for Federal Office
1. Realtors PAC	$2,474,133
2. Association of Trial Lawyers of America PAC	2,428,300
3. American Federation of State, County, and Municipal Employees PAC	2,374,950
4. American Medical Association PAC	2,336,281
5. Democratic Republican Independent Voter Education Committee (Teamsters)	2,183,250
6. Dealers Election Action Committee of the National Automobile Dealers Association	2,107,800
7. United Auto Workers Voluntary Community Action Program	1,915,460
8. International Brotherhood of Electrical Workers Committee on Political Education	1,884,470
9. National Education Association PAC	1,853,390
10. BUILD—PAC of the National Association of Home Builders	1,807,240
11. Committee on Letter Carriers PAC	1,760,496
12. Machinists Non-Partisan Political League	1,637,300
13. National Rifle Association Political Victory Fund	1,633,211
14. United Parcel Service of America PAC	1,527,149
15. United Food and Commercial Workers Active Ballot Club	1,505,951
16. American Federation of Teachers Committee on Political Education	1,415,400
17. Laborers Political League	1,413,850
18. Carpenters Legislative Improvement Committee	1,372,423
19. National Association of Life Underwriters PAC	1,336,000
20. National Beer Wholesalers Association PAC	1,301,719

Note: Some numbers were rounded by the FEC.
Source: Federal Election Commission, "Top 50 PACs, Contributions to Candidates," accessed at *http://www.fec. gov/press/paccnt98,* November 21, 1999.

Table 7.1 have extensive lobbying operations in Washington. The point is that for most organized interests, lobbying with campaign money is just one small part of a larger strategy that encompasses many lobbying techniques.[79] To demonstrate this fact, one recent study reported that the average organized interest that made monetary contributions to candidates and parties also used sixteen other lobbying techniques. Further, the organized interests that made PAC contributions used more lobbying techniques than those that did not. These findings suggest that monetary contributions complement other lobbying techniques. Lobbyists know that their primary weapon is not money but information—information that might persuade policymakers to vote their way. They also know that information is useless if they do not get to deliver it to policymakers. One way to ensure that a policymaker will receive a lobbyist's information and pay it some attention is to contribute money to his or her campaign or party. Money may not win a policymaker over, but at least it gets a lobbyist's foot in the door. Lobbyists and organized interests realize that most elected officials are very busy and do not have time to meet with everyone who asks for their attention. Thus, lobbyists try to ensure access by contributing money.[80] As author Alan Rosenthal reports in his study of state lobbying, lobbyists consistently report that campaign contributions buy "the assurance that [a lobbyist's] issues will get a fair hearing."[81]

The desire of organized interests to buy access is best demonstrated by the propensity of PACs to contribute money primarily to incumbents—policymakers with whom their parent organizations deal regularly.[82] Some PACs are less reluctant to support challengers than others. Citizen group and labor union PACs, for example, regularly support challengers. Nonetheless, they too tend to concentrate their efforts on incumbents. Table 7.3, which contains information on the allocation of PAC contributions to members of Congress over the past seven election cycles, shows that the vast majority of PAC contributions accrue to incumbent legislators. The tendency for organized interests and their PACs to support incumbents when they contribute money directly to candi-

TABLE 7.3 PAC Contributions to Candidates for Federal Office by Candidate Status, 1985–1998

	Incumbents	Challengers	Open Seats
1985–1986	$ 96,200,000 (69%)	$19,900,000 (14%)	$23,800,000 (17%)
1987–1988	118,200,000 (74%)	18,900,000 (12%)	22,200,000 (14%)
1989–1990	125,800,000 (79%)	16,200,000 (10%)	17,100,000 (11%)
1991–1992	135,300,000 (72%)	22,900,000 (12%)	30,700,000 (16%)
1993–1994	137,200,000 (72%)	19,000,000 (10%)	33,400,000 (18%)
1995–1996	146,400,000 (67%)	31,600,000 (15%)	39,800,000 (18%)
1997–1998	170,900,000 (76%)	22,100,000 (12%)	27,000,000 (12%)

Note: Numbers were rounded by the FEC.
Sources: Federal Election Commission, "PAC Activity Increases in 1995–96 Election Cycle" (April 22, 1997), p. 1, accessed at *http://www.fec.gov/press/pacye96*, June 23, 1999; Federal Election Commission, "FEC Releases Information on PAC Activity for 1997–98" (June 8, 1999), accessed at *http://www.fec.gov/press/pacye98*, November 24, 1999.

dates is visible at all levels of government.[83] This means that even when organized interests prefer the challenger to the incumbent, they tend to contribute to the incumbents in order to improve their relationships with sitting policymakers. This tendency for organized interests to support incumbents is quite frustrating to challengers. Throughout the past two decades, for example, Republicans in Congress expressed frustration at the fact that many corporate PACs, their ostensible political allies, contributed heavily to Democratic incumbents. Republicans felt that by doing so, corporate PACs were "shooting themselves in the foot." Corporate PACs, however, felt differently. They maintained that because Democrats were in charge, they had to support them, or their interests would go unrepresented.

The desire to ensure access is also demonstrated by the tendency of PACs to contribute most of their money to the most powerful policymakers. Within the House and Senate, for example, PACs support party leaders (e.g., the Speaker of the House, the Senate majority leader) and people on the most powerful committees (e.g., those who write tax laws and make appropriations) much more than rank-and-file legislators.[84]

The role of money in buying access to powerful policymakers was quite evident during the mid-1990s, when it was revealed that many soft money contributors to the Democratic National Committee were invited to spend the night at the White House in the famous Lincoln bedroom. President Clinton and Vice President Gore, both prodigious soft money fund raisers, also hosted White House "policy discussions" over coffee for big soft money donors.[85] It is difficult to prove that soft money donors received any specific policy concessions from the president, the vice president, or the Democratic party. But the president's admission that some big contributors to the party received a free night in the Lincoln bedroom was proof enough to many that Democratic policymakers could be bought for a price.

A More Favorable Government

Campaign money can help an organized interest secure a government it likes. Organized interests that lobby with campaign money may be pragmatic, but they are not stupid. This means that they seldom support policymakers who are openly hostile to them. Probably not a single labor union, for example, would support archconservative Dick Armey (R, Texas) just because he is a powerful incumbent. And few business PACs other than Ben and Jerry's PAC are going to give socialist House member Bernie Sanders (I, Vermont) large sums of money. Thus, although organized interests are likely to support incumbents and power brokers, they are not likely to support incumbents and power brokers who have a consistent record of bashing them.

What then do organized interests do if the makeup of the government is not to their liking? Do they continue to buy access to policymakers whom they know will never come around to their way of thinking? Some do, but others do not. One option for the organized interest that is not happy with the current makeup of the government is to support candidates in *open seat elections*—elections that have no incumbent. The value of an open seat contribution is that it does not offend a powerful incumbent yet allows an organized interest to support a candidate that shares its political views. As you can see from Table 7.3, open seat contributions are more common than contributions to challengers.

Studies have shown that campaign contributions can significantly influence a nonincumbent's chances of being elected. Thus, PAC contributions to candidates in open seat elections can have a large impact on election outcomes.[86] Open seat elections were vital to the Republican takeover of the House of Representatives in 1994. Without powerful Democratic incumbents opposing them, many Republican House candidates received lots of PAC money and won election.

Small Favors

Finally, campaign money can buy organized interests small favors. A campaign contribution may not change a legislator's overall point of view, but it may cause him or her to insert a short amendment into a large piece of legislation, push harder for a specific proposal than he or she otherwise might have, or put in a good word for an organized interest. These things do not represent huge changes in behavior, but they can mightily help an organized interest.[87]

CAMPAIGN MONEY: IS THERE NEED FOR REFORM?

Critics in politics, the media, and the public alike continue to express distrust and disdain for the practice of lobbying with money. Why? On what basis do critics object to campaign contributions? Are the critics' objections off-base, or do they have merit? Before concluding this chapter, we will briefly examine the moral and ethical implications of lobbying with campaign money by addressing these questions.

Critics have raised four major concerns about organized interest campaign contributions. First, they think that campaign money skews representation toward moneyed interests by affecting which candidates can run for, and ultimately win, elected office. The argument goes like this. If money is absolutely critical to being elected, it is possible that candidates who do not appeal to big money donors might never run for office regardless of their other qualifications. If this occurs, government officials will increasingly come to represent not the entirety of their constituencies but rather those portions of their constituencies that are able to provide them with the money they need to win elections. This criticism is particularly troubling because the vast majority of organized interests that lobby with campaign money are business-related organized interests—organized interests that already have a considerable advantage in organized interest representation. Currently, for example, 42 percent of all federal PACs are affiliated with individual corporations, and another 15 percent are affiliated with trade associations.[88] In all, corporate and trade association PACs accounted for approximately two-thirds of all PAC contributions to federal candidates during the 1997–1998 election cycle.[89]

A second and closely related objection to lobbying with campaign money is that it makes some people and interests—specifically, those with lots of money to spend on electoral campaigns—more influential in elections than others. This seems to violate the one person–one vote principle that is the bedrock of American democracy. In essence, this argument goes, people and interests with lots of money have more influence over election outcomes than people and interests without lots of money. And since elections are the primary way that ordinary citizens express their policy preferences, this is a bad thing.

Third, despite academic studies to the contrary, many critics believe that campaign contributions *do* influence the way policymakers behave. Some analysts have argued that although contributions may not buy votes, they may buy less noticeable but nonetheless important favors for big money donors. Congressional scholars Richard Hall and Frank Wayman, for example, have observed that monetary contributions and other forms of campaign help may be effective at the margins of policymakers' behavior. Campaign money may, for example, convince a legislator to withhold an amendment in a committee markup, provide a lobbyist with important information on legislative procedures, or do other things that are seemingly minor but nonetheless important to organized interests.[90] Or, as Charles Keating's critics have argued, campaign contributions may buy a contributor a certain amount of goodwill that translates into small favors here and there and add up to big changes in the end. If this is the case, campaign contributions are influential despite some evidence that they are not.

Finally, some critics believe that massive organized interest contributions to electoral campaigns increase public cynicism by convincing people that all politicians are for sale.[91] The rise of soft money has fed this cynicism. Nothing else feeds cynicism, however, like reports that policymakers more or less extort money from lobbyists. Although it is certainly true that lobbyists run around begging policymakers for things, it is also true that policymakers run around begging lobbyists for things—especially campaign contributions. As if deliberately to feed the fires of public cynicism, Democratic lawmakers in my home state of Tennessee recently took this "virtual extortion" to new heights. In a series of meetings held over two weeks at a hotel in the capital city of Nashville, Democratic party leaders summoned lobbyists one by one and politely suggested that they make contributions. Lobbyists were told that the amount each contributed would be posted on a bulletin board at the autumn retreat of the House Democratic Caucus, thus reminding legislators which lobbyists had been supportive and which had not.[92]

In sum, lobbying with campaign money is controversial because it raises the specter of bribery. While Americans have always been suspicious of big money in politics, there is evidence that they are more cynical today than ever before—partially due to the enormous amounts of campaign cash flowing to both major parties from organized interests.[93] In recent years, concerns about the deleterious effects of big money in politics have led to numerous reform proposals. The most prominent proposal surfaced in 1999, when Senators John McCain (R, Arizona) and Russell Feingold (D, Wisconsin) floated a comprehensive plan to overhaul the federal campaign finance system. The McCain-Feingold bill, which was actually a scaled-back version of a bill first offered in 1996, contained three components: it would ban all soft money, ban most forms of issue advocacy, and provide incentives for candidates for federal office to limit their spending.[94] The bill failed to pass in 1999, but McCain and Feingold promise to resurrect it.

How do organized interests and their defenders answer their critics? Defenders of the current system offer several rebuttals. One argument that policymakers often make is that lobbying with campaign money is okay because they would never allow themselves to be bought. Policymakers' denials to this effect are generally offered with a healthy dose of righteous indignation. Recently, for example, when Republican Arizona state representative Jean McGrath was asked about her relationships with the business groups that gave her thousands of dollars, she responded: "I'm insulted that you could even think that I could be bought with a contribution."[95] A similar argument is made by policymakers who maintain that they receive money only from organized interests that share their basic philosophy, and thus contributions are just a happy coincidence rather than something to worry about. One of Jean McGrath's colleagues in the Arizona House, Republican "Rusty" Bowers, made this argument when he told a reporter: "The people that contribute to me do not drive my vote. However, once you establish a voting record, people who agree with you are more likely to contribute to your campaign."[96]

Another common response to critics' barbs, one that organized interests regularly offer, is that contributing money to policymakers, far from being an extreme evil, is an important and unfairly maligned form of political participation. A lobbyist for the cable industry used this argument recently when confronted with questions regarding his group's contributions, which totaled over $400,000, to Illinois state legislators prior to their approval of a bill that allowed cable companies to charge customers a five dollar late fee: "You have to believe that [making a campaign contribution] is a legitimate part of democracy and the political process."[97] A labor lobbyist active in New York State politics gave a similar explanation for her group's huge campaign contributions: "We represent thousands of hard-working men and women. . . . [Our contributions] help give our members a collective voice so they can shape policy."[98] In short, organized interests are quick to say that contributing money is a form of legitimate political participation.

The Get-as-much-as-you-can-burg Address

DANZIGER 7-17-99
LOS ANGELES TIMES SYNDICATE
www.danzigercartoons.com

Of the money, by the money, and for the money? Many Americans fear that policy-makers prostitute themselves to the organized interests that help them get elected. In this editorial cartoon, Congress is portrayed as a grinning overweight man grown fat with monetary contributions. *Danziger, Los Angeles Times.*

Another common defense of the current system is that it is not really as bad as critics say it is. Economist Robert J. Samuelson is probably the most prominent proponent of this point of view. Lobbying with campaign money, Samuelson argues, is not really "out of control" at all. He points out that campaign spending at all levels of government during the 1995–1996 election cycle totaled $4 billion. Although this seems like a lot of money, he argues, it represents only one-twentieth of 1 percent of the national income. This, he argues, is "a small price for democracy."[99] Samuelson also notes that after adjusting for inflation, campaign spending in 1996 represented only a 28 percent increase over spending in 1986, hardly, he says, the explosion that critics say it is.

Along the same lines, some analysts have pointed out that PACs—the most controversial types of organized interests—are not really all that important in the big scheme of things. For one thing, they are not the main source of money for electoral campaigns. In the 1997–1998 congressional elections, for example, PACs accounted for only 25 percent of contributions to candidates.[100] Defenders of the current system also note that although PACs are numerous, many are shoestring operations that exist in name only. During the 1997–1998 election cycle, for example, 38 percent of all federally registered PACs spent less than $5,000, and nearly 75 percent spent less than $50,000.[101] PACs are even less active in state and local elections.

Perhaps the most common defense of campaign contributions is the one offered by the most prominent defender of the current system, Senator Mitch McConnell (R, Kentucky). McConnell, who speaks for many other Republicans in Congress, argues that although the system is not perfect, the proposed solutions would actually make things worse.[102] McConnell and his supporters are fond of saying, for example, that public financing of federal elections, a remedy that Ralph Nader and other liberal activists favor, is nothing more than an unfair tax on ordinary citizens. Similarly, McConnell often points out that contribution bans and spending limits violate people's First Amendment rights. In fact, the Supreme Court more or less sanctioned this view when it declared campaign spending a form of speech in its famous *Buckley v. Valeo* (1976) decision. Recently McConnell stated, "One thing you can be certain of, when you hear the three words campaign finance reform—somebody is trying to take away your right to speak. They want speech police."[103]

So where does this leave us? On the one hand, there are good reasons to be suspicious of lobbying with campaign money. It appears that money sometimes makes people do things that they otherwise might not do. Recent revelations about soft money contributors to the Democratic party illustrate how the unending chase for money can lead to corruption and malfeasance. By late 1999, it became clear that several fund raisers for the Democratic party had illegally laundered money in their quest for big soft money contributions. Some of the money contributed to the party, it turned out, originally came from foreign citizens and entities before being passed on to party officials. Taking money from an illegal source and passing it on to a party committee is against the law. By early 2000, several Democratic fund raisers had either pleaded guilty or been found guilty of various corruption charges.[104]

On the other hand, despite periodic scandals and revelations of corruption, it is possible to go overboard in attacking campaign spending. Academic studies have consistently shown that campaign contributions by themselves seldom influence the behavior of policymakers. Moreover, the recent case of the tobacco industry suggests that lobbying with campaign money can go only so far. Despite massive donations to candidates of both parties and the parties themselves over the past two decades, the tobacco industry was unable to avoid a historic settlement that forced it to pay state governments $368 billion in return for some protection against lawsuits.[105]

In the end, we must conclude that campaign contributions, especially in conjunction with other lobbying efforts, may reap rewards for the organized interests that can afford to make them. So does the system need to be reformed? Are the critics of campaign spending on the mark? The answer seems to be: partially. I say this because virtually everybody—even the people who have benefited most from the current campaign finance system—concedes that big money in politics is a problem. Change is almost certain to come eventually, but probably later than sooner.

CONCLUSION: LOBBYING WITH CAMPAIGN MONEY

Giving money directly to policymakers in an attempt to influence their decisions is bribery, and therefore against the law. Nonetheless, organized interests lobby with campaign money to an astounding degree. They do so in six ways: they contribute money to candidates, spend independently, make in-kind contributions, bundle, contribute money to political parties, and engage in election issue advocacy. By far the most common way that organized interests lobby with campaign money is by contributing money to candidates for public office. Campaign contributions generally flow through PACs—special types of organized interests that are set up solely to collect money from individuals and spend it on electoral campaigns. PACs, though far from dominant sources of campaign money, are perhaps the most controversial types of organized interests in the United States. The specter of moneyed interests' bankrolling campaigns and spending millions to affect public policy worries many Americans. Only time will tell if the current system of campaign finance—a system that allows organized interests great latitude to lobby with money—will survive. For now, however, it is safe to say that organized interests will continue to be an important source of campaign money.

What's Next

We are not quite through with our look at how organized interests attempt to influence public policy. Although media tend to focus on direct lobbying and lobbying with money, organized interests have become quite adept at another type of lobbying: indirect lobbying. This is where we are headed next.

EXERCISES

1. Choose one of the U.S. senators from your state. How much money did he or she receive in PAC contributions during the latest election cycle? Which PACs gave the most money? Next, investigate the senator's voting record and committee memberships and see if you can determine why the senator received support from the particular PACs that he or she did.
2. The 1996 elections were the first in which organized interests engaged in substantial election issue advocacy. Relying on news accounts of election

issue advocacy campaigns, answer the following questions. Which specific organized interests engaged in election issue advocacy? In your opinion, why did they do so? What forms did their election issue advocacy take? Did these organized interests engage in other forms of campaign activity as well?

RESEARCH RESOURCES

Publications

Books. To learn more about a specific PAC, consult *CQ's Federal PACs Directory* (Washington, D.C.: Congressional Quarterly Press), which is published periodically. Every presidential and congressional election is followed by a spate of books that attempt to make sense of it. Some of the best books on the elections of 1996 are Paul R. Abramson, John H. Aldrich, and David W. Rhode, *Change and Continuity in the 1996 and 1998 Elections* (Washington, DC: Congressional Quarterly Books, 1999); John C. Green, ed., *Financing the 1996 Election* (Armonk, NY: M. E. Sharpe, 1999); and Larry Sabato, ed., *Toward the Millennium: The Elections of 1996* (Reading, MA: Addison-Wesley, 1999). For books on the most recent election, search your library databases or library card catalogue.

Web Resources

Campaigns and Elections *magazine. Campaigns and Elections* is a monthly magazine that provides "how-to" campaign information for candidates, organized interests, political consultants, and political parties. The magazine's web site, located at *www.campaignline.com,* contains articles on all facets of campaigns and elections.

Campaign finance sites. A number of organizations provide on-line information about campaign finance, candidates, elections, and voting. Project Vote Smart, for example, is a nonpartisan, nonprofit organization with a national library of factual information on tens of thousands of candidates for public office (including those for state and federal positions). The organization's web address is *www.vote-smart.org.* Similarly, the Center for Responsive Politics (CRP) contains an on-line database of information about where candidates for state and federal office get their money. The CRP's web address is *www.opensecrets.org.*

Candidate web sites. Many candidates have their own web sites. Some of these sites contain detailed information about where the candidate gets money and how he or she spends it. Search for these sites using an Internet search engine.

The FEC. The official web site of the FEC, located at *www.fec.gov,* contains detailed information on campaign finance, including information on where candidates, parties, and PACs get their campaign money.

Notes

1. The meeting was called by Senator Donald Riegle (D, Michigan), who surprised the others by not showing up. Riegle, however, did show up at a number of other meetings, and he also made several calls on Keating's behalf. The five senators, who came to be known as the "Keating Five," were never charged with criminal wrongdoing.

2. John R. Cranford, "Ex-Lobbyist Paints Murky Picture of Buying Access on the Hill," *Congressional Quarterly Weekly Report,* December 22, 1990, pp. 4197–4199.

3. Anthony Corrado, "Financing the 1996 Elections," in Gerald M. Pomper, Walter Dean Burnham, Anthony Corrado, Marjorie Randon Hershey, Marion R. Just, Scott Keeter, Wilson Carey McWilliams, and William G. Meyer, eds., *The Election of 1996* (Chatham, NJ: Chatham House, 1997), p. 135.

4. Federal Election Commission, "Financing the 1996 Presidential Campaign," accessed at *http://www.fec.gov/pres96/presgen1,* November 21, 1999.

5. Candice J. Nelson, "Money in the 1996 Elections," in William Crotty and Jerome E. Mileur, eds., *The Election of 1996* (New York: Dushkin/McGraw-Hill, 1997), chap. 12.

6. Federal Election Commission, "FEC Reports on Congressional Fundraising for 1997–1998" (April 28, 1999), accessed at *http://www.fec.gov/press/canye98,* November 13, 1999.

7. Ibid.

8. Ibid.

9. Robert Hardt, Jr., "Ruth's $4.5M Bucks Poll Trend That Favors Rudy," *New York Post,* August 9, 1998.

10. Jay Jochnowitz, "It's Jennings, and It's a Landslide," *Albany Times Union,* September 10, 1997, p. 1.

11. Ronald J. Hrebenar, *Interest Group Politics in America* (3rd ed.) (Armonk, NY: M. E. Sharpe, 1997), p. 210.

12. Gregory Weaver, "State Campaign Costs Rise to Alarming Levels," *Indianapolis Star,* March 9, 1997, p. B1.

13. Dennis Chaptman, "Sykes Leads Butler in Campaign Cash," *Milwaukee Journal Sentinel,* February 1, 2000, p. 1B.

14. Jonathan Rauch, *Government's End: Why Washington Stopped Working* (New York: Public Affairs, 1999), pp. 88–89; Frank J. Sorauf, *Inside Campaign Finance: Myths and Realities* (New Haven, CT: Yale University Press, 1992), pp. 30–37.

15. Brooks Jackson, "Financing the 1996 Campaign: The Law of the Jungle," in Larry J. Sabato, ed., *Toward the Millennium: The Elections of 1996* (Needham Heights, MA: Allyn and Bacon, 1997), pp. 248–249.

16. Paul Allen Beck, *Party Politics in America* (8th ed.) (New York: Longman, 1997), pp. 277–278; Jackson, "Financing the 1996 Campaign," p. 234.

17. It is beyond the scope of this book to examine the entire American system of campaign finance. See Sorauf, *Inside Campaign Finance*.

18. Ibid., pp. 2–7.

19. Ibid., pp. 2–3.

20. Herbert Alexander and Monica Bauer, *Financing the 1988 Election* (Boulder, CO: Westview Press, 1991), chap. 1.

21. Sorauf, *Inside Campaign Finance: Myths and Realities* (New Haven, CT: Yale University Press, 1992), p. 4.

22. *Buckley v. Valeo,* 424 U.S. 1 (1976).

23. John R. Wright, *Interest Groups and Congress: Lobbying, Contributions, and Influence* (Boston, MA: Allyn and Bacon, 1996), p. 120.

24. FEC Advisory Opinion 75–23, December 3, 1975.

25. Larry J. Sabato, *PAC Power: Inside the World of Political Action Committees* (New York: Norton, 1984), p. 10.

26. Federal Election Commission, "PAC Count, 1974 to Present," accessed at *http://www.fec.gov/press/paccount,* March 13, 1999.

27. Federal Election Commission, "FEC Issues Semi-Annual Federal PAC Count," accessed at *http://www.fec.gov/press/pcnt799,* November 16, 1999.

28. Federal Election Commission, "PAC Activity Increases in 1995–1996 Election Cycle" (April 22, 1997), p. 1, accessed at *http://www.fec.gov/press/pacye96,* March 13, 1999.

29. Federal Election Commission, "FEC Releases Information on PAC Activity for 1997–98" (June 8, 1999), accessed at *http://www.fec.gov/press/pacye98,* October 29, 1999.

30. Federal Election Commission, "Financing the 1996 Presidential Campaign," p. 1, accessed at *http://www.fec.gov/pres96/presgen1,* May 3, 1999.

31. Federal Election Commission, "Congressional Fundraising and Spending Up Again in 1996" (April 14, 1997), accessed at *http://www.fec.gov/press/canye96,* March 13, 1999.

32. Federal Election Commission, "FEC Reports on Congressional Fundraising for 1997–98" (April 28, 1999), accessed at *http://www.fec.gov/press/canye98,* November 1, 1999.

33. Alan Rosenthal, *The Third House: Lobbyists and Lobbying in the States* (Washington, DC: Congressional Quarterly Press, 1993), p. 133.

34. James D. King and Helenan S. Robin, "Political Action Committees in State Elections," *American Review of Politics* 16 (Spring 1995): 63.

35. Clive S. Thomas and Ronald J. Hrebenar, "Political Action Committees in the States: Some Preliminary Findings" (paper presented at the annual meeting of the American Political Science Association, Washington, DC, September 1991).

36. Anne Scott, "Facts About PACs," *Business Record,* December 9, 1996, p. 1.

37. Judy Keen, "States a Testing Ground for Campaign Finance Reform," *USA Today,* May 2, 1997, p. 1A.

38. Richard Coe, "Expose the Flow of Campaign Money to the Light," Alabama *Anniston Star,* December 31, 1996.

39. Ann O'M. Bowman and Richard C. Kearney, *State and Local Government* (3rd ed.) (Boston, MA: Houghton Mifflin, 1996), pp. 130–131. See also Ray Gibson and Rick Pearson, "Campaign Spending Hits New Heights in Illinois," *Chicago Tribune,* February 1, 1997, p. 5; Tom Precious, "Special Interests Donate Millions to State Lawmakers," *Albany Times Union,* March 14, 1997.

40. Sorauf, *Inside Campaign Finance: Myths and Realities* (New Haven CT: Yale University, 1992), p. 180.

41. Federal Election Commission, "PAC Activity in 1994 Elections Remains at 1992 Levels" (March 31, 1995), p. 5; King and Robin, "Political Action Committees in State Elections," pp. 61–77.

42. Federal Election Commission, "PAC Activity Increases in 1995–96 Election Cycle."

43. Federal Election Commission, "FEC Releases Information on PAC Activity for 1997–1998."

44. Frank J. Sorauf, "Adaptation and Innovation in Political Action Committees," in Allan J. Cigler and Burdett A. Loomis, eds., *Interest Group Politics* (4th ed.) (Washington, DC: Congressional Quarterly Press, 1995), p. 178.

45. Ibid.

46. Ibid., p. 181.

47. Ibid.

48. *Congressional Quarterly's Federal PAC Directory* (Washington, DC: Congressional Quarterly, 1998), p. 368.

49. Paul S. Herrnson, "The National Committee for an Effective Congress: Liberalism, Partisanship, and Electoral Innovation," in Robert Biersack, Paul S. Herrnson, and Clyde Wilcox, eds., *Risky Business?* (Armonk, NY: M. E. Sharpe, 1994), pp. 39–55.

50. Scot Lehigh and Frank Phillips, "White House Taps Mass. Native Who Blazed Trails for Women," *Boston Globe,* February 5, 1999, p. B3.

51. See Anthony J. Nownes and Patricia Freeman, "Interest Group Activity in the States," *Journal of Politics* 60:1 (February 1998): 92.

52. Clyde Wilcox and Wesley Joe, "Dead Law: The Federal Election Finance Regulations, 1974–1996," *PS: Political Science and Politics* 30 (March 1998): 14–17; David Magleby, ed., *Outside Money: Soft Money and Issue Advocacy in the 1988 Congressional Elections* (Lanham, MD: Rowman and Littlefield, 2000).

53. Paraphrased from Mark J. Rozell and Clyde Wilcox, *Interest Groups in American Campaigns: The New Face of Electioneering* (Washington, DC: Congressional Quarterly Press, 1999), p. 113.

54. Ibid., p. 139.

55. Ibid., p. 140.

56. David Magleby, "Interest Group Election Ads," in Magleby, ed., *Outside Money: Soft Money and Issue Advocacy in the 1988 Congressional Elections* (Lanham, MD: Rowman and Littlefield, 2000), p. 46.

57. Paul S. Herrnson, "Parties and Interest Groups in Postreform Congressional Elections," in Allan J. Cigler and Burdett A. Loomis, eds., *Interest Group Politics* (5th ed.) (Washington, DC: Congressional Quarterly Press, 1998), pp. 158–159.

58. Adapted from Rozell and Wilcox, *Interest Groups in American Campaigns: The New Face of Electioneering* (Washington, DC: Congressional Quarterly Press, 1999), p. 126.

59. Magleby, "Interest Group Election Ads," p. 51.

60. David Cantor, "The Sierra Club Political Committee," in Robert Biersack, Paul S. Hernnson, and Clyde Wilcox, *After the Revolution: PACs, Lobbies, and the Republican Congress* (Boston, MA: Allyn and Bacon, 1999), pp. 113–114.

61. Ibid., p. 113.

62. Magleby, "Interest Group Election Ads," p. 45.

63. Ibid., p. 46.

64. Ibid., p. 51.

65. Wilcox and Joe, "Dead Law," p. 17.

66. Rozell and Wilcox, *Interest Groups in American Campaigns: The New Face of Electioneering* (Washington, DC: Congressional Quarterly Press, 1999), p. 142.

67. Kenneth R. Mayer, "Taking a Closer Look at the Issue of Issue Ads: Emphasis Should Be on Fund Disclosure, Not Limiting Speech," *Wisconsin State Journal*, November 7, 1999, p. 2B.

68. Diana Dwyre, "Spinning Straw into Gold: Soft Money and U.S. House Elections," *Legislative Studies Quarterly* 21 (August 1996): 410.

69. Ibid., pp. 410–411.

70. Common Cause, "Soft Money: What Is It and Why Is It a Problem," accessed at *www.commoncause.org/laundromat/softmoney,* November 28, 1999.

71. Jackson, "Financing the 1996 Campaign," p. 236.

72. Federal Election Commission, "FEC Reports on Political Party Activity for 1997–1998" (April 9, 1999), accessed at *http://www.fec.gov/press.ptyye98.html,* November 23, 1999.

73. Connie Cases, "Dems, GOP Raised $881 Million," Associated Press News Service, January 11, 1997, p. 1.

74. Ibid.

75. Brooks Jackson, *Honest Graft: Money and the American Political Process* (New York: Knopf, 1988), p. 295.

76. See Janet Grenzke, "Shopping in the Congressional Supermarket: The Currency Is Complex," *American Journal of Political Science* 33 (1989): 1–24; John R. Wright, "PACs, Contributions, and Roll Calls: An Organizational Perspective," *American Political Science Review* 79 (1985): 400–414; John R. Wright, "Contributions, Lobbying, and Committee Voting in the U.S. House of Representatives," *American Political Science Review* 84 (1990): 417–438. There are, of course, those who believe that campaign money does substantially alter policymakers' behavior. See John P. Frendreis and Richard W. Waterman, "PAC Contributions and Legislative Behavior: Senate Voting on Trucking Deregulation," *Social Science Quarterly* 66 (June 1985): 401–412; Stephen Moore, Sidney M. Wolfe, Deborah Lindes, and Clifford Douglas, "Epidemiology of Failed Tobacco Control Legislation," *Journal of the American Medical Association,* October 19, 1994, p. 1171.

77. Sorauf, *Inside Campaign Finance: Myths and Realities* (New Haven, CT: Yale University Press, 1992), pp. 74–77.

78. Paul S. Herrnson, "Interest Groups, PACs and Campaigns," in Paul S. Herrnson, Ronald G. Shaiko, and Clyde Wilcox, eds., *The Interest Group Connection: Electioneering, Lobbying, and Policymaking in Washington* (Chatham, NJ: Chatham House, 1998), p. 41.

79. Anthony J. Nownes, "The People Who Lobby State Government," unpublished manuscript (1997).

80. Herrnson, "Interest Groups, PACs and Campaigns," p. 42; Laura I. Langbein, "Money and Access: Some Empirical Evidence," *Journal of Politics* 48 (November 1986): 1052–1062.

81. Rosenthal, *The Third House: Lobbyists and Lobbying in the States* (Washington, DC: Congressional Quarterly Press, 1993), p. 139.

82. Herrnson, "Interest Groups, PACs and Campaigns," pp. 41–42.

83. Rosenthal, *The Third House: Lobbyists and Lobbying in the States* (Washington, DC: Congressional Quarterly Press, 1993), p. 136.

84. Roger H. Davidson and Walter J. Oleszek, *Congress and Its Members* (4th ed.) (Washington, DC: Congressional Quarterly Press, 1994), pp. 79–83; Paul S. Herrnson, "Interest Groups, PACs and Campaigns," pp. 41–42; Wright, *Interest Groups and Congress: Lobbying, Contributions, and Influence* (Boston, MA: Allyn and Bacon, 1996), chap. 5.

85. Marianne Holt, "The Surge in Party Money in Competitive 1998 Congressional Elections," in Magleby, ed., *Outside Money*, p. 26.

86. Gary C. Jacobson, *Money in Congressional Elections* (New Haven, CT: Yale University Press, 1980), p. 51.

87. See Richard L. Hall and Frank W. Wayman, "Buying Time: Moneyed Interests and the Mobilization of Bias in Congressional Committees," *American Political Science Review* 84 (September 1990): 797–820; Wright, "Contributions, Lobbying, and Committee Voting in the U.S. House of Representatives," pp. 417–438.

88. Federal Elections Commission, "PAC Financial Activity" (n.d.), accessed at *www.fec.gov/press/pacsum98,* November 12, 1999.

89. Federal Election Commission, "Contributions from PACs by Type of PAC" (n.d.), accessed at *www.fec.gov/press/allsum98,* November 12, 1999.

90. Hall and Wayman, "Buying Time: Moneyed Interests and the Mobilization of Bias in Congressional Committees," *American Political Science Review* 84 (September 1990), pp. 797–820.

91. Sabato and Simpson, *Dirty Little Secrets.*

92. Jeff Woods, " 'Shakedown' Angers State Lobbyists," *Nashville Banner,* July 22, 1997.

93. Sabato and Simpson, *Dirty Little Secrets,* pp. 3–8.

94. M. Margaret Conway and Joanne Connor Green, "Political Action Committees and Campaign Finance," in Cigler and Loomis, eds., *Interest Group Politics* (5th ed.), p. 210.

95. Michael Murphy and Kris Mayes, "Invisible Legislature: Lobbying in Arizona," *Arizona Republic,* December 22, 1996, p. A12.

96. Ibid.

97. Rick Pearson, "Ante Up: The Springfield Money Game," *Chicago Tribune,* November 9, 1997, p. 1.

98. Precious, "Special Interests Donate Millions to State Lawmakers."

99. Robert J. Samuelson, "Campaign Finance Hysteria," *Washington Post,* October 8, 1999, p. A29.

100. Federal Election Commission, "FEC Reports on Congressional Fundraising for 1997–98."

101. Federal Election Commission, "PACs Grouped by Total Spent" (n.d.), accessed at *http://www.fec.gov/press/pacsp98,* November 30, 1999.

102. Bob Hohler, "Soft Money Ban Is Called No Cure-all; As Senate Takes Up Funding Bill, Some Point to Potential for Abuse," *Boston Globe,* October 19, 1999, p. A1.

103. Ann Scott Tyson, "Bitterest Foe of Fund-raising Overhaul Draws His Sword," *Christian Science Monitor,* October 19, 1999, p. 1.

104. David S. Cloud, "U.S. Moves to Toughen Fund Probe," *Wall Street Journal,* March 16, 2000, p. A28; Pete Yost, "Hsia Found Guilty of Arranging $100,000 Donation to Democrats," Associated Press Newswires, March 2, 2000.

105. Samuelson, "Campaign Finance Hysteria," p. A29.

8 ▷ Indirect Lobbying

Knoxville, Tennessee
Early 1994

I am sitting in my living room watching television. My favorite program goes to commercial break. The camera nervously approaches an angst-ridden yuppie couple, Harry and Louise, sitting at their kitchen table poring over documents. They worry aloud that President Clinton's proposed comprehensive health care reform package might make their health care less affordable and less effectual. "Under Clinton's plan," the wife breathlessly asks her husband, "will we be able to choose our own doctor?" The answer is ominously obvious.[1] At the end of the commercial, a voice urges me to contact my representatives in Washington to express my opposition to President Clinton's plan. At the bottom of the screen, I see who is paying for this commercial: the Health Insurance Association of America (HIAA), a trade association that represents small to medium-sized insurance companies. In late 1994, Clinton's plan is ignominiously shelved after Congress refuses to support its key provisions.

It makes sense to assume that organized interests lobby only government officials. After all, government officials make public policy. Who else would organized interests lobby? The answer, it turns out, is *you and me*. The commercial that interrupted my favorite program was aimed not at government officials but at television viewers—ordinary citizens who generally have no direct role in making public policy. This sort of lobbying, lobbying that is aimed at citizens rather than policymakers, is called *indirect lobbying* and is the subject of this chapter.

We begin by exploring what indirect lobbying is. As you will see, the goal of indirect lobbying is the same as that of direct lobbying: to influence public policy. Next, we ask: Why do organized interests engage in indirect lobbying? The answer to this question lies in the very nature of our representative democracy. From here, we examine the techniques by which organized interests lobby citizens. As with direct lobbying, organized interests have a number of distinct techniques at their disposal. We conclude with a look at recent trends in indirect lobbying. Although indirect lobbying has been around for a long time, it is more common than ever before.

WHAT IS INDIRECT LOBBYING?

Indirect lobbying is defined as lobbying aimed at citizens rather than public officials.[2] It is important to note that some people refer to indirect lobbying as *grass-roots lobbying,* which is defined as lobbying aimed at ordinary citizens that is designed to mobilize them to contact legislators or other decision makers.[3] I prefer the term *indirect lobbying* because not all lobbying that is aimed at citizens is designed to mobilize them to contact legislators and other policy-

Meet Louise In 1993 and 1994, the Health Insurance Association of America aired a series of television advertisements featuring "Harry and Louise," a fictitious couple who worried out loud that President Clinton's health care reform plan would degrade the quality of their health care. *Courtesy of Health Insurance Association of America (HIAA).*

makers. Some is designed to shape attitudes and opinions. In short, the general definition of grass-roots lobbying is simply too narrow to encompass all the forms of lobbying examined in this chapter.

The very definition of indirect lobbying begs the following question: Why would an organized interest lobby citizens rather than public officials? The answer is that organized interests know that ordinary citizens profoundly affect public policy. In fact, one of the bedrock principles of American democracy is that ordinary people are the ultimate source of government authority.

Ordinary citizens influence public policy outcomes in three particularly important ways. First, they choose policymakers. The founders of this country created a government of representatives by which ordinary citizens do not have a chance to vote on most public policy issues directly. Rather, they vote for the people who vote on public policy issues directly. The mechanism by which voters choose policymakers—elections—provides them with a means by which to induce policymakers to be responsive or punish them for failing to respond.[4] Second, citizens pressure policymakers to do or not to do certain things. The Constitution guarantees American citizens the right to make their opinions known to policymakers. In practice, this means that by participating in political parties, contacting public officials, attending rallies and protests, and joining organized interests, citizens can influence the decisions of policymakers. Although policymakers do not always respond to citizen pressure, generally they consider ordinary citizens' opinions when they make public policy decisions—mostly because they know that their jobs depend on it.[5] Finally, citizens sometimes make public policy directly by voting in initiative or referendum campaigns. An *initiative* is a proposed law that is placed directly on a ballot for citizen approval. Although there is no federal initiative process, twenty-four states allow citizens to vote on initiatives. Under the initiative, ordinary citizens can place issues on the state ballot by gathering the requisite number of signatures on an initiative petition.[6] A *referendum* is a proposed law that has been passed by the legislature but requires citizen approval before it can be implemented. Twenty-one states have provisions that allow citizens to petition to force a popular vote on bills enacted by the state legislature through a referendum.[7] Some local governments allow both initiatives and referendums. Initiatives and referendums are not all that common, but they are becoming more so. In 1998 alone, there were sixty-four initiatives and referendums on ballots in sixteen states.[8]

In sum, indirect lobbying is aimed at citizens rather than public officials. Organized interests lobby citizens because they know that citizens often have a profound impact on public policy outcomes. Although ordinary citizens do not often vote on public policy issues directly, they indirectly influence the direction of government policy.

INFLUENCING PUBLIC POLICY THROUGH INDIRECT LOBBYING: CHANGING ATTITUDES, CHANGING BEHAVIOR

The ultimate goal of all indirect lobbying is the same: to affect public policy. The more immediate goal, however, is to do one or both of the following: influence people's opinions and encourage people to contact policymakers to make their opinions known. If an indirect lobbying effort successfully does either or both of these, it has the potential to affect public policy.

Lobbying to Affect Public Opinion

Some indirect lobbying efforts attempt to shape people's attitudes and opinions about an issue or series of issues. This type of indirect lobbying is called *lobbying to affect public opinion.* The underlying premise is that because attitudes and opinions are eventually translated into public policy, it makes sense to try to affect them.[9] A great deal of research shows that attitudes and opinions about political issues and candidates affect how people vote, how often they vote, and to what extent they participate in other political activities, such as contacting public officials, engaging in protest, joining organized interests, and contributing money to candidates for public office. In short, to shape opinions about political issues is indirectly to shape public policy.

An example will illustrate how lobbying to affect public opinion works in practice. Mobil Oil, one of the nation's leading petroleum companies, has engaged in lobbying to affect public opinion for decades. It regularly places advertisements in the *New York Times* and other national newspapers that are designed to shape people's attitudes and opinions. The advertisements look much like standard editorials and generally appear in the opinion section of newspapers. Mobil's political advertisements are different from their regular consumer advertisements in that they do not say, "Buy Mobil gasoline." Rather, they contain the company's thoughts and ideas about energy policy in the United States. Mobil hopes that its advertisements will affect people's opinions on energy-related manners. Further, it hopes that these opinions will eventually manifest themselves in political activity that will produce public policy favorable to the company, such as voting for a candidate who shares Mobil's views or opposing a bill that Mobil opposes.

In order for lobbying to affect public opinion to work, citizens must be receptive and responsive to the information they receive from organized interests. Because myriad factors determine each individual's political attitudes and opinions, we cannot say for certain whether they are. Nonetheless, there are two good reasons to believe that citizens may be receptive and responsive to the information they receive from organized interests.[10] First, research on advertising indicates that most people are willing to consider information from outside sources when making up their minds about particular issues.[11] In fact, the whole premise of advertising is that people are open to the messages they receive from outside sources. Second, it appears that campaign advertisements—advertisements that have a lot in common with advocacy advertisements—shape the attitudes, opinions, and behavior of some voters.[12] Although most people ignore campaign advertisements, a substantial minority of Americans actually responds to them. In sum, research on advertising and campaigning suggests that lobbying to affect public opinion has some chance of success.

Lobbying for Contact

Some indirect lobbying efforts are intended to encourage citizens to make their opinions known to policymakers. This type of indirect lobbying, called *lobbying for contact,* involves getting ordinary citizens to pressure policymakers to support an organized interest's agenda.[13] The premise is that because policymakers—especially elected officials—want to keep their jobs, they will respond to the desires of ordinary people.[14]

The National Rifle Association's (NRA) campaign against the Brady bill in the early 1990s provides a good example of how lobbying for contact works in practice. In late 1992, President Clinton began a push for legislation that required a five-day waiting period for the purchase of handguns. Congress debated the legislation in 1993. During the fierce battle over the law, the NRA sent millions of letters to its members, urging them to contact members of Congress and express opposition to the bill. The NRA believed that if millions of ordinary citizens expressed strong opposition to the Brady bill, Congress would be unlikely to pass it. Although the bill became law in 1994, the NRA almost succeeded in derailing it despite overwhelming public support.[15]

Lobbying efforts designed to encourage people to make their views known to policymakers rest on the assumption that citizens are willing to make their views known to policymakers. Are they? The answer is an emphatic yes. Each year about one-third of all adult Americans—over 50 million people—contact a public official about a policy issue. In fact, as Figure 8.1 shows, contacting public officials is the third most common form of political participation in the United States. Citizens do not limit their contact to elected officials. It is not unheard of for citizens to contact bureaucrats and even judges. In fact, the federal government and all states allow citizen participation in the administrative rule-making process by allowing citizens to comment on proposed rules and regulations, as well as take part in some judicial proceedings.

Perhaps even more important than the fact that citizens are willing to contact policymakers is that they are more willing to do so if they are asked to do so.[16] Stories of indirect lobbying campaigns that successfully mobilized people to contact policymakers are legion. During the battle over President Clinton's health care reform proposal in 1993–1994, for example, the National Federation of Independent Business (NFIB) managed to generate 500,000 letters to members of Congress.[17] And in a recent battle over gun control legislation, the NRA managed to produce 3 million progun telegrams to members of Congress in three days.[18]

Stories like these leave no doubt that indirect lobbying campaigns can be successful in generating public pressure on policymakers. Whether this public pressure influences the behavior of policymakers and thus the direction of public policy is, of course, an entirely different question, which we explore in some detail in Chapter 9.

There are several ways that citizens can make their views known to policymakers. First, they can write letters, place telephone calls, or send faxes. Virtually every public official in the United States has an office at which he or she

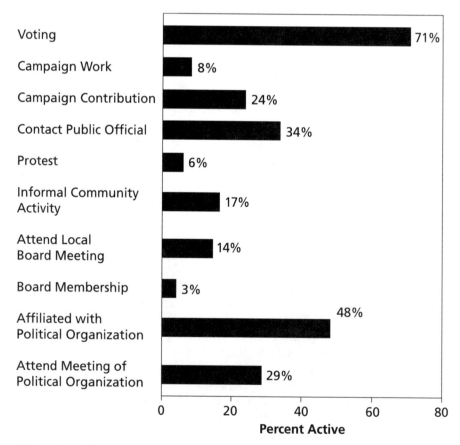

FIGURE 8.1 Political Activities of Ordinary Citizens

Source: Sidney Verba, Kay Lehman Schlozman, and Henry E. Brady, *Voice and Equality: Civic Voluntarism in American Politics* (Cambridge, Mass.: Harvard University Press, 1995), p. 51.

can receive mail, telephone calls, and fax messages, and most public officials also have e-mail addresses. And virtually every member of Congress, as well as many state legislators, governors, and local officials, have their own web sites. No one knows for certain how many letters, telephone calls, and faxes policymakers receive each year, but the number is surely in the hundreds of millions. Political scientist Kenneth Goldstein recently estimated that members of Congress received over 150 million pieces of mail during one recent (1993–1994) congressional session.[19] Surely the president, state, and local officials received hundreds of millions more. Although few public officials open their own mail, answer their own telephone, or fetch their own faxes, make no mistake that they pay close attention to messages they receive from their constituents.

Citizens can also make their views known by meeting with policymakers face to face. How easy it is to set up a meeting with a public official depends. For influential constituents—corporate executives, small business owners, and community leaders, for example—it may be fairly easy.[20] For ordinary citizens, it is difficult but not impossible. Although few public officials meet with every individual who requests a meeting, many policymakers are willing to meet with particularly vocal and persevering citizens.[21] Elected officials, for example, regularly meet with constituents at public forums and meetings. In addition, public officials of all stripes attend organized interest-orchestrated "lobby days." Most organized interests believe that personal meetings are the most effective ways for citizens to communicate their opinions and attitudes to policymakers.[22]

The advantages of personal meetings are manifold. First, they allow citizens to establish a relationship with a policymaker that may lead to consistent access. Second, they allow citizens to make their case forcefully and emotionally. Letters, faxes, and telephone calls are not effective media for the transmission of emotion and passion. Third, they allow citizens to put a human face on an issue. It is one thing for a legislator to get 1,000 telephone calls from schoolteachers. It is quite another for a legislator to see 1,000 school teachers and their children milling about the Capitol steps.

Another way that citizens can make their views known to policymakers is by engaging in *protest,* an event at which citizens gather together and make their case by creating a public spectacle. Protest was the method of choice for civil rights and antiwar activists in the 1960s, many of whom felt that their letters, telephone calls, and personal entreaties to public officials were being ignored. More recently, antiabortion activists and their opponents have used protest. For example, every year on January 23, the anniversary of the controversial *Roe v. Wade* Supreme Court decision that effectively legalized abortion in this country, organized interests on both sides of the abortion debate stage massive demonstrations in Washington, D.C.[23] One of the biggest recent protests took place on the twenty-fifth anniversary of *Roe v. Wade* in 1989, when a coalition of prochoice organized interests descended on Washington in a three-day March to Washington that featured over 300,000 protesters, as well as appearances by celebrity spokespeople including Jane Fonda, Glenn Close, and Leonard Nimoy (Spock from *Star Trek*).[24] Not to be outdone, a number of prolife organized interests held their own Washington protest a year later, which featured Cardinal John O'Connor and tens of thousands of protesters.[25] Protest may not seem to have much in common with letters, faxes, and telephone calls, but its goal is the same: to make citizens' views known to public officials. One way to think of it is like this: if writing, calling, faxing, and meeting are the polite conversation of citizen contact with policymakers, protest is the screaming and shouting.

Citizens can also make their opinions known by engaging in *dramatics*. Dramatics are similar to protest but are generally more carefully orchestrated and more provocative. The best way to define dramatics is by example. Again, organized interests active in the battle over abortion produce the best examples. Throughout the 1980s, antiabortion activists regularly showed up at protests with child-sized coffins draped in velvet and trash cans filled with doll parts covered with red paint. Their desire was to shock people and attract media attention. Their histrionics did both.[26] More recently, an antiabortion activist showed up at a protest brandishing a fetus in a jar.

Finally, citizens may make their opinions known by presenting petitions to policymakers. The typical petition contains a brief statement followed by places where people can sign to indicate their support for the statement. For example, I was recently given a petition that contained a statement to the effect that the undersigned believed the governor should provide more state funding for public parks. I was informed that once 1,000 people signed the petition, it would be mailed to the governor's office.

Lobbying to Affect Public Opinion and Lobbying for Contact

Some indirect lobbying efforts are designed both to encourage citizens to make their views known to policymakers and to shape people's attitudes and opinions. The HIAA's campaign against President Clinton's health care reform package that began this chapter is a good example. By demonizing the very idea of "government-run health care," the HIAA attempted to shape opinions about health care issues. And by asking people who were against the plan to contact their representatives in Congress, the HIAA encouraged people to make their views known to policymakers.

THE INFORMATIONAL BASIS OF INDIRECT LOBBYING

All indirect lobbying efforts, like all direct lobbying efforts, entail the provision of information. However, unlike direct lobbying, indirect lobbying entails the provision of information to citizens, not policymakers. Generally this information is policy analysis. The policy analysis that organized interests provide to citizens is considerably less complex and technical than the policy analysis they provide to policymakers. Nonetheless, the goal of providing information is the same: to win people over to the organized interest's way of thinking.

If indirect lobbying is successful—that is, it convinces people of the rightness of an organized interest's cause or convinces them to contact policymakers—it also indirectly provides information to policymakers. An indirect lobbying effort that produces citizen pressure on policymakers, for example, provides important political information to public officials about how people are likely to vote in the next election. In fact, political scientist John Wright says that the best way to think of indirect lobbying campaigns is as "field experiments in electoral mobilization."[27] Similarly, indirect lobbying efforts that successfully affect opinions and attitudes eventually produce political activity that provides political information to policymakers.

Any time an organized interest decides to engage in indirect lobbying, it must decide exactly whom it is going to lobby, that is, whom it is going to provide information to. An organized interest that engages in indirect lobbying essentially has three options: lobby the mass public, the attentive public (some subsection of the larger population that is concerned with a particular issue or series of issues), or only members, activists, and sympathizers. Some people call this *narrowcasting*—focusing narrowly rather than broadly. Several factors determine to which audience an organized interest directs its indirect lobbying efforts. One is cost. Not surprisingly, the more people an organized interest wishes to reach, the more expensive it is. Many organized interests that would like to reach the mass public cannot do so because it is too expensive. Another factor that determines which audience an organized interest targets in an indirect lobbying campaign is the immediate goal of the campaign. When organized interests wish to change the attitudes and opinions of large numbers of people, they generally focus broadly. And when they lobby for contact, they generally focus more narrowly on members and sympathizers they have reason to believe will respond positively to their appeals. Focusing more broadly runs the risk of mobilizing opponents as well as supporters. Finally, which audience an organized interest targets is determined to some extent by the level of success of its direct lobbying efforts. Organized interests that are not successful in their direct lobbying efforts have an incentive to "broaden the scope of conflict" by getting more people involved.[28] One way to get more people involved is to lobby citizens.

Because the goal of indirect lobbying is to reach citizens, organized interests often seek media attention for their indirect lobbying efforts.[29] Media attention can increase the number of people an organized interest reaches in an indirect lobbying campaign. There are three ways that organized interests can attract media attention: notify news outlets of their activities, give interviews on radio and television, and do something outrageous that is certain to attract media attention. The publicity that comes from media coverage can attract new supporters to an organized interest's cause, generate enthusiasm among current supporters, and cause policymakers to take notice. The value of media coverage was particularly apparent during the civil rights movement of the 1960s. The citizen groups at the forefront of that movement successfully mobilized tens of thousands of citizens to make their views known to policymakers and attracted media attention, which eventually galvanized public support for the civil rights movement.

TECHNIQUES OF INDIRECT LOBBYING

The Classics

Indirect lobbying has been around forever. Almost fifty years ago in *The Governmental Process*, political scientist David Truman noted that "a primary concern of all organized political interest groups in the United States is the character of the opinions existing in the community." As such, Truman continued, organized interests of all kinds engage in "program[s] of propaganda, though rarely so labeled, designed to affect opinions concerning the interests" of the organization. Truman also concluded that organized interests "frequently urge members to participate" in the political process by making their views known to policymakers.[30] Truman basically said what the previous section in this chapter did: organized interests often try to influence public policy by lobbying to affect public opinion *and* lobbying for contact.[31]

In Truman's time, there were relatively few ways for organized interests to reach citizens. Today there are dozens of ways. In this section, we briefly examine the classic techniques of indirect lobbying—techniques that have been around for a long time. The most common of these are contacting people directly, distributing brochures and pamphlets, advertising in newspapers and magazines, and sending direct mail.

Contacting People Directly

One of the most time-honored indirect lobbying techniques is contacting people directly. Throughout most of American history, organized interests have used personal encounters to lobby citizens. Civil rights groups in the 1950s and 1960s, for example, relied heavily on personal encounters to convince people of the rightness of their cause and to mobilize people to march, boycott, and sit in.[32] In fact, peer pressure played an important role in getting many people to participate in civil rights demonstrations and protests. Of course, throughout most of the eighteenth and nineteenth centuries, contacting people directly was one of the only ways for organized interests to lobby citizens. In the absence of telephones, televisions, computers, and fax machines, organized interests had few options.

Contacting people directly remains an important way for organized interests to contact citizens. One organization that has made extensive use of this technique is the environmental citizen group Greenpeace, which is famous for its door-to-door indirect lobbying and membership campaigns. Greenpeace activists regularly fan out all over the United States and knock on doors for their cause.

Distributing Brochures and Pamphlets

Another seasoned indirect lobbying technique is distributing brochures and pamphlets. Throughout this century, organized interests have used brochures and pamphlets both to make their case to the public and to encourage citizen participation. In the late 1940s, for example, the American Medical Association (AMA) distributed brochures and pamphlets in opposition to President Harry Truman's compulsory federal health insurance plan. One AMA tract entitled *The Voluntary Way Is the American Way* tried to convince citizens that Truman's plan was wrongheaded. The pamphlet read: "If the doctors lose their freedom today—if their patients are regimented tomorrow who will be next? YOU WILL BE NEXT!"[33] The tendentious brochure explained that the "socialization" of health care could lead to the socialization of the entire American economy. It also argued that the "socialization" of medicine in Germany eventually led to horrific Nazi medical experiments. The AMA's brochure clearly was designed to mold attitudes and opinions about health care issues. It also explicitly encouraged citizens to contact their representatives in Congress.

Most brochures and pamphlets bear a striking resemblance to the AMA's early prototype. Like it, most use inflammatory language and appeal to widely accepted values like freedom, liberty, and fairness. Nothing is more popular in pamphlets and brochures, however, than fear mongering, which seeks to convince people that they must act in order to stave off impending doom. A brochure I recently received from a citizen group called Action on Smoking and Health (ASH), for example, begins: "Smoking Hurts. . . . You are a smoker whether you like it or not. In fact, 99.98% of Americans smoke!"[34] The brochure goes on to explain that most Americans do not in fact smoke but are "forced to inhale other people's tobacco smoke." Smoking, it concludes, constitutes a serious health problem for all Americans, so citizens should demand changes in public policy.

Advertising in Newspapers and Magazines

Another venerable indirect lobbying technique is advertising in newspapers and magazines. Print advertisements have been around for many decades. In 1949, for example, a trade association of privately owned power companies placed an advertisement in a number of national magazines stating that private power companies were overregulated and should be left alone by the federal government, which was threatening to adopt further regulations.[35]

Stylistically and substantively, print advertisements are similar to brochures and pamphlets. For example, most print advertisements appeal to widely accepted norms and values and use fear as a motivator. One of the largest print advertising campaigns ever took place during the battle over the North American Free Trade Agreement (NAFTA) in 1993. NAFTA, which sought to improve trilateral trade between Mexico, Canada, and the United States, was opposed vigorously by environmental citizen groups and labor unions. In the midst of the congressional debate over the trade agreement, a short-term coalition of environmental citizen groups mounted a multimillion-dollar print advertising campaign. The cornerstone of this campaign was a series of advertisements that appeared in national newspapers such as the *New York Times* and the *Washington Post*. One such advertisement, which took up a full page in the *New York Times,* began, as most other print advertisements do, with a warning: "ENVIRONMENTAL CATASTROPHE, CANADA TO MEXICO. 8 Fatal Flaws of NAFTA."[36] The text of the advertisement was full of disquieting and fear-inducing words and phrases. For example, it stated that NAFTA would create a "toxic hell" in Texas border towns, and it warned that the inevitable result of NAFTA would be "environmental devastation and joblessness." The advertisement concluded with the following instructions: "*As currently written, NAFTA is not fixable and will cause disaster* [italics in original]. Help us fight against it. Use the coupons below. Thank you." The coupons were three "cut along the dotted line" boxes that could be cut out and sent directly to policymakers. Each contained a brief statement of opposition to NAFTA and a place for the name and address of the sender. One coupon was addressed to the House majority leader, Richard Gephardt, and one to President Clinton's director of public affairs. The third allowed the sender to write in the name of his or her House member.

Sending Direct Mail

Another common indirect lobbying technique is sending direct mail. Although direct mail has not been around as long as brochures and print advertisements, it has been used extensively by organized interests for at least twenty-five years. A number of organized interests use direct mail to recruit members and raise money. Many also use it to lobby indirectly.

Like direct mail campaigns designed to recruit members, indirect lobbying direct mail campaigns begin with a mailing list. Most of the time the mailing list consists solely of names of members. Sometimes, however, it also contains names of nonmembers who are sympathetic to the organized interest's cause. Next, each person on the mailing list is sent a letter that describes the problem at hand and then issues a call to action that suggests what specific action can and should be taken to solve the problem.

Direct mail expert R. Kenneth Godwin notes that most direct mail lobbying letters share two important traits.[37] First, like many print advertisements and brochures, they "use fear or guilt to motivate recipients"[38] and stress "the darker side of politics, portraying the opposition with strong negative descriptors such as 'bureaucrats,' 'left-wing hippies,' 'destroyers,' and 'so-called minorities.'"[39] Second, direct mail letters demand that people act immediately.[40]

New Modes of Reaching Citizens

Although indirect lobbying has been around for a long time, a number of prevalent indirect lobbying techniques are relatively new. Among these new techniques are advertising on television, appearing on television programs, running television programs, advertising on radio, appearing on radio programs, running radio programs, sending the "new" direct mail, calling people on the telephone, using the Internet, and publishing research reports. Most of these new techniques were borne of changes in telecommunications technology.

Using the Television: Advertising, Programming, and Talking

There are several ways that organized interests use television to lobby citizens. One way is by running television commercials. The HIAA's "Harry and Louise" spot, described at the start of this chapter, is a good example of a television commercial used to lobby citizens. In terms of content, television advertisements tend to resemble print advertisements: they use fear as a motivator and appeal to widely accepted values. Stylistically, however, television advertisements are unique in that they allow organized interests to make use of striking visual images.[41]

Organized interests also lobby citizens by running television programs. No other force in American politics has had more success with television programming than the Christian Right. Throughout the 1970s and 1980s, Jerry Falwell used his nationally syndicated television show, *Old Time Gospel Hour,* to lobby citizens on a wide variety of issues.[42] Today the dominant force in television lobbying is Pat Robertson. For several years, Robertson has used his "700 Club" to preach on everything from school prayer and abortion to income taxes and campaign finance reform.

Another way that organized interests use television to lobby citizens is by getting important group personnel on the air. Television has become an important medium for political debate.[43] Most of the debate takes place on talk shows like CNN's *Crossfire,* PBS's *The McLaughlin Group,* and CNBC's *Hardball.* When these shows first appeared, they tended to rely on a limited stable of pundits, including George Will, Morton Kondracke, and Michael Kinsley, who made their living endlessly editorializing about political issues. Today representatives from organized interests often appear on such programs. If the hosts of *Crossfire,* for example, want people to help them debate global warming, they might call a staff scientist from the Sierra Club, a citizen group that favors stronger environmental regulations, and an economic analyst from the U.S. Chamber of Commerce, a trade association that opposes more environmental regulations. Organized interests consider television talk shows important avenues for reaching citizens, and they often put talk show hosts on notice that they are willing to appear on their shows.

Using the Radio: Advertising, Programming, and Talking

Organized interests use radio much like they use television. During the battle over health care reform, for example, the HIAA ran radio commercials similar to its television commercials. Organized interests also run radio programs. For example, the conservative Christian organization Focus on the Family sponsors radio programs on Christian-oriented radio stations throughout the country. Finally, organized interests often get group personnel to appear on radio talk shows. Many conservative organized interests, for example, try to convince Rush Limbaugh, Oliver North, and G. Gordon Liddy to put their personnel on the air.

Calling People on the Telephone

Organized interests lobby indirectly by calling people on the telephone. The telephone, of course, has been around for a very long time, but its use as an indirect lobbying tool is a relatively recent phenomenon. In the past two decades, as long-distance rates have fallen, organized interests have come to rely increasingly on the telephone to lobby citizens. Telephone lobbying, indirect lobbying expert R. Kenneth Godwin observes, is similar to telephone selling.[44]

As if to provide me with evidence to support Godwin's point, an environmental citizen group recently called and asked me to contact my member of Congress about a bill pending. The call began as most telephone solicitations do: "Hello, Mr. Nownes," a pleasant female voice said. "I hate to take up your valuable time, but I was hoping to talk to you about an issue of great importance to environmentalists such as yourself." The caller went on to explain that Congress was debating important environmental legislation and concluded by asking me to call my member of Congress to express support for the legislation.

Telephone lobbying is easier today than it used to be. Special computer programs allow organized interests to call large numbers of people at a relatively low cost. One such program automatically selects names and telephone numbers from a massive CD-ROM database according to specifications dictated by the user. The program also dials numbers automatically, delivers a recorded message to whomever answers, and even connects the call's recipient directly to the office of his or her member of Congress.

Sending the "New" Direct Mail

Advances in communications technology have also changed the face of an old form of indirect lobbying: sending direct mail. Computers have made direct mail more personalized. Before computers, organized interests sent identical form letters to the people they wanted to reach. Today organized interests send different letters to different people. By using large databases, organized interests can find out what issues interest each letter recipient and emphasize those issues in their mailings. In addition, organized interests can use powerful computers to personalize a letter's salutation.[45]

Today's direct mailings are also more sophisticated. They contain more graphics and color than in the past, and because computers can put stamps on envelopes and print addresses in cursive, the mailing looks more like personal mail than "junk mail." The greater sophistication and personalization of direct mail increase the probability that an individual will open a direct mailing rather than throw it away on receipt.

Using the Internet

One of the newest indirect lobbying techniques is using the Internet. Several thousand organized interests now have their own web sites.

To see how organized interests use their web sites for indirect lobbying purposes, consider an example: the Christian Coalition's web site.[46] When I accessed it, at the top of the first screen of text was the title "Christian Coalition Worldwide" framed in color next to the coalition's logo. Below the title was a news headline: "Supreme Court Allows States to Legally Protect Unborn Babies." This headline, I learned, changes periodically but always concerns an issue that is important to the coalition. Like most other web sites, this one contains something akin to a table of contents that guides viewers. There are two ways that the Christian Coalition uses its web site to lobby citizens. First, it includes on its site a permanent section entitled "Contact Congress," which tells visitors how to contact members of Congress. A viewer who clicks on the Contact Congress icon is sent to a different screen that details how to contact any member of Congress by mail, telephone, fax, e-mail, telegraph, or in person. Second, the coalition flashes important "action alert" messages on its web site—messages that essentially are on-line print advertisements urging viewers to take action on a specific policy proposal. Because updating a web site is easy, the coalition can react quickly to political events and place new action alert messages on its page any time it wishes.

Organized interests use the Internet to lobby indirectly also by sending e-mail. Many organized interests have special list servers that enable them to send e-mail to large numbers of people simultaneously. In general, organized interests use e-mail much like they use regular direct mail: they send letters to raise money, goad people into action, or do both. New members of an organized interest are generally asked for their e-mail address as well as street address.

Although e-mail indirect lobbying is in its infancy, there is good reason to believe that it will become increasingly prevalent. First, e-mail is easy. List servers allow organized interests to send letters to huge numbers of people at the flip of a switch. Second, e-mail is inexpensive. Finally, e-mail allows an organized interest to react immediately. A direct mail, telephone, or door-to-door indirect lobbying campaign may take days or weeks to get off the ground. In contrast, an e-mail indirect lobbying campaign can be devised and carried out in a few hours.

Publishing Research Reports

Finally, organized interests lobby indirectly by publishing research reports. Research reports are similar to pamphlets and brochures but are generally longer and more sophisticated and generally contain policy analysis. They became especially prominent in the 1970s, as the federal government began dealing with highly complex and technical policy issues for the first time. Think tanks are more likely than other types of organized interests to lobby through the publication of research reports, but other types of organized interests have taken up publishing research reports as well.[47]

To illustrate how organized interests lobby indirectly through the publication of research reports, consider an example. Recently the consumer products company Procter and Gamble (P&G) relied heavily on research reports in a policy battle over one of its products. By early 1998, P&G had spent more than $300 million to develop the fat substitute olestra.[48] Before it could use olestra in any of its food products, however, it had to get approval from the Food and Drug Administration (FDA). Approval was by no means a sure thing. The company's own tests had revealed that olestra produced a number of side effects, including, in the company's own words, "anal leakage" and "fecal urgency."[49]

P&G realized that in order for olestra to be approved by the FDA and accepted by the public, it had to convince people that it was not dangerous to their health. To do this, it mounted a sophisticated indirect lobbying campaign. In 1995, as the FDA began to evaluate the safety of olestra, P&G commissioned a number of well-known scientists to study the product. Not surprisingly, virtually all of the studies that the company commissioned showed that olestra was next to harmless. The papers that reported scientists' happy findings were given to the FDA, of course, but were also published in scientific journals and given to the media.[50]

In 1995 and 1996, P&G held a number of public forums and scientific events at which scientists sponsored by the company discussed the health benefits of olestra. The proceedings of one conference on olestra were subsequently published in the highly respected *Annals of the New York Academy of Science.* By 1996, a number of research reports supportive of olestra were floating around the country. These research reports were designed to convince policymakers at the FDA to approve olestra. In this sense, the research reports were tools of direct lobbying. But because P&G also distributed its reports to scientists, the media, and other interested parties, they were also tools of indirect lobbying. P&G clearly hoped that its research would lead to public acceptance of olestra, and perhaps even lead ordinary citizens to pressure the FDA to approve olestra. In the end, the FDA approved olestra.

Determining Which Indirect Lobbying Technique to Use

Organized interests can reach citizens in a number of ways. This, of course, begs the following question: What factors determine which indirect lobbying techniques an organized interest uses? Two factors in particular seem to be important. First, of course, is cost. If an organized interest does not have much money, it most likely will eschew expensive techniques such as running television advertisements and rely instead on contacting people directly or distributing brochures. The other important factor is the number of people an organized interest wishes to reach. If it is targeting millions of people, its best bet is probably to advertise on television. In contrast, if it wishes to reach only a few hundred people, direct mail, telephone calls, e-mails, or faxes are better bets.

TRENDS IN INDIRECT LOBBYING

The future of indirect lobbying is impossible to predict. Nonetheless, several developments are already apparent. First, indirect lobbying is more common than ever before. Second, the rise of indirect lobbying has given rise to an indirect lobbying industry. Finally, indirect lobbying has become highly controversial.

Increasing Prevalence of Indirect Lobbying

Indirect lobbying is more prevalent than ever before.[51] Today, as Table 8.1 shows, 80 percent of Washington organized interests and 86 percent of state organized interests engage in some form of indirect lobbying. These numbers represent a huge expansion of indirect lobbying since the 1950s, 1960s, and 1970s.[52] We do not have surveys from the 1950s, 1960s, and 1970s to indicate precisely how much indirect lobbying has increased, but case studies, historical accounts, and surveys from the 1980s and 1990s clearly show that more organized interests engage in more indirect lobbying than ever before.[53] In a recent review article on contemporary organized interest politics, political scientists

TABLE 8.1. Proportion of Respondents Reporting That They Engage in Three Indirect Lobbying Techniques

Technique	States (N = 595)	Washington (N = 175)
Mounting grass-roots lobbying efforts	83	80
Talking to the media	74	86
Running advertisements in media about position	18	31

Note: Each respondent was asked to indicate which of the techniques he or she had used in the past year.
Sources: The state data come from Anthony J. Nownes and Patricia K. Freeman, "Interest Group Activity in the States," *Journal of Politics* 60:1 (February 1998). The Washington data come from Kay Lehman Schlozman and John T. Tierney, *Organized Interests and American Democracy* (New York: Harper and Row, 1986), p. 150.

Allan Cigler and Burdett Loomis concluded that "what has changed most" in organized interest politics since the mid-1970s "is the sheer magnitude, sophistication, and cost of grassroots politicking."[54]

Organized interests increasingly have turned to indirect lobbying for two reasons. First, they have come to realize that indirect lobbying works. In the 1960s and 1970s, organized interests of all kinds began to note that indirect lobbying could produce results. They saw, for example, that by taking to the streets, civil rights groups forced the revocation of discriminatory laws and policies. And so many organized interests that previously had eschewed indirect lobbying—especially businesses and trade associations that were hurt by stricter government regulations—decided to give it a try. Second, organized interests have turned to indirect lobbying because advances in communications and computer technology have made it easier than in the past. Today, with the press of a button, an organized interest can call, write, fax, or e-mail almost anybody in the United States. In the past, if an organized interest wanted to contact a person directly, it had to look in the telephone book and either call, write, or drop by. Today organized interests have access to huge databases that allow them to contact people at home or at work with relative ease. Moreover, they have a plethora of tools with which to reach people. Forty years ago, organized interests could not reach citizens by television, fax, or computer. Finally, technology has made many forms of indirect lobbying less expensive. For example, telephoning people is less expensive than ever before. Deregulation and innovative technologies like WATS lines have made telephoning citizens relatively cheap and easy.

The Rise of Indirect Lobbying Firms

Not surprisingly, the rise of indirect lobbying has led to the rise of indirect lobbying firms. In Washington, as well as in states and cities across the country, an adjuvant industry has arisen to meet the needs of organized interests that wish to mount indirect lobbying campaigns. One of the most successful indirect lobbying firms in Washington is the Clinton Group, which sells its services to liberal organized interests. To get an idea of what indirect lobbying firms do, consider how the Clinton Group might help a liberal citizen group like the National Organization for Women (NOW) that opposes a Supreme Court nominee because of his or her opposition to abortion rights:

> The Clinton Group will take the membership rolls of the group and match names to phone numbers. It might also use its computer to cross-reference magazine subscriptions, data on personal purchasing habits, and precincts with particular voting and income profiles to come up with a bigger list of sympathetic people.
>
> At the company's phone bank in Louisville, Kentucky, a computer dials the numbers. When someone answers, an operator comes on the line and explains NOW's position, offering to transfer the caller, at no charge, to the White House switchboard or local member of Congress.[55]

The Clinton Group works almost exclusively for left-leaning and moderate organized interests. Washington is also home to the powerful Bonner and Associates, an indirect lobbying firm that works mostly for corporations and trade associations. During the Clinton years, Bonner and Associates became a multimillion-dollar firm as industries of all kinds sought help in beating back various proposals to reform the nation's health care system.[56] Firms like the Clinton Group and Bonner and Associates offer a wide range of indirect lobbying services to organized interests. The ubiquity of indirect lobbying firms makes it easier than ever for organized interests to lobby citizens.

Indirect lobbying has generated a great deal of controversy because of the ease with which organized interests can mount phony indirect lobbying campaigns. To give you an idea of what I mean by phony, consider the following case. In 1995, with the help of Washington lobbyist Bob Beckel, a trade association called the Competitive Long Distance Coalition, which consisted of MCI, Sprint, and AT&T, mounted a massive indirect lobbying campaign designed to stop legislation designed to make it easier for local telephone companies to offer long-distance service. The coalition telephoned MCI, Sprint, and AT&T customers, asked them if they favored "competition" in the long-distance telephone industry, and then sent up to four telegrams to members of Congress on behalf of each person who answered yes.[57] The coalition succeeded in generating over 500,000 telegrams. About half were fake. Many contained bogus names and signatures, and some were signed by people who were dead. This is not an isolated case. Every year, organized interests mount indirect lobbying campaigns that produce fake "grass-roots" communications from citizens. Such indirect lobbying efforts are often referred to as "astroturf" (meaning "phony grass") lobbying campaigns.

Phony indirect lobbying campaigns raise some troubling questions. Generally it is easy for a policymaker to check up on a lobbyist who contacts him or her directly. In most places, lobbyists are required to register—that is, to disclose for whom they work and how they can be reached. Thus, if a lobbyist calls a legislator and says, "My name is Tom Jones, and I work for Amalgamated Controls Inc.," the legislator can easily find out if there is such a company, and if there is, if Jones actually works for it. It also is often relatively easy for a policymaker to verify the information that lobbyists provide. For example, if Jill Loby tells a legislator that her company has four plants in the legislator's district, the legislator can ask friends, confidants, and even other lobbyists if this is true. In sum, it is easy for policymakers to check up on the people who lobby them directly.

In contrast, it is difficult for policymakers to check up on the ordinary citizens who contact them during indirect lobbying campaigns. A successful indirect lobbying campaign might produce tens or even hundreds of thousands of telephone calls, letters, faxes, or e-mails, and it would be impractical and impossible for a policymaker to determine if each one of these communications was genuine. Another reason it is difficult for policymakers to check up on the people who lobby them indirectly is that the information that citizens provide to policymakers during indirect lobbying campaigns is generally opinion, not factual in nature, and is thus impossible to verify in any objective sense. In short, policymakers have to take it for granted that people actually mean what they say.

The point here is this: although it is difficult to mount phony direct lobbying efforts, it is easy to mount phony indirect lobbying efforts. Not only does computer technology make it easier than ever before for an organized interest to simulate the effects of a real indirect lobbying campaign, policymakers seldom have the resources to check out the thousands of letters, telegrams, telephone calls, and faxes they receive each day. Nonetheless, policymakers have become more savvy at distinguishing between real and phony indirect lobbying efforts. They have come to recognize, for example, the telltale signs of bogus indirect lobbying campaigns. One is sudden and overwhelming public outcry about a particular issue. Another is multiple letters, faxes, phone calls, or e-mails from the same source. Nonetheless, fraudulent indirect lobbying remains a problem.

CONCLUSION: INDIRECT LOBBYING AND THE PROVISION OF INFORMATION

Indirect lobbying is defined as lobbying that is aimed at citizens rather than public officials. There are two general types of indirect lobbying: lobbying to affect public opinion and lobbying for contact. The former is designed to influence people's attitudes and opinions, the latter to encourage people to contact policymakers and make their opinions known. Both types have the same ultimate goal: to affect public policy.

Indirect lobbying, like direct lobbying, entails the provision of information. However, when they lobby indirectly, organized interests provide information to citizens rather than policymakers. This information is generally policy analysis, although it is considerably less complex and technical than that which organized interests provide to policymakers. If indirect lobbying is successful—that is, it convinces people of the rightness of an organized interest's cause or convinces them to contact policymakers—it also provides information to policymakers. Generally it is political information about how people are likely to vote in the next election.

Organized interests lobby citizens in a number of ways. Among the classic techniques are meeting with people face to face, distributing brochures and pamphlets, running print advertisements, and sending direct mail. Among the more contemporary techniques are advertising on television, advertising on radio, running programs on television, running programs on radio, appearing on television talk shows, appearing on radio talk shows, using the Internet, and publishing research reports.

In the past twenty to thirty years, indirect lobbying has become more common, has given rise to an indirect lobbying industry, and has created a great deal of controversy. These trends are likely to continue.

What's Next

We have examined what organized interests are, where they come from, and what they do, but we have more or less ignored what impact they have on public policy. I have done this for a reason: examining influence without understanding the nature, prevalence, and extent of organized interest activity is hopeless. We cannot ignore the question of influence any longer. Few other issues in American politics are more enduring, controversial, and important than the issue of organized interest influence. This issue is the subject of the next, and penultimate, chapter.

EXERCISES

1. Pick an organized interest, and find its web site. What types of information are on the web site? Does the organization use its site for indirect lobbying? How?
2. Speculate as to how the World Wide Web might affect indirect lobbying in the future. In your opinion, what are some of the benefits of the web as an indirect lobbying medium? What are some of the drawbacks?

RESEARCH RESOURCES

Publications

Books. To learn more about indirect lobbying, read one or more of these books: Kenneth M. Goldstein, *Interest Groups, Lobbying, and Participation in America* (London: Cambridge University Press, 1999); Ken Kollman, *Outside Lobbying: Public Opinion and Interest Group Strategies* (Princeton, N.J.: Princeton University Press, 1998); and Darrell M. West and Burdett A. Loomis, *The Sound of Money: How Political Interests Get What They Want* (New York: Norton, 1998).

Web Resources

Lobbying firms. Because many lobbying firms offer indirect lobbying services to their clients, they are good sources of information on the goals, logistics, and uses of indirect lobbying. Here are the web addresses for some Washington-based lobbying firms that offer indirect lobbying services: Pinpoint Communications, *www.pinpointc.com;* Podesta.com, *www.podesta.com;* Raintree Communications, *www.policyvoice.com;* and the Wexler Group, *www.wexlergroup.com.*

Organized interest web sites. For more information on how to find an organized interest's web site, consult the Web Resources section at the end of Chapter 1.

Notes

1. See Darrell M. West, Diane J. Heith, and Chris Godwin, "Harry and Louise Go to Washington: Political Advertising and Health Care Reform," *Journal of Health Policy, Politics, and Law* (Spring 1996): 35–68.

2. Allan J. Cigler and Burdett A. Loomis, "Contemporary Interest Group Politics: More Than 'More of the Same,'" in Allan J. Cigler and Burdett A. Loomis, eds., *Interest Group Politics* (4th ed.) (Washington, DC: Congressional Quarterly Press, 1995), p. 395.

3. Burdett A. Loomis, "A New Era: Groups at the Grassroots," in Allan J. Cigler and Burdett A. Loomis, eds., *Interest Group Politics* (Washington, DC: Congressional Quarterly Press, 1983), pp. 170–171.

4. James G. Gimpel, "Grassroots Organizations and Equilibrium Cycles in Group Mobilization and Access," in Paul S. Herrnson, Ronald G. Shaiko, and Clyde Wilcox, eds., *The Interest Group Connection: Electioneering, Lobbying, and Policymaking in Washington* (Chatham, NJ: Chatham House, 1998), p. 101.

5. See John W. Kingdon, *Congressmen's Voting Decisions* (2nd ed.) (New York: Harper and Row, 1981); David R. Mayhew, *Congress: The Electoral Connection* (New Haven, CT: Yale University Press, 1974).

6. David M. Hedge, *Governance and the Changing American States* (Boulder, CO: Westview Press, 1998), p. 32.

7. Ibid., p. 33.

8. Thad L. Beyle, *State and Local Government: 1999–2000* (Washington, DC: Congressional Quarterly Press, 1999), p. 31.

9. Morris P. Fiorina, *Retrospective Voting in American National Elections* (New Haven, CT: Yale University Press, 1981); D. Roderick Kiewiet, *Macroeconomics and Micropolitics: The Electoral Effects of Economic Issues* (Chicago: University of Chicago Press, 1983). See also Sidney Verba, Kay Lehman Schlozman, and Henry E. Brady, *Voice and Equality: Civic Voluntarism in American Politics* (Cambridge, MA: Harvard University Press, 1995).

10. See Burdett A. Loomis and Eric Sexton, "Choosing to Advertise: How Interests Decide," in Cigler and Loomis, eds., *Interest Group Politics* (4th ed.), pp. 193–214.

11. See Charles E. Gengler and Thomas J. Reynolds, "A Structural Model of Advertising Effects," in Andrew A. Mitchell, ed., *Advertising Exposure, Memory, and Choice* (Hillsdale, NJ: Erlbaum, 1993); Chris Enyinda Iheany, "An Econometric

Analysis of Multimedia Effects on Consumers' Purchase Decisions at the Super-market Level Using Scanner-Derived Data" (Ph.D. diss., University of Tennessee, 1995).

12. Stephen Ansolabehere and Shanto Iyengar, *Going Negative: How Attack Ads Shrink and Polarize the Electorate* (New York: Free Press, 1995); Edwin Diamond and Stephen Bates, *The Spot: The Rise of Political Advertising on Television* (Cambridge, MA: MIT Press, 1992).

13. Clyde Wilcox, "The Dynamics of Lobbying the Hill," in Herrnson, Shaiko, and Wilcox, eds., *The Interest Group Connection: Electioneering, Lobbying, and Policymaking in Washington* (Chatham, NJ: Chatham House, 1998), p. 90.

14. Ibid., p. 96.

15. See Peter H. Stone, "Under the Gun," *National Journal,* June 5, 1993, pp. 1334–1338.

16. Verba, Schlozman, and Brady, *Voice and Equality: Civic Voluntarism in American Politics* (Cambridge, MA: Harvard University Press, 1995), chap. 5.

17. Cigler and Loomis, "Contemporary Interest Group Politics: More Than 'More of the Same,'" in Cigler and Loomis, eds. *Interest Group Politics* (Washington, DC: Congressional Quarterly Press, 1995), p. 402.

18. Ibid., p. 395.

19. Kenneth M. Goldstein, "Tremors Before the Earthquake: Grassroots Communication to Congress Before the 1994 Election" (paper delivered at the annual meeting of the American Political Science Association, Chicago, September 1995), p. 4.

20. William P. Browne, *Cultivating Congress: Constituents, Issues, and Interests in Agricultural Policymaking* (Lawrence: University of Kansas Press, 1995).

21. Wilcox, "The Dynamics of Lobbying the Hill," p. 97.

22. See Common Cause's web site for details: *http://www.commoncause.org/get_involved/contact-1.*

23. Laura Woliver, "Abortion Interests: From the Usual Suspects to Expanded Coalitions," in Allan J. Cigler and Burdett A. Loomis, eds., *Interest Group Politics* (2nd ed.) (Washington, DC: Congressional Quarterly Press, 1986), pp. 327–342.

24. Alissa Rubin, "Interest Groups and Abortion Politics in the Post-Webster Era," in Allan J. Cigler and Burdett A. Loomis, eds., *Interest Group Politics* (3rd ed.) (Washington, DC: Congressional Quarterly Press, 1991), p. 244

25. Ibid., p. 245. See also Raymond Tatalovich, *The Politics of Abortion in the United States and Canada: A Comparative Study* (Armonk, NY: M. E. Sharpe, 1997); Dallas A. Blanchard, *The Anti-Abortion Movement and the Rise of the Religious Right: From Polite to Fiery Protest* (New York: Twayne, 1994).

26. Marjorie Randon Hershey, "Direct Action and the Abortion Issue: The Political Participation of Single-issue Groups," in Cigler and Loomis, eds., *Interest Group Politics* (2nd ed.), pp. 27–45.

27. John R. Wright, *Interest Groups and Congress: Lobbying, Contributions, and Influence* (Boston, MA: Allyn and Bacon, 1996), p. 90.

28. See E. E. Schattschneider, *The Semisovereign People: A Realist's View of Democracy in America* (New York: Holt, Rinehart, and Winston, 1960).

29. Christopher H. Foreman, Jr., "Grassroots Victim Organizations: Mobilizing for Personal and Public Health," in Cigler and Loomis, eds., *Interest Group Politics* (4th ed.), pp. 33–53.

30. David Truman, *The Governmental Process: Political Interests and Public Opinion* (2nd ed.) (New York: Knopf, 1971), pp. 213, 389.

31. Some interesting early studies of indirect lobbying include Lewis E. Gleeck, "96 Congressmen Make Up Their Minds," *Public Opinion Quarterly* 4 (Spring 1940): 3–24; and Rowena Wyant and Herta Herzog, "Voting Via the Senate Mailbag," *Public Opinion Quarterly* 5 (Fall and Winter 1941): 359–382.

32. Dennis Chong, *Collective Action and the Civil Rights Movement* (Chicago: University of Chicago Press, 1991).

33. *The Voluntary Way Is the American Way* (Chicago: American Medical Association National Education Campaign, 1949).

34. *Let's Take Action on Smoking and Health* (Washington, DC: Action on Smoking and Health, n.d.).

35. Truman, *The Governmental Process: Political Interests and Public Opinion* (2nd ed. (New York: Knopf, 1971), p. 232.

36. This advertisement appeared in the *New York Times,* September 21, 1993, p. A11.

37. R. Kenneth Godwin, "Money, Technology, and Political Interests: The Direct Marketing of Politics," in Mark P. Petracca, ed., *The Politics of Interests: Interest Groups Transformed* (Boulder, CO: Westview Press, 1992), pp. 308–325.

38. R. Kenneth Godwin, *One Billion Dollars of Influence* (Chatham, NJ: Chatham House, 1988), p. 24.

39. Godwin, "Money, Technology, and Political Interests: The Direct Marketing of Politics," in Mark P. Petracca, ed., *The Politics of Interests: Interest Groups Transformed* (Boulder, CO: Westview Press, 1992), p. 311.

40. Ibid., p. 310.

41. Neil Postman, *Amusing Ourselves to Death* (New York: Penguin Books, 1985).

42. Loomis, "A New Era: Groups at the Grassroots," in Cigler and Loomis eds., *Interest Group Politics* (Washingtion, DC: Congressional Quarterly Press, 1983), p. 173.

43. Eric Alterman, *Sound and Fury: The Washington Punditocracy and the Collapse of American Politics* (New York: HarperCollins, 1992).

44. Godwin, "Money, Technology, and Political Interests: The Direct Marketing of Politics," in Mark P. Petracca, ed., *The Politics of Interests: Interest Groups Transformed* (Boulder, CO: Westview Press, 1992), p. 310.

45. Ibid.

46. *http://www.cc.org,* accessed July 31, 1998.

47. James G. McGann, "Academics to Ideologues: A Brief History of the Public Policy Research Industry," *PS* 4 (September 1992): 734–735.

48. Kenneth Silverstein, *Washington on $10 Million a Day: How Lobbyists Plunder the Nation* (Monroe, ME: Common Courage Press, 1998), p. 58.

49. Ibid.

50. Ibid., p. 63.

51. Cigler and Loomis, "Contemporary Interest Group Politics: More Than 'More of the Same,'" in Cigler and Loomis, eds., *Interest Group Politics* (4th ed.) (Washington, DC: Congressional Quarterly Press, 1995), p. 395.

52. Ibid., pp. 394–395.

53. Darrell M. West and Burdett A. Loomis, *The Sound of Money: How Political Interests Get What They Want* (New York: Norton, 1999); Cigler and Loomis, "Contemporary Interest Group Politics: More Than 'More of the Same,'" in Cigler and Loomis, eds., *Interest Group Politics* (4th ed.) (Washington, DC: Congressional Quarterly Press, 1995), pp. 393–405.

54. Cigler and Loomis, "Contemporary Interest Group Politics: More Than 'More of the Same,'" in Cigler and Loomis, eds., *Interest Group Politics* (4th ed.) (Washington, DC: Congressional Quarterly Press, 1995), p. 395.

55. Ibid., p. 396.

56. Stephen Engleberg, "A New Breed of Hired Hands Cultivates Grass-Roots Anger," *New York Times*, March 17, 1995.

57. Wilcox, "The Dynamics of Lobbying the Hill," p. 98.

The Influence
of Organized Interests

Washington, D.C.
August 2, 1996

After months of debate, Congress approves a bill that increases the minimum wage from $4.25 to $5.15 per hour.[1] John F. Sturm, president of the Newspaper Association of America (NAA), is ecstatic. After the bill passes, Sturm boasts: "This is probably the best thing that has happened to the [newspaper] industry from a legislative standpoint in anyone's memory."[2] Why is the head of the newspaper industry's main trade association so giddy about a minimum wage increase that ostensibly increases the cost of doing business? The reason is that tucked deep within the bill is an arcane provision that allows newspaper publishers to treat distributors and carriers as independent contractors rather than employees. To most Americans, this is a matter of semantics, but to newspaper publishers, it is a huge windfall. The legal reclassification of distributors and carriers enables publishers to avoid paying workers' social security benefits and other employment taxes. The NAA's Sturm proudly proclaims that the bill will "save a lot of newspapers a lot of money in the future."[3]

Why was Congress so generous to the newspaper industry? One possible answer is lobbying. For years before the minimum wage increase, the newspaper industry had lobbied relentlessly for special tax treatment. Among the lobbyists retained by the industry in the early 1990s were Tony Podesta, the brother of President Clinton's staff secretary, John Podesta; Vernon Jordan, the director of Dow Jones and a close friend of President Clinton; and Tommy Boggs, superstar lobbyist and son of late House majority leader Hale Boggs.[4] And to make sure that its lobbying efforts were well received, the newspaper industry doled out generous campaign contributions. During the 1995–1996 election

TABLE 9.1 Public Opinion About the Responsiveness of American Government, 1980–1998 Question: "Would you say the government is pretty much run by a few big interests looking out for themselves or that it is run for the benefit of all the people?"

Answer	1980	1988	1992	1994	1996	1998
Few big interests	70%	64%	75%	76%	70%	64%
Benefit of all	21	31	20	19	27	32
Don't know/depends	9	5	4	5	3	4

Source: National Election Studies, Center for Political Studies, University of Michigan, *The NES Guide to Public Opinion and Electoral Behavior* (Ann Arbor: University of Michigan, Center for Political Studies, 1995–1998), accessed at *http://www.umich.edu/~nes/nesguide/tab_exam)*, December 7, 1999.

cycle alone, media and communications sources contributed $53.2 million to federal candidates and political parties.[5]

It is a matter of faith among many Americans that organized interests like the NAA regularly get their way in Washington. As Table 9.1 attests, public opinion polls show that most Americans believe that policymakers respond more to the needs of "a few big interests" than to ordinary Americans. Are the public's perceptions accurate? Do organized interests and their lobbyists dominate American government and politics? Or are accounts of organized interest influence mere hyperbole? These questions cut to the very heart of American democracy. After all, a government for organized interests and by organized interests is exactly what the founders of this country did not want. In this chapter, we examine what political scientists have learned about organized interest influence. We begin with a look at the difficulties inherent in assessing the impact of lobbying on policy outcomes. From here, we examine some theories that purport to explain the role of organized interests in the policymaking process. Finally, we ask: When do organized interests get their way?

THE THORNY QUESTION OF ORGANIZED INTEREST INFLUENCE

The story at the start of this chapter seems to be a straightforward account of organized interest influence. The newspaper industry tirelessly lobbied for a special tax break. Then a few years later, Congress and the president caved in and gave the industry what it wanted. It seems to be an open and shut case. Right?

Wrong. In reality, it is very difficult to determine precisely what role organized interests played in the adoption of the newspaper tax break, for three reasons. First, the ultimate decision to enact the tax break had numerous causes, not just one. In the end, this policy decision, like most other policy decisions, was the result of a multifaceted and complex process. The decision involved literally thousands of political actors, each with a different mixture of motives. Among those actively involved were the president and his aides, hundreds of members of Congress, hundreds of congressional staffers, and scores of lobbyists. Because so many actors were involved, it is difficult to determine precisely how much influence each actor or set of actors exerted. Second, in most cases it is very difficult to distinguish influence from agreement. It is not uncommon for public officials to do precisely what organized interests want them to do simply because they agree with them. This is agreement. But it looks a lot like influence. In cases like this, it is difficult to determine precisely how much influence organized interests exert. Finally, "access" and "activity" do not necessarily mean "influence." In other words, just because a group is there, or has lots of money, or has lots of contacts does not mean it is influential. It may be tempting to equate presence and activity with influence, but it is unwise. Sometimes organized interests do a lot and get little in return. For example, in the past twenty years, organized interests representing tobacco companies have spent hundreds of millions of dollars on lobbying. In 1997 alone, the five biggest American tobacco companies spent $30 million on lobbying.[6] They have repeatedly testified before Congress, met personally with policymakers of all kinds, engaged in litigation, contributed millions of dollars to candidates and political parties, and engaged in issue advocacy campaigns. None of this enabled the tobacco industry to avoid a historic settlement that forced tobacco companies to pay state governments $368 billion.

This section is a caveat—a warning that the question of organized interest influence is a thorny one. It is not easy to figure out exactly how much power organized interests exert over policy outcomes. All policy decisions have multiple causes, not just one, and it is hard to separate agreement from influence. Moreover, sometimes smoke does not mean fire. In other words, presence and activity do not automatically add up to influence.

PLURALISM: PUTTING ORGANIZED INTERESTS ON THE MAP

Despite James Madison's warnings about the mischiefs of faction, it was not until the middle of the twentieth century that social scientists began to study organized interest influence in earnest. Most scholars more or less ignored organized interests until then because they did not see them as important players in the political process.[7] For approximately the first 150 years of our history, political scientists focused the bulk of their attention on governmental actors, because they viewed organized interests and other extragovernmental actors as more or less peripheral to the political process.[8]

At midcentury all of this began to change. As organized interests proliferated in the 1940s and 1950s, political scientists began to take note of their role in policymaking. One of the first political scientists to address the question of organized interest influence was David Truman. In his influential book *The Governmental Process* (1951), Truman found that millions of Americans joined organized interests to further their political goals and that these organized interests were key players in the political process.[9] In virtually every public policy battle that Truman investigated, he found the fingerprints of organized interests and their lobbyists. In case after case, Washington policymakers interacted extensively with organized interests before reaching their final decisions. Truman stopped short of concluding that organized interests dominated the policymaking process, but he strongly insinuated that policymakers were quite responsive to the desires of organized interests.

In the ten to fifteen years after Truman's *Governmental Process* was published, several scholars weighed in on the question of organized interest influence. Most agreed with Truman that organized interests were active and influential in most major policy decisions. Truman and others who shared this view came to be known as *pluralists*.[10] Their basic perspective on organized interest politics became known as *pluralism*. Pluralists differed from most previous scholars of American politics in two respects: they recognized that organized interests were deeply immersed in policymaking at all levels of government, and they did not view organized interests as threats to American democracy. Unlike Madison and other critics of organized interests, pluralists argued that organized interests were essentially harmless. They believed that organized interests represented real people with reasonable political demands and therefore were legitimate vehicles by which citizens communicated their views to government officials. Researchers in the pluralist tradition portrayed lobbyists as benevolent transmitters of information from citizens to policymakers.[11]

Pluralism reached its apex with the publication of political scientist Robert Dahl's book *Who Governs?* in 1961. Dahl studied policymaking in the city of New Haven, Connecticut, and found that although organized interests were often active and influential, they were far from injurious to democracy. First, Dahl found, different organized interests participated in different policy decisions. As such, no single organized interest or set of organized interests dominated New Haven politics. Second, Dahl concluded that New Haven politics was relatively open. In other words, virtually any organized interest was allowed to participate if its claims were legitimate and mainstream. In short, if a group of citizens wanted to be influential, they had the opportunity; no one was shut out of the governmental process. Third, Dahl concluded that organized interests represented real people and thus were important institutions linking citizens and government.[12]

Not all early scholars of organized interests shared pluralists' optimism. Political sociologist C. Wright Mills, for example, argued that government policymakers listened solely to the demands of a very narrow stratum of exclusive organized interests that represented rich and powerful people—people Mills called "the power elite."[13] Because the power elite were better represented than ordinary citizens, Mills argued, policy decisions were skewed toward the interests of the rich and famous. People who shared Mills's views about organized interests came to be known as *elitists,* and Mills's basic perspective on organized interest politics became known as *elitism.* Although many sociologists accepted Mills's basic premise that American politics was elitist in nature, most political scientists accepted the pluralist interpretation. Dahl, Truman, and other pluralists were the preeminent political scientists of their time. As such, their empirical studies were well received and convinced most other political scientists that pluralism provided an accurate portrayal of the role of organized interests in policymaking.

In the end, although some scholars disagreed with their rather sanguine view of American politics, pluralists showed once and for all that organized interests were important players in American politics. At the time, it was a powerful insight. Before pluralists began to examine the role of organized interests in policymaking, most social scientists had viewed policy decisions solely as manifestations of government activity.

SUBGOVERNMENTS AND POLICY DOMAINS

Pluralists showed that organized interests were deeply involved in policymaking at all levels of government. But the question remained: How involved were they? Did they actually influence the decisions of policymakers, or did they operate at the fringes of American politics? As organized interests continued to proliferate throughout the 1960s and 1970s, political scientists grappled with these questions in an attempt to discern the true nature and extent of organized interest influence.

At about the same time that pluralists spread the word about organized interest involvement in policymaking, a group of scholars formulated a new theory of organized interest influence called *subgovernment theory.*[14] After studying how policy was made in a number of different issue areas, subgovernment theorists concluded that each policy area at each level of government had its own *subgovernment*—a limited number of organized interests, legislators, and key bureaucrats who interacted on a stable, ongoing basis to produce policy outcomes in a particular issue area.[15] Political scientist John Wright provides an example of how a subgovernment works. On the issue of veterans' affairs, he argues, "House and Senate Veterans' Affairs Committees in Congress, the Veterans Administration, and organizations such as the American Legion and the Veterans of Foreign Wars (VFW) work[ed] together in developing policies on education, health care, and housing for veterans."[16] Similarly, on agriculture issues at the national level, members of the House and Senate Agriculture Committees, organized interests such as the American Farm Bureau Federation and the National Council of Farmer Cooperatives, and bureaucrats from the U.S. Department of Agriculture (USDA) interacted regularly to make farm policy. Because the shape of a subgovernment resembles that of a triangle, many subgovernment theorists called subgovernments "iron triangles."

According to subgovernment theory, the policy decisions that come out of subgovernments are self-serving; they "specifically reward the primary constituencies of the [subgovernment's] participants, often to the detriment of the public at large."[17] The agriculture subgovernment, for example, created farm subsidy programs that benefited farmers, who got cash payments from the national government; members of the House and Senate Agriculture Committees who curried favor with their constituents by providing them with monetary subsidies; and USDA bureaucrats, who got to keep their jobs as long as farm programs existed. Similarly, the veterans' affairs subgovernment made policies that guaranteed direct payments to veterans. Veterans' groups were happy with the payments, as were bureaucrats from the Veterans Administration whose jobs depended on continued government programs, and members of Congress who got to tell their constituents that they were doing right by veterans.

The implications of subgovernment theory are obvious: organized interests are equal partners in government policymaking. In all issue areas at all levels of government, subgovernment theory holds that organized interests work side by side with policymakers to make public policy. This, of course, makes them extremely powerful. Moreover, subgovernment theory implies that virtually all organized interests are powerful. According to subgovernment theory, every organized interest has its own subgovernment. For example, organized interests representing truckers are part of the transportation subgovernment, organized interests representing health care providers are part of the health care subgovernment, and teachers' unions are part of the education subgovernment. In a process known as logrolling—a sort of "you scratch my back and I'll scratch yours" arrangement in which everyone butts out of everyone else's subgovernment—virtually all organized interests exercise power in the issue area most important to them. Unlike pluralists, subgovernment theorists were quite pessimistic about American politics and policymaking. For example, they were highly critical of the policy outcomes produced by subgovernments. The problem with subgovernment policymaking, according to subgovernment theorists, was this: the opinions of ordinary citizens were more or less ignored by policymakers. Because as we learned in Chapter 3 some interests are not represented by organized interests, some interests are ignored by government officials.

Subgovernment theory is an intuitively attractive theory with several strengths. It is simple and straightforward and rightly acknowledges that public policy decisions are the result of ongoing interactions between organized interests and policymakers from lots of different governmental institutions. Moreover, it recognizes that most organized interests have relatively narrow policy concerns. Finally, it correctly notes that organized interests often work together—with each other as well as with policymakers—to get what they wanted.

Unfortunately, subgovernment theory, which was quite popular in the late 1960s and early 1970s, had one fatal flaw: it ignored certain realities of American

Lobbyists party with policymakers Subgovernment theory holds that policymakers have preternaturally close relationships with lobbyists. One reason the theory resonates with many people is that policymakers often do hob-knob with lobbyists at swank events like this campaign fund-raiser. *Crandall/The Image Works.*

politics. First, it ignored the fact that many issue areas are rife with conflict, both among organized interests and between organized interests and other political actors. For example, contrary to subgovernment theory, many organized interests lobby Congress against the farm subsidies that are pushed by the members of the agriculture subgovernment. Taxpayers' citizen groups, for example, lobby against subsidies because they lead to higher taxes, and consumer citizen groups lobby against subsidies because they increase food prices. Second, subgovernment theory falsely portrayed policymaking as a neat, stable, and orderly process. If there is one thing that we know about public policymaking, it is that it is not neat, stable, and orderly. As political scientist William Browne has noted, "There's always been far too much going on in American politics for [subgovernment] theory to be accurate. . . . And the goings-on have always been so disorderly, almost chaotic."[18] Finally, subgovernment theory incorrectly suggested that virtually all organized interests got what they wanted from government. This is not true and never has been. The real world of organized interest politics comprises both winners and losers. Organized interests do not merely reciprocate with one another and live happily ever after. Sometimes their interests conflict. Seldom does public policy make everyone happy.

By the mid-1970s, most political scientists recognized that subgovernment theory was fatally flawed. Even many of those who thought that the theory did a reasonable job of portraying policymaking in the 1960s and early 1970s recognized by the late 1970s and early 1980s that the proliferation of organized interests made subgovernment policymaking virtually impossible. By the mid-1970s the search for a better theory was under way.

One of the more popular theories went something like this: public policy was made not in small, exclusive subgovernments but rather in large and permeable *policy domains*—"well-understood and established policy area[s], or a community of players."[19] Each issue area has its own policy domain, which comprises the actors who interact to make public policy on the domain issue. Policy domains were seen as profoundly different from subgovernments. First, policy domains are much larger and more permeable, consisting not of a handful of actors but rather of hundreds, if not thousands, of different political actors.[20] It is no accident that the concept of policy domains gained credence during the mid-1970s, when the number of organized interests involved in policymaking skyrocketed. Second, policy domains are much more conflictual than subgovernments. Domain theorists argued that because public policy is made in open and permeable domains or "networks," organized interests often enter into open conflict with one another as they press competing claims on government. Finally, policy domains are utterly mutable. Subgovernment theory portrayed relationships among organized interests and between organized interests and other political actors as stable and long lasting. In contrast, policy domain theorists maintained that relationships among organized interests and between organized interests and other political actors are anything but stable. In domains, things change constantly as new players moved in and out and issues change and evolve. In the end, no domain looks exactly the same two days in a row. Politics simply changes too quickly and too unpredictably for that.

There is no question that policy domain theorists do a better job of describing the realities of contemporary policymaking than subgovernment theorists do. Political scientists agree that in most issue areas, public policy is made in large, permeable, ever-changing policy domains. The concept of a policy domain is appealing because it acknowledges that politics is messy and unpredictable. This is a sobering thought for the scholar of organized interest influence because it means that each public policy battle is unique. Therefore, every specific public policy decision is likely to be the result of a different set of factors and forces. This means that an organized interest that succeeds in getting what it wants today may not be successful in getting what it wants tomorrow and that a lobbying technique that works today may not work tomorrow. Most important, it means that life as an organized interest is highly unpredictable.

In the end, we must conclude that organized interest influence is situational—that is, it varies dependent on the specific set of circumstances. To put it another way, the answer to the question, "How influential are organized interests," is, "It depends." Sometimes organized interests are able to get what they want from government; sometimes they are not. It all depends on the situation—the unique combination of factors that exists at a given time in a given place.

The primary lesson of this section is that politics is simply too messy, unpredictable, and protean to allow for easy generalizations about organized interest influence. Subgovernment theorists attempted to make such generalizations but ultimately failed because they did not fully appreciate the disorderliness of American politics.

THE CONDITIONS OF ORGANIZED INTEREST INFLUENCE

The only reasonable answer to the question, How influential are organized interests? is, "It depends." This, of course, begs the following question: On what does it depend? This section is devoted to answering this question. Specifically, it asks: Under what conditions are organized interests most likely to exert influence over public policy outcomes?

This question is probabilistic in nature; that is, it does not pretend that we can know with certainty either when organized interests will and will not influence public policy outcomes or precisely how much total influence organized interests exert. The policy process is so unpredictable and disordered that definitive statements about organized interest influence are very difficult to formulate. The best we can do is stipulate six conditions under which organized interests may exert substantial influence.

Condition 1: Organized interests have a high probability of affecting policy outcomes when they face little or no opposition from other political actors.[21] Organized interests often ask policymakers for things to which no one objects. Businesses, for example, often ask policymakers for minor changes in laws and regulations. Because these changes affect no one but the businesses that lobby for them, no one objects. In such cases, organized interests often get what they want. Government policymakers are in a no-lose situation if they go along with organized interests in situations like this: they can simultaneously make organized interests happy by acceding to their demands and avoiding upsetting anyone.

But when an organized interest or set of organized interests asks for something to which someone objects, its chances of success immediately plummet. This implies two things. First, organized interests exercise little power in regard to other political actors (e.g., members of Congress, bureaucrats, the president) in situations when lots of other political actors are involved. In short, when there are numerous players involved in a policy decision, the power of any specific actor or set of actors tends to decrease. Second, a specific organized interest stands a much higher chance of affecting a policy outcome if no other organized interests oppose its demands.

Condition 2: Organized interests have a high probability of affecting policy outcomes when they lobby on issues about which the public and the media know and care little.[22] For the most part, organized interests and lobbyists do their work in relative obscurity. This works to their advantage. The example at the beginning of this chapter is a case in point. If millions of Americans were aware that the newspaper industry was about to get special treatment from the federal government, they might have been perturbed. Some citizens may have called or written to someone in Washington to express their dissatisfaction. As it happened, however, few Americans knew about the newspaper industry's tax break. While the newspapers and their trade associations busily lobbied in Washington, the public and the media paid attention to other issues. In such situations—where the public and the media are not paying attention—government policymakers can simultaneously make organized interests happy by giving them what they want and avoid offending ordinary citizens.[23]

Condition 3: Organized interests have a high probability of affecting policy outcomes when they lobby on issues that are highly technical or complex.[24] Technical issues are those that few ordinary people understand—for example, motor freight regulation, corporate taxation, and banking regulation. Each of these issues is extremely technical and complex. Banking regulation, for example, concerns issues such as what services banks can and cannot offer, the differences between banks and savings and loans, and the investment opportunities that lending institutions can offer. On issues such as these, organized interests can be enormously influential. One reason is that the public seldom cares about or understands highly technical and complex issues. This means that organized interests concerned with these issues can go about their business with little attention from either the public or the media. The other reason is that on highly technical and complex issues, government policymakers are highly dependent on organized interest lobbyists for information. On technical issues on which they lack expertise, policymakers often defer to organized interests, which have information that they value.[25] This, of course, has a tendency to improve organized interests' chances of getting what they want. Think of it in this way: a policymaker who wants information about banking regulation must go to the people who are most likely to have it: banks and bankers. If the policymaker relies solely on this information to make decisions, he or she is likely to make decisions that favor the banking industry.

An example here is illustrative. The savings and loan (S&L) crisis of the 1980s, which cost taxpayers billions of dollars, was precipitated by changes in banking laws that allowed S&Ls to invest federally insured deposits in risky ventures, such as commercial real estate. The policy changes that led to the crisis were pushed through Congress by S&L lobbyists who felt that the changes would be good for business. In the end, they were wrong. But one of the reasons that they were able to get what they wanted from Congress was that the issue on which they were lobbying was highly technical. Neither policymakers nor the public really understood the issues. Therefore, the public raised no opposition to the S&Ls' plans to change lending laws. And policymakers lacked the expertise necessary to understand the implications of what S&Ls were asking for, so they relied heavily on the information provided to them by S&L lobbyists—information that turned out to be far from objective.

Condition 4: Organized interests have a high probability of affecting policy outcomes when they lobby policymakers who are undecided on an issue. On many issues, policymakers have their own ideas about what to do. It is hard to imagine, for example, a member of Congress, state legislator, or state governor who does not have strong opinions about abortion, gun control, or taxes. Moreover, even when policymakers do not have their own opinions about issues, they are likely to be influenced by their party affiliation, ideology, friends, or constituents. In cases where policymakers have their own ideas about what they should do, organized interests do not stand much of a chance of influencing policy outcomes.

Sometimes, however, policymakers do not have strong opinions. Although most policymakers are generalists—that is, they have opinions on a wide range of issues—no single policymaker can know the ins and outs of all issues. In such cases, organized interests can be influential. It is much easier to influence people who are undecided on an issue than to influence people who are strongly committed to one thing or another. In addition, a policymaker who is undecided on an issue is probably open to information from organized interests, especially if he or she does not have alternative sources of information.

Condition 5: Organized interests have a high probability of affecting policy outcomes when they lobby on issues that are nonpartisan and nonideological.[26] Some issues—abortion, the death penalty, taxes, and school prayer come to mind—excite ideological and partisan controversy. Both parties have well-defined positions on such issues, and conservatives and liberals have long-standing and consistent differences on them. On issues like these, organized interests are likely to have little influence. Instead, factors like party affiliation, ideology, constituent opinion, and pressure from colleagues are likely to determine what policymakers do. This is not to say that organized interests that lobby on such issues are completely powerless. But it is to say that organized interests probably take a back seat to other factors.

Some issues, however, are neither partisan nor ideological and do not excite or inflame partisan and ideological differences. On issues like these, organized interests can exert a great deal of influence. Consider, for example, the issue of disability rights. On this issue, the two parties do not have long-standing, easily identifiable differences. In fact, recent history suggests that both parties support the same types of disability rights policies and programs. This is the reason that the Americans with Disabilities Act (1991) was passed overwhelmingly by a Democratic Congress and then signed by Republican president George Bush. Issues surrounding veterans' benefits are also nonpartisan and nonideological. Neither party wants to take a public position against veterans' benefits, and liberals and conservatives do not have well-defined differences on the issue.

Research has found that on issues like disability rights and veterans' affairs, organized interests can exert substantial influence over policy outcomes.[27] Few policymakers have strong views on such issues, they often do not have to worry about toeing a party line, and there is no cost in going along with organized interests on such issues. Policymakers can safely do what veterans' groups and disability groups ask them to do without alienating anybody.

In sum, organized interests are more likely to exert influence in some situations than in others. Even if one or more of these six conditions exists, there is no guarantee that organized interests will be influential. American politics is too unpredictable to allow for definitive conclusions about organized interest power.

WHAT ABOUT LOBBYING?

Many of the conditions that determine whether policymakers respond to organized interests are out of their control. It goes without saying, however, that to capitalize on these conditions, an organized interest must lobby. In other words, an organized interest must try to influence public policy in order to do so. But not all lobbying is created equal. It turns out that regardless of the objective conditions that face a specific organized interest, some lobbying strategies and tactics are more effective than others are. In this section, we ask: Which ones? The approach here is similar to that taken in the last section: a probabilistic approach to examining what organized interests can do to improve their chances of affecting public policy outcomes. Political scientists have discovered that some types of lobbying behavior are more likely to lead to success than others.

Strategy 1. Organized interests can improve their chances of success by entering into coalitions with other organized interests. It is impossible to underestimate the value of coalition building. In a recent guide to lobbying, political veterans Bruce Wolpe and Bertrom Levine argue that "the exacting measure of success [in lobbying] is the ability to create, join, or manage coalitions united behind a public policy proposal."[28] First, coalitions are beneficial because they lend credibility to an organized interest's demands. If lots of organized interests want something, chances are it will receive serious consideration from policymakers. If, however, only one organized interest wants something, policymakers may be leery. Second, coalitions dampen conflict. Organized interests stand a much better chance of success when they face little or no opposition from other political actors—including other organized interests. By gathering into coalitions, organized interests can defuse conflict. Third, coalitions allow organized interests to pool their resources to create effective lobbying campaigns. By doing this, each coalition participant spends a bit less than it might have had it worked alone.[29]

Coalitions are so important that organized interests of all kinds now regularly seek out coalition partners before they even begin lobbying policymakers. The battle over the North American Free Trade Agreement (NAFTA) in 1993 demonstrates how ubiquitous coalition politics has become. During the battle, organized interests on both sides of the issue formed massive coalitions to lobby policymakers and the public. On one side was a huge coalition of labor, environmental, and consumer organizations. On the other was a colossal coalition of corporations, trade associations, and conservative think tanks. Recent battles over health care reform and campaign finance reform have also featured huge active coalitions on both sides.[30]

Strategy 2. Organized interests can improve their chances of success by seeking issue niches. An *issue niche* is defined as a narrow, highly specific issue identity that allows an organized interest to avoid competition and conflict with other organized interests.[31] A hypothetical example will clarify just what an issue niche is and how it can help an organized interest get what it wants.

Let us assume that a number of soybean farmers form an organized interest. All of the farmers favor monetary subsidies for soybean farmers but oppose monetary subsidies for wheat and cotton and mohair. The soybean farmers call their organization Farmers Against Ridiculous Monetary Subsidies (FARMS). FARMS hires lobbyists and rents office space in Washington. When Congress begins debating a new farm bill, FARMS lobbies for soybean subsidies but against wheat, cotton, and mohair subsidies. FARMS soon learns that wheat, cotton, and mohair subsidies are quite popular with wheat, cotton, and mohair commodity groups, which lobby hard against FARMS. By the end of its first month in Washington, FARMS has made a lot of enemies among wheat, cotton, and mohair commodity groups. FARMS's enemies eventually form an anti-FARMS coalition and hire a lobbyist to follow FARMS's lobbyist around and tell people that he's "full of it." FARMS has another problem besides unpopularity: it is broke. Because it lobbies on four different issues, it spreads itself very thin.

At the end of its first year, FARMS has lots of enemies and is short on funds. Consequently, it cannot lobby very effectively. What can FARMS do? One answer is to scale back its demands. For FARMS, this means ending its lobbying campaigns against wheat, cotton, and mohair subsidies and concentrating on soybeans. This makes sense for several reasons. First, it saves FARMS millions of dollars. Second, it allows FARMS to stop making enemies in Washington. Not surprisingly, when FARMS drops its opposition to the demands of other farm groups, it becomes much more popular with those groups. Finally, scaling back its demands allows FARMS to focus on the issue of most interest to its members: federal subsidies for soybean farmers. Because there are few organized interests concerned with soybeans, FARMS becomes the preeminent soybean organization in Washington. Other farm groups do not oppose it because it has dropped its opposition to them. Policymakers are more open to FARMS's demands because the group has few enemies. And FARMS is a much more effective lobbying organization because it no longer spreads itself too thin. FARMS does one thing—lobby on soybean-related issues—and does it well. In sum, FARMS has found a niche—a narrow but comfortable place where it can thrive. This niche allows FARMS to avoid conflict, build a policy identity, and preserve resources.[32]

In effect, when an organized interest seeks a niche, it is scaling back its demands until it finds something that it thinks it can get as opposed to something it probably would not be able to get. This allows an organized interest to avoid conflict. In most cases, an organized interest would rather go to work on a sure thing than enter a battle it may lose. Most organized interests choose their battles carefully—avoiding those they think they may lose and entering only those they think they can win. This is the essence of niche-seeking behavior.

Strategy 3. Organized interests can improve their chances of success by doing a lot. Scaling back demands does not mean scaling back activity. Chapters 5 through 8 showed that the typical organized interest does a lot, and all this activity makes sense. The biggest study of organized interest influence ever conducted shows that the more an organized interest does, the more likely it is to get what it wants.[33] In other words, doing more is better than doing less. This does not mean that an organized interest should lobby on lots of different issues or enter into lots of different policy battles. But when it does decide to enter a policy battle, it should do everything it possibly can. Doing a lot means several things. It means targeting policymakers across institutions and levels of government—that is, lobbying multiple branches of government as well as multiple levels of government. It also means lobbying multiple actors within each institution of government. If an organized interest lobbies Congress, for example, it should lobby lots of legislators and committees rather than just one or a few.

The value of doing more means that money is increasingly essential to an organized interest's success. It is not the case that organized interests with lots of money always win and those without money always lose, but money can increase an organized interest's chances of success.[34] The more money an organized interest has, the more lobbyists it can hire, the more policymakers it can see, the more levels and institutions of government it can approach, and the more lobbying it can do.

Strategy 4. Organized interests can improve their chances of success by contributing money to policymakers' campaigns. Money does not buy policymakers, but it can buy access to policymakers. Policymakers pay more attention to organized interests that give them money than they do to organized interests that do not give them money.[35] This does not mean that organized interests that lobby with campaign money always get what they want or that organized interests that do not lobby with campaign never get what they want. It does mean, however, that if an organized interest does not lobby with campaign money, its ability to interact with policymakers is limited. And the ability to interact with policymakers—to present them with information—is absolutely crucial to an organized interest's success. The value of campaign contributions highlights the importance of money in lobbying. The more money an organized interest has, the more policymakers it can support. And the more policymakers it can support, the more doors are open to its lobbyists.

Strategy 5. Organized interests can improve their chances of success by getting ordinary citizens to do their work for them. Policymakers know that going against the wishes of their constituents is political suicide. This is why organized interests engage in indirect lobbying in the first place: to convince policymakers that the public is on their side. Studies have shown that lobbying the public can be extremely effective. If an organized interest can convince lots of ordinary citizens to contact policymakers in support of its position, it stands a good chance of getting what it wants.[36]

An organized interest's ability to mobilize the public on its behalf rests on two factors. First, it must have the money to lobby the public. Lobbying the public is not cheap; advertisements, direct mail, and telephone lobbying cost a lot of money. Second, an organized interest must have the support of substantial numbers of ordinary people. Lobbying the public works only if at least some ordinary people are receptive to an organized interest's message. Some organized interests know that they can mobilize a substantial number of citizens on their behalf. The National Rifle Association, the National Education Association, and the AFL-CIO have been highly successful at mobilizing members to contact policymakers on their behalf. What these organizations have in common is the ability to tap a large membership. Organized interests that have few or no members lack a ready-made base of ordinary citizens whom they can lobby. They may, however, have a sense of whether the public supports or opposes them. They can use public opinion polls, surveys, and media accounts to predict how people will respond if they lobby the public. Any time an organized interest thinks it can successfully mobilize lots of ordinary citizens, it will be tempted to do so.

There is something paradoxical about the effect of public opinion on organized interest behavior: sometimes it compels organized interests to go to great lengths *not* to get the public involved. For example, organized interests representing the newspaper industry tried hard not to publicize their campaign for a tax break. They worried that if the public knew about the details of the tax break, people would not support their position. So rather than lobby the public, the newspaper industry did just the opposite: it lobbied quietly behind the scenes and attempted to avoid publicity.

An organized interest that thinks it might lose a particular policy battle has an incentive to get the public involved, for if the public agrees with the potential loser, it may help turn the tide in the organization's favor. In contrast, an organized interest that thinks it will win a particular policy battle has no incentive to get the public involved. If the organization is probably going to win anyway, why run the risk of mobilizing opposition?

WHEN ORGANIZED INTERESTS GO HEAD TO HEAD: THE IMPORTANCE OF MONEY AND PUBLIC SUPPORT

In the section before last, we examined the conditions under which organized interests are most likely to be influential. If only a few or none of these conditions exist in a specific policy battle, organized interests are not likely to be major players. However, if two or more of these conditions exist, organized interests are likely to exert substantial influence over the eventual policy outcome.

Let us assume that a policy battle is under way in which conditions are ripe for organized interest influence. The issue before Congress is nonideological, nonpartisan, technical, and complex in nature; policymakers are undecided on the issue; and the public is uninterested and uninformed. Now imagine that a handful of organized interests are active on the issue. If in this situation all of the organized interests are on the same side, it is likely that their collective view will prevail. But what happens if half of the organized interests have one view and the other half has an opposing view? Which side is likely to prevail?

In many cases, the side with the most money prevails. In a recent book on lobbying, organized interest scholars Darrell M. West and Burdett A. Loomis argue that money is often crucial in determining who wins and who loses when organized interests go head to head.[37] West and Loomis found that in most policy battles, big spenders have several advantages over less profligate organized interests. First, they can afford to hire the best, most experienced lobbyists. Second, they have better access to policymakers because they can afford to make massive campaign contributions. Third, they can engage in a wide variety of lobbying activities, and as we learned in the previous section, doing more tends to produce results. Fourth, they can afford to keep the pressure on over a longer period of time. Finally, and perhaps most important, they can engage in expensive indirect lobbying campaigns that more needy organized interests cannot afford. In the end, West and Loomis contend that money is often the key determinant of who wins and who loses when organized interests go head to head.

Money, however, does not always prevail. An even more important asset than money is public support. Thus, all is not lost for less wealthy organized interests that are locked in battle with well-heeled, free-spending organized interests.

Poor organized interests can win if they can get the public on their side. This is one of the lessons of the civil rights movement of the 1950s and 1960s.

The goals of the civil rights movement were initially unpopular with both the public and government policymakers. Moreover, opponents of civil rights were well organized and had many resources at their disposal. To bolster their position, organizations such as the NAACP and the Southern Christian Leadership Conference sought to attract public support for their goals. In fact, one of Dr. Martin Luther King's primary tactics was to provoke physically violent reactions from police officers who confronted civil rights protesters. This, he believed, would turn public opinion against segregationists and would convince the majority of Americans that the civil rights groups' goals were legitimate and worthy of support. King was right. As television and newspaper accounts showed America that segregationists were unprincipled and violent, public support shifted toward the civil rights groups. Eventually the government listened and passed landmark civil rights legislation in the 1960s. A great deal of research suggests that mobilizing public opinion is the only feasible option for organized interests that lack the resources to lobby government officials directly.[38]

Another resource that can trump money is members. An organized interest with lots of members, even if it does not have lots of money, has a chance to defeat better-funded organized interests. This is one of the lessons of the environmental movement. Environmental citizen groups such as the Sierra Club, the National Wildlife Federation, and the Audubon Society have far fewer resources than the corporate organized interests with which they often do battle. However, these groups and many others like them have something that corporate and trade groups do not: individual members. Individual members are important because they vote. Elected officials do not like to upset the voters on whom they depend for their jobs. Environmental citizen groups, despite their relative lack of money, are often able to convince Congress that ignoring them will be politically costly. Interestingly, the power of members helps explain the phenomenal success of the National Rifle Association, which many consider the most powerful organized interest in the history of the United States. It is not money that makes the NRA so powerful; it is members. The NRA has a well-deserved reputation for delivering on Election Day. The NRA's strength is based on the perception that gun enthusiasts are single-issue voters capable of swinging elections against candidates who advocate any form of gun control.[39]

Finally, in a battle between organized interests, one resource that often helps determine who wins and who loses is allies within government. In her studies of the women's movement, political scientist Anne N. Costain noted that the women's movement of the 1960s eventually produced spectacular successes despite strong opposition from other organized interests and an initial lack of public support for its goals. How did this happen? For one thing, the fledgling women's movement of the early 1960s contacted women in government who helped women's groups recruit new members, publicize women's concerns, and hold government-sanctioned conferences on women's issues. This not only strengthened the organized interests that composed the women's movement, but also worked gradually to change public opinion toward women's issues. In the end, allies in government worked hand in hand with the women's movement to help the movement achieve its goals. Allies in government both strengthen organized interests internally and work within government to achieve their goals.[40]

In sum, when organized interests go head to head, a few factors appear to affect the outcome of the battle. First, there is money. In many cases, the side with the most money wins. However, if the side with the most money is opposed by an organized interest or set of organized interests with either public support, numerous members, or allies within government, it may lose. One thing is certain: any time an organized interest is rich and has many members, allies in government, and public support, it is likely to get its way.

CONCLUSION: HOW POWERFUL ARE ORGANIZED INTERESTS?

Public opinion polls and surveys show that overwhelming majorities of Americans believe that "special interests" dominate government decision making. Are the public's perceptions accurate? Do organized interests get what they want from government while the views of ordinary citizens are virtually ignored? Our answer to this question represents a bit of an anticlimax, for in the end we must say, "It depends."

The primary message of this chapter is that sometimes organized interests get what they want from government, and sometimes they do not. The real world of politics, as scholars of policy domains have noted, is too messy, contentious, and unpredictable to support broad and sweeping generalizations about the power and influence of organized interests. Each public policy decision is the result of an exceedingly complex and multifaceted process that involves many factors. Organized interest lobbying is just one of these factors. In some policy battles—those, for example, where the public is unengaged and uninvolved—organized interests typically exert tremendous influence over policy outcomes. In other policy battles—those, for example, that involve highly salient, ideologically charged issues or those where the public is heavily involved and highly engaged—organized interests typically exert little or no influence.

In the end, it is clear that organized interests are powerful players in American politics. As pluralists noted fifty years ago, they are left out of very few policy battles. It is just as clear, however, that organized interests do not dominate and control American politics. Despite considerable public cynicism, there is plenty of evidence that policymakers do what their constituents want them to do, even if this conflicts with the desires of powerful organized interests. This is one reason, in fact, that organized interests spend so much time and money engaging in indirect lobbying.

EXERCISE

1. In your opinion, what is the most powerful organized interest in the United States? On what did you base your answer? Make an argument by presenting evidence that the organized interest you have identified is more powerful than any other organized interest in the United States.

RESEARCH RESOURCES

Publications

Fortune magazine. Every year *Fortune* publishes a story on the most influential organized interests in Washington. The article for this year (or last year) may give you some ideas for research topics.

Web Resources

Fortune magazine. Fortune's web site is located at *www.fortune.com.*
Polling organizations. To find out what your fellow Americans think about organized interests, check out these web sites run by some of the largest and most prestigious polling organizations in the United States: *www.gallup.com, www.roper.com,* and *www.zogby.com.*

Notes

1. The Small Business Jobs Protection Act increased the minimum wage in two phases. The first phase, effective October 1, 1997, raised the minimum wage from $4.25 to $4.75. The second phase, effective October 1, 1997, raised the minimum wage from $4.75 to $5.15. See David Skidmore, "Clinton Signs Minimum Wage Bill with Campaign-Style Flourish," *U.S. News and World Report On Line,* August 20, 1996, accessed at *http://www.usnews.com/usnews/wash/ap820wag,* September 14, 1998.

2. Kenneth Silverstein, *Washington on $10 Million a Day: How Lobbyists Plunder the Nation* (Monroe, ME: Common Courage Press, 1998), p. 86.

3. Arthur E. Rowse, "A Lobby the Media Won't Touch," *Washington Monthly* (May 1998): 12.

4. Ibid., pp. 12–13.

5. Ibid., p. 10.

6. Darrell M. West and Burdett A. Loomis, *The Sound of Money: How Political Interests Get What They Want* (New York: Norton, 1999), p. 49.

7. Two exceptions are E. Pendleton Herring, *Group Representation Before Congress* (Baltimore, MD: Johns Hopkins University Press, 1929); and Peter H. Odegard, *Pressure Politics: The Story of the Anti-Saloon League* (New York: Columbia University Press, 1928).

8. See, for example, Frank Goodnow, *Politics and Administration: A Study in Government* (New York: Macmillan, 1900); William A. Schaper, "What Do Students Know About American Government?" *Proceedings of the American Political Science Association* 2 (1905): 207–228; Woodrow Wilson, *Congressional Government* (Boston, MA: Houghton Mifflin, 1885).

9. David Truman, *The Governmental Process: Political Interests and Public Opinion* (New York: Knopf, 1951).

10. Other pluralist works include Earl Latham, *The Group Basis of Politics* (Ithaca, NY: Cornell University Press, 1952); Robert Golembiewski, "The Group Basis of Politics: Notes on Analysis and Development," *American Political Science Review* 54 (December 1960): 962–971.

11. See Raymond A. Bauer, Ithiel de Sola Pool, and Lewis A. Dexter, *American Business and Public Policy: The Politics of Foreign Trade* (New York: Atherton Press, 1963); Lester Milbraith, *The Washington Lobbyists* (Chicago: Rand-McNally, 1963); Andrew M. Scott and Margaret A. Hunt, *Congress and Lobbies: Image and Reality* (Chapel Hill, NC: University of North Carolina Press, 1965).

12. Robert A. Dahl, *Who Governs?* (New Haven, CT: Yale University Press, 1961).

13. See C. Wright Mills, *The Power Elite* (New York: Oxford University Press, 1956). See also Peter Bachrach and Morton S. Baratz, "Two Faces of Power," *American Political Science Review* 56 (December 1962): 947–952. For a more recent study, see John Gaventa, *Power and Powerlessness* (Urbana: University of Illinois Press, 1980).

14. See Douglas Cater, *Power in Washington* (New York: Vintage Books, 1964); J. Leiper Freeman, *The Political Process* (New York: Random House, 1955); Ernest Griffith, *Impasse of Democracy* (New York: Harrison-Hilton Books, 1939).

15. This is paraphrased from Jeffrey M. Berry, "Subgovernments, Issue Networks, and Political Conflict," in Richard A. Harris and Sidney M. Milkis, eds., *Remaking American Politics* (Boulder, CO: Westview Press, 1989), pp. 239–260.

16. John R. Wright, *Interest Groups and Congress: Lobbying, Contributions, and Influence* (Boston, MA: Allyn and Bacon, 1996), p. 169.

17. William P. Browne, "Policy and Interests: Instability and Change in a Classic Issue Subsystem," in Allan J. Cigler and Burdett A. Loomis, eds., *Interest Group Politics* (2nd ed.) (Washington, DC: Congressional Quarterly Press, 1986), p. 185.

18. William P. Browne, *Groups, Interests, and U.S. Public Policy* (Washington, DC: Georgetown University Press, 1998), p. 213.

19. Ibid., p. 216.

20. See Hugh Heclo, "Issue Networks and the Executive Establishment," in Anthony King, ed., *The New American Political System* (Washington, DC: American Enterprise Institute, 1979), p. 102. Heclo uses the term *issue network* instead of *policy domain,* but the concepts are similar.

21. William P. Browne, "Organized Interests and Their Issue Niches: A Search for Pluralism in a Policy Domain," *Journal of Politics* 52 (May 1990): 477–509; Robert H. Salisbury, John P. Heinz, Edward O. Laumann, and Robert L. Nelson, "Iron Triangles: Similarities and Differences Among the Legs" (paper presented at the annual meeting of the American Political Science Association, Washington, DC, September 1988).

22. See E. E. Schattschneider, *The Semisovereign People: A Realist's View of Democracy in America* (New York: Holt, Rinehart, and Winston, 1960); John E. Chubb, *Interest Groups and the Bureaucracy* (Stanford, CA: Stanford University Press, 1983); M. Margaret Conway, "PACs in the Political Process," in Allan J. Cigler and Burdett A. Loomis, eds., *Interest Group Politics* (3rd ed.) (Washington, DC: Congressional Quarterly Press, 1991), pp. 199–216; Richard Harris, "Politicized Management: The Changing Face of Business in American Politics," in Harris and Milkis, eds., *Remaking American Politics,* pp. 261–288; Woodrow Jones, Jr., and K. Robert Keiser, "Issue Visibility and the Effects of PAC Money," *Social Science Quarterly* 68 (March 1987): 170–176.

23. For details on the public's lack of interest in politics, see Michael X. Delli Carpini and Scott Keeter, *What Americans Know About Politics and Why It Matters* (New Haven, CT: Yale University Press, 1996); Russell Neuman, *The Paradox of Mass Politics: Knowledge and Opinion in the American Electorate* (Cambridge, MA: Harvard University Press, 1986).

24. See Browne, "Organized Interests and Their Issue Niches"; Chubb, *Interest Groups and the Bureaucracy*; William P. Welch, "Campaign Contributions and Legislative Voting: Milk Money and Dairy Price Supports," *Western Political Quarterly* 35 (December 1982): 478–495; John R. Wright, "Contributions, Lobbying, and Committee Voting in the U.S. House of Representatives," *American Political Science Review* 84 (June 1990): 417–438.

25. John Mark Hansen, *Gaining Access: Congress and the Farm Lobby, 1919–1981* (Chicago: University of Chicago Press, 1991).

26. Alan Rosenthal, *The Third House: Lobbyists and Lobbying in the States* (Washington, DC: Congressional Quarterly Press, 1993), pp. 208–215; Richard Scotch, *From Goodwill to Civil Rights: Transforming Federal Disability Policy* (Philadelphia: Temple University Press, 1985).

27. On disability rights issues, see Scotch, *From Goodwill to Civil Rights.* On veterans' issues, see Salisbury, Heinz, Laumann, and Nelson, "Iron Triangles: Similarities and Differences Among the Legs" (paper presented at the annual meeting of the American Political Science Association, Washington, DC, September 1988).

28. Bruce Wolpe and Bertram J. Levine, *Lobbying Congress: How the System Works* (2nd ed.) (Washington, DC: Congressional Quarterly Press, 1996), p. 42. See also Kevin Hula, "Rounding Up the Usual Suspects: Forging Interest Group Coalitions in Washington," in Allan J. Cigler and Burdett A. Loomis, eds., *Interest Group Politics* (4th ed.) (Washington, DC: Congressional Quarterly Press, 1995), pp. 239–258; Lawrence S. Rothenberg, *Linking Citizens to Government: Inter-*

est Group Politics at Common Cause (New York: Cambridge University Press, 1992).

29. Hula, "Rounding Up the Usual Suspects: Forging Interest Group Coalitions in Washington," in Allan J. Cigler and Burdett A. Loomis, eds. *Interest Group Politics* (4th ed.) (Washington, DC: Congressional Quarterly Press, 1995), p. 246.

30. Allan J. Cigler and Burdett A. Loomis, eds., "From Big Bird to Bill Gates: Organized Interests and the Emergence of Hyperpolitics," in Allan J. Cigler and Burdett A. Loomis, eds., *Interest Group Politics* (5th ed.) (Washington, DC: Congressional Quarterly Press, 1998), pp. 389–401.

31. This is paraphrased from Browne, "Organized Interests and Their Issue Niches," pp. 184–185.

32. Ibid., pp. 501–503.

33. John P. Heinz, Edward O. Laumann, Robert L. Nelson, and Robert H. Salisbury, *The Hollow Core: Private Interests in National Policy-Making* (Cambridge, MA: Harvard University Press, 1993), chap. 11.

34. Anthony J. Nownes and Patricia K. Freeman, "Interest Group Activity in the States," *Journal of Politics* 60:1 (February 1998).

35. Christine DeGregorio, "Assets and Access: Linking Lobbyists and Lawmakers," in Paul S. Herrnson, Ronald G. Shaiko, and Clyde Wilcox, eds., *The Interest Group Connection: Electioneering, Lobbying, and Policymaking in Washington* (Chatham, NJ: Chatham House, 1998), pp. 137–153; Richard A. Smith, "Interest Group Influence in the U.S. Congress." *Legislative Studies Quarterly* 20 (February 1995), pp. 89–139.

36. James G. Gimpel, "Grassroots Organizations and Equilibrium Cycles in Group Mobilization and Access," in Herrnson, Shaiko, and Wilcox, eds., *The Interest Group Connection: Electioneering, Lobbying, and Policymaking in Washington* (Chatham, NJ: Chatham House, 1998).

37. West and Loomis, *The Sound of Money: How Political Interests Get What They Want* (New York: Norton, 1999), pp. 228–230.

38. David J. Garrow, *Protest at Selma* (New Haven, CT: Yale University Press, 1978); Kenneth Kollman, *Outside Lobbying: Public Opinion and Interest Group Strategies* (Ann Arbor: University of Michigan Press, 1998); Thomas L. Gais and Jack L. Walker, "Pathways to Influence in American Politics," in Jack L. Walker, ed., *Mobilizing Interest Groups in America: Patrons, Professions, and Social Movements* (Ann Arbor: University of Michigan Press, 1991).

39. Kelly Patterson, "The Political Firepower of the National Rifle Association," in Cigler and Loomis, eds., *Interest Group Politics* (5th ed.), pp. 135–139; Kelly Patterson, "Political Firepower," in Robert Biersack, Paul Herrnson, and Clyde Wilcox, eds., *After the Revolution: PACs and Lobbies in the Republican Congress* (Boston, MA: Allyn and Bacon, 1999), pp. 66–76; Clyde Wilcox, "The Dynamics of Lobbying the Hill," in Herrnson, Shaiko, and Wilcox, eds., *The Interest Group Connection: Electioneering, Lobbying, and Policymaking in Washington* (Chatham, NJ: Chatham House, 1998), pp. 98–99.

40. Anne M. Costain, "Social Movements as Interest Groups: The Case of the Women's Movement," in Mark P. Petracca, ed., *The Politics of Interests: Interest Groups Transformed* (Boulder, CO: Westview Press, 1992), pp. 285–307.

Conclusion: The Role of Organized Interests in American Politics

The dilemma for democracy is that not everyone has equal access to the financial resources necessary for . . . elaborate [lobbying] efforts. If there were rough equity among various interests, money would not be so problematic. However, when a few interests have large amounts of money and many have little, democracy is threatened. . . . [Large, well-heeled] organized interests fare disproportionately well in a policy-making process dominated by cash.

Darrel M. West and Burdett A. Loomis, *The Sound of Money:
How Political Interests Get What They Want*

Organized interests not only fit the moderate pace of the U.S. policy process and mainstream American society, they also fit specifically because of what their lobbyists do with the resources they have. Successful factions have won in politics and policy making not by forcing narrow values on the rest of the nation. Rather, they've won largely by reflecting the sentiments, values, institutions, and accumulated policy traditions that make up and support American governments.

William P. Browne, *Groups, Interests and U.S. Public Policy*

Organized interest scholars Darrell West and Burdett Loomis, on the one hand, and William Browne, on the other, clearly have radically different views of contemporary organized interest politics in the United States. As the quotations attest, West and Loomis believe that organized interest politics at the turn of the millennium represents a threat to American democracy. In contrast, Browne contends that organized interests fit nicely within the policy process and reflect American democracy rather than threaten it. Which of these views is correct? Are organized interests benign reflections of democracy? Or are they malignant irritants on the body politic? We now return to these questions—questions with which we began this book. First, we seek to explain the paradox of organized interests. Second, we look for a resolution to the paradox of organized interests. Finally, we ask: Is organized interest politics in need of reform?

EXPLAINING THE PARADOX OF ORGANIZED INTERESTS

Why do laypeople and scholars alike express ambivalence about organized interests? Why do most ordinary Americans both support *and* fear organized interests? Why do some scholars view organized interests as important and beneficial aspects of representative government, while others view them as heinous and destructive manifestations of selfishness? We will attempt to provide answers to all of these questions. As you will see, at the heart of the answers to all three is this simple truth: organized interests embody both what is admirable *and* what is abhorrent about American democracy. Ultimately it is this fact that explains the paradox of organized interests.

Organized Interests as Admirable Manifestations of Democracy

Few Americans would admit that they see organized interests as admirable. Yet for most of us, our actions speak louder than our words: we join organized interests at a substantially higher rate than citizens in other countries. Moreover, despite occasional scandals, we trust organized interests and their lobbyists to represent us before government. This is why we continue to join and otherwise support them. It is also why we continue to respond to their appeals for political action. Ironically, despite the bad reputation that organized interests have, the bulk of the evidence suggests that we are right to trust them. Chapters 4 through 8 demonstrate that most lobbyists, most of the time, are professional, honest, and ethical. The typical lobbyist is nothing like the caricatured imagined lobbyist who shows up in editorial cartoons and tabloid television news stories. Lobbyists, it appears, seldom rely on arm-twisting, bribes, and chicanery to get their way. Rather, they depend on information.

Pluralists may have gone overboard in suggesting that the American political system was one in which interests were represented equally before government. But as Chapters 1 and 2 demonstrate, the variety of interests currently represented by organized interests is nothing short of breathtaking. The sheer number and variety of organized interests active in the United States today has led many learned observers to suggest that America at the turn of the millennium is closer than ever to achieving the pluralist ideal of equal organized interest representation before government. In 1995, for example, political scientist James Q. Wilson, who began studying organized interests in the 1940s, remarked: "Back then [in the 1940s], we were told that America had a pluralist system in which almost everybody was represented. It wasn't true. Today it is."[1] Chapter 3's emphasis on biases within the organized interest universe augurs against wholeheartedly accepting Wilson's rosy view of contemporary organized interest politics. Nevertheless, there is no question that large numbers of Americans from across the ideological spectrum can count on organized interests to represent their views faithfully before government.

Contrary to the bad press that organized interests often get, organized interests have helped make America a better place. Consider, for example, the organized interests that formed the core of the civil rights movement. For most of the twentieth century, these organizations worked tirelessly to change this country's civil rights laws—laws that discriminated against nonwhites in education, employment, housing, voting, and much more. Only after decades of hard work did these organized interests achieve their goals—goals that we can now see were perfectly legitimate, commendable, and worthy. In short, organized interests that helped end overt discrimination in America can rightfully claim to have "done good." And this is not an isolated example. Organized interests can claim at least partial credit for advancing wildly popular measures that have safeguarded the environment, provided income assistance for the truly needy, helped people move from welfare to work, made automobiles safer, mandated long prison terms for habitual violent criminals, and lowered taxes on the working poor. In sum, contrary to what some people might say about organized interests, sometimes they do good work. In a democracy, there is something admirable about groups of citizens working together to change laws that they see as unjust and unwise. Often organized interests are the vehicles through which they do so.

The notion that organized interests dominate policymaking in America and regularly drown out the voices of ordinary Americans is not accurate. As Chapter 9 shows, policymakers seldom accommodate organized interests if it means alienating ordinary citizens. In the end, a policymaker who must choose between his or her constituents and powerful organized interests will virtually always choose constituents.

What then accounts for the widespread notion that organized interests thwart democracy? One explanation is that we sometimes forget that politics inherently involves winners and losers. When our side wins, we tend to attribute it not to organized interests but rather to political leaders we admire and to the power of ordinary citizens like ourselves to "speak truth to power." In other words, we say that "democracy worked." When our side loses, however, we look to place blame, and often organized interests shoulder that blame. A related explanation is that politicians often encourage us to believe that organized interests run roughshod over majority preferences. When policies go wrong, politicians do not blame themselves, nor do they blame the voters on whom they rely to keep their jobs. Rather, they blame organized interests. It is easy and it is convenient. All of this notwithstanding, objective observers of organized interest politics must acknowledge that organized interests

Advocacy can lead to positive change Organized interests sometimes have a positive impact on public policy. For example, the National Child Labor Committee, which commissioned this photograph in 1911 to raise public awareness of the horrendous conditions facing child miners, was instrumental in passing legislation that outlawed child labor early in the twentieth century. *Courtesy George Eastman House.*

sometimes contribute to democracy. They are not, as some suggest, unmitigated evil.

We must conclude that organized interests are indeed admirable manifestations of democratic government. For one thing, organized interests—selfish though they may be—represent citizens like you and me. We may not all be represented equally, but most of us are represented to some extent by some organized interests. Second, organized interests and their lobbyists generally work well within the boundaries of the law to achieve their goals. Sensationalistic news stories to the contrary, most organized interest activity is legal and legitimate. Third, organized interests do not dominate policymaking in America. Policy outcomes generally have multiple causes. Organized interests, just as James Madison desired, have a difficult time winning when they face substantial opposition from large numbers of citizens. In other words, they often take a back seat to ordinary citizens. Finally, organized interests sometimes promote and achieve positive change. The next time Congress passes a law that you support, consider this: there were probably dozens of organized interests working to ensure its passage.

Organized Interests as Abhorrent Vehicles of Selfishness

Any reasonable observer of American politics would conclude that organized interests also embody some of what is wrong with American politics. First, they are inherently selfish. The typical organized interest represents a narrow constituency, and as organized interests have proliferated, these constituencies have become narrower than ever before. This presents a problem: that most organized interests have no regard for the public interest. To make matters worse, because organized interests deluge government officials with their demands, it is hard for them to look out for the public interest. In the end, the sheer number and variety of organized interests means that although there is an organized interest looking out for every narrow constituency, there is no organized interest looking out for the country as a whole. This lack of unity, often exacerbated by organized interests themselves when they emphasize threats, anxieties, and dangers in their appeals for public support, undermines community and increases cynicism.

A second problem with organized interests is that they are not created equal. Thomas Jefferson is deservedly famous for his statement in the Declaration of Independence that "all men are created equal." Equality, of course, is the cornerstone of American democracy. To this day, each American citizen has one vote and one vote only. This means that Microsoft chairman Bill Gates casts one vote just like you and I do. But many Americans feel that organized interest politics undermines the cherished one person–one vote principle. As Chapters 1 and 2 show, voting is but one form of political participation. Supporting organized interests is another. And when it comes to organized interest representation, equality is not the rule. As Chapter 3 shows, some interests are better represented by organized interests than others. Moreover, constituencies that are already doing well—arguably the constituencies with the least credible claims on government—are disproportionately well represented. Of course, being well represented by an organized interest does not necessarily guarantee success in the public policy process, but it certainly helps. In sum, the fact that some citizens by dint of their superior representation by organized interests seem to have a louder voice than others strikes many Americans as profoundly undemocratic.

As for the activities of organized interests, critics note that just because something is legal does not mean that it is right. For example, it may be perfectly legal for an organized interest to take a policymaker on a junket, give this person gifts, buy him or her meals, and donate unlimited sums of money to his or her party, but this does not make it admirable. In fact, it is troubling that some people—namely, well-paid lobbyists who work for well-heeled organized interests—have special access to policymakers. After all, when is the last time *you* played golf with your senator or had a drink with your state representative? Lobbyists do these things every day.

Does having special access to policymakers make a difference? Yes and no. On the one hand, as Chapter 9 suggests, it is rare for organized interests to get what they want when they face serious and substantial opposition from the public. On the other hand, in many cases, organized interests do not face serious and substantial opposition from the public. Most lobbyists, most of the time, do their work in obscurity. They, of course, are working on issues of great interest to the organized interests that pay them. To a lobbyist for a large trucking company, for example, regulations concerning how much weight trucks can carry over interstate highways are of utmost importance. But the average citizen remains unaware of the issue. Thus, in this case, citizens are out of the loop on legislation that may have serious consequences for traffic safety. Their concerns may not be represented at all before government.

The point here is this: just because organized interests do not always get their way does not mean that they are harmless. Certainly organized interests lose when they face serious opposition from the public, but on most issues, the public is not activated. Not surprisingly, ordinary citizens spend more time worrying about their jobs, their families, and the rest of their lives than about every piece of legislation that comes before Congress, the state legislature, or the city council. In the end, because so much of what government does is of only minor interest to most citizens, organized interests often get what they want from government. This leaves citizens asking: If I am not paying particularly close attention to every issue, who is looking out for me?

Finally, a number of recent developments in organized interest politics seem to justify anxiety about organized interest power. First, there is soft money. As we discussed in Chapter 7, organized interests are essentially allowed to contribute unlimited sums of money to political parties. These unlimited contributions are exactly the sorts of contributions that Congress ostensibly eliminated in the 1970s. Not surprisingly, polls show that vast majorities of Americans believe that soft money contributions affect the decisions of policymakers.[2] Indeed, it would be naive to believe otherwise. Second, there is election issue advocacy. Like soft money, election issue advocacy is a way for organized interests to get deeply involved in electoral campaigns, seemingly in violation of campaign finance laws. Election issue advocacy is even more troubling than soft money because it does not have to be disclosed. In other words, an organized interest can spend as much money as it wants on behalf of or in opposition to a candidate, and it is not required to disclose a thing. This raises the troubling specter of elections dominated not by ordinary citizens or even candidates but rather by well-heeled organized interests that are unidentifiable. In this scenario, accountability is impossible.

A RESOLUTION TO THE PARADOX OF ORGANIZED INTERESTS?

In sum, there is evidence to support both views of organized interests. So which view is correct? Ultimately we must conclude that both views are correct. On the one hand, organized interests play important, legitimate, and worthwhile roles in American politics. They raise new issues, push for desirable policies, and represent ordinary citizens. On the other hand, organized interests can represent a threat to democracy. They behave selfishly, skew representation toward certain views, and sometimes convince policymakers to do things that may not be in the best interest of the country as a whole.

How can organized interests be both threatening and admirable? The answer lies in the nature of democracy. Organized interests reflect democracy, and democracy itself is both admirable and threatening. On the one hand, democracy can lead to tyranny, injustice, or unwise public policy. In a democratic system, there is always the chance that a majority can oppress a minority. This is what happened for much of our history when a majority of white citizens acted to deprive a minority of nonwhite citizens of their civil rights and liberties. On the other hand, democracy can bring about justice, fairness, and wise public policy. In a democratic system, there is always the chance for a majority to throw out policies that they find unjust and unfair. This is what happened when civil rights laws were changed in the 1960s to ensure equal protection of the law for nonwhite citizens.

In short, the hallmark of democratic government is that it is quite responsive to citizens' desires. Herein lies the danger; herein lies the beauty. Responsiveness is dangerous because sometimes we want things that deprive others of their rights. It is also dangerous because sometimes we want things that will turn out to be bad for us in the end. But responsiveness is also beneficial. It means that we have control over our own destinies. Unlike people in totalitarian countries, *we* decide what is the best path for us. It is also beneficial because it means we can correct past mistakes. If we do something that leads to disaster, we can fix it. To put it briefly, organized interests have all the strengths and weaknesses, all the ups and downs, all the costs and benefits of democracy itself. This is not surprising given that organized interests are *us*. Ultimately they represent the causes we support and the institutions that educate us and sell us products and services.

Is There Need for Reform?

In the end, because organized interests are reflections of democracy itself, the paradox of organized interests cannot be completely resolved without drastically compromising the core principles of American government. Here is what

Americans exercising their rights Most Americans cherish their ability to express themselves politically without fear of government suppression. Here, anti–World Trade Organization protesters exercise their First Amendment rights on the streets of Seattle in 1999. *AP/Wide World Photos.*

James Madison wrote in Federalist No. 10 about the possibility of banning organized interests:

> Liberty is to faction what air is to fire, an aliment without which it instantly expires. But it could not be a less folly to abolish liberty, which is essential to political life, because it nourishes faction than it would be to wish the annihilation of air, which is essential to animal life, because it imparts to fire its destructive agencies.[3]

Madison felt that any attempt to ban organized interests would compromise the principles embodied in the Constitution. Of course, as we noted in Chapter 1, he was well aware of the dangers that organized interests could pose. He believed that the best way to guard against undue organized interest influence was to create a republican system that dispersed power widely among separate branches and levels of government in a large and diverse society. We must conclude that Madison's solution to the paradox of organized interests is the only feasible solution in a democratic society.

Madison's solution to the potential threat of organized interest tyranny has worked to the extent that no single organized interest or small set of organized interests has ever managed to commandeer the machinery of American government. Yet his solution has not worked entirely. Rightfully or not, large numbers of American citizens feel that their government cannot be trusted, that it is overly responsive to the wishes of special interests, and that the regulations concerning organized interests are inadequate to control them. This is a problem because distrust of government is often accompanied by withdrawal from politics. Widespread abandonment of politics is a very real threat to democracy. After all, people are the *demos* in *democracy*. If people do not participate in politics, decisions will be based largely on the wishes of organized interests.

All of this begs the following question: Should anything be done to regulate organized interests? Certainly any serious restrictions on organized interest activity must be dismissed out of hand, but commonsense restrictions meant to ensure accountability and restore people's trust in American government seem more than reasonable. In closing, I suggest two modest reforms that could serve the purpose of allowing organized interests broad latitude to participate in American politics while still serving the goal of removing any serious threats of organized interest tyranny.

First, organized interests should be forced to disclose all of their activities. A full disclosure regime would require them to divulge where they get their money and how they spend it. Thus, any organization that spends *any* money or time lobbying government at *any* level of government would be required to account for its activities publicly. These records could be made available to the public, perhaps on the Internet, where anyone who wishes to can examine them. Of course, regulations that require organized interests to detail their every move would be burdensome and unrealistic. It seems reasonable, however, to force organized interests to disclose precisely what laws and policies they lobby for and against, how much money they spend on lobbying, and, especially, how much campaign money they contribute and to whom.

The primary rationale for a disclosure regime is that it would allow citizens to decide for themselves if organized interests are out of control. It would allow citizens to see for themselves what pressures are put on their representatives, and it would allow them to see how their representatives respond to this pressure. If a citizen decides that his or her representative is being unduly influenced by organized interests, that person is then free to hold that representative accountable.

Some would argue that we already have a disclosure regime. Current laws and regulations require organized interests to register with the federal government if they lobby, and campaign finance laws require organized interests to report all of their campaign contributions. But the current system of disclosure is full of loopholes. First, regulations vary from place to place, and many states and cities require no disclosure whatsoever. Second, some sorts of organized interest activity are not subject to extant disclosure rules. As we saw in Chapter 7, election issue advocacy is completely unregulated. This means that organized interests can spend as much money as they want on behalf of or in opposition to a candidate for virtually any office in America. Clearly this violates the spirit of free and open elections. It does not give voters access to important information about what candidates stand for, where their support is coming from, or who is bankrolling their campaigns. Finally, the disclosure laws that currently exist are not "user friendly." Although organized interests in most places must register with the government and report some of their activities, obtaining these records is often very difficult. For example, if you wish to know precisely where the National Rifle Association or the American Civil Liberties Union gets its money, you must either rely on the organization's annual report, which is often incomplete, or you must order a copy of its federal income tax form from the Internal Revenue Service. Ostensibly these forms are available to the public, but the IRS is exceedingly slow in providing them, and they are costly to obtain.

In sum, full disclosure is an eminently sensible reform. Although it would require all fifty states, the federal government, and all local governments to pass new laws, it is probably worth all the work. It does not favor any specific types of organized interests over any others, and it does not prohibit any specific activities. Most important, it lets citizens decide for themselves if organized interests have gone too far. Accountability is essential to the functioning of American government. As long as organized interests and the public officials they target are allowed to hide or obscure their activities, citizens have less of the information they need to make informed choices about who will lead them.

A second reform that seems reasonable is the restriction of organized interest soft money. Soft money contributions are exactly the types of unlimited, unregulated contributions that the authors of the Federal Election Campaign Act worked so hard to prohibit. Massive organized interest soft money contributions cannot help but lead many Americans to believe that their policymakers are for sale. Indeed, this fear was behind the public outcry over Bill Clinton's "sale" of the Lincoln bedroom to large soft money donors. One specific soft money regulation seems particularly sensible: soft money that comes directly from organized interest treasuries should be prohibited. The problem with these types of contributions is that they do not come from individual voters. It is one thing for organized interests to use their treasuries to fund ongoing lobbying. But elections in the United States should be sacred; they are contests that elevate voters, not institutions. PACs are required to get their money from voters. So at the very least we know that their activities are funded entirely by the very citizens who ultimately decide the outcome of elections. Soft money, however, violates the sanctity of the electoral process by essentially allowing institutions and organizations—entities that are not allowed to vote—to play an exceedingly large role in our elections. As a society, we have decided that institutions and organizations have the right to press their concerns on government officials. But allowing them free rein in elections is tantamount to giving them the right to vote.

The primary argument in favor of allowing organized interest soft money contributions is that they are constitutionally protected forms of free speech. This argument is facile. The Constitution grants a broad range of freedoms and civil liberties to individuals, *not* institutions. The authors of the Bill of Rights were worried about undue government interference in the lives of American citizens. They may have had reservations about government involvement in the affairs of institutions, but these reservations were not part and parcel of the Bill of Rights. Indeed, applying the Bill of Rights to institutions does not really make much sense. Can an institution "bear arms"? Does an institution "freely assemble"? Can an institution "exercise a religion"? Of course not. The argument here is not that government should be able to do whatever it wishes to regulate and control the activities of institutions. Rather, it is that the Bill of Rights should not be read so as to preempt any government attempts to rein in the activities of institutions in the election process.

Several other possible reforms seem quite reasonable, including a ban on gifts and junkets. Both of these reforms strike me as reasonable, workable, and meaningful. In addition, they strike at the heart of what troubles Americans most about organized interests: subterfuge and money. Currently large majorities of American citizens say that the system of organized interest regulation needs to be overhauled. There is no public outcry for reform, however, because such reform is low on the priority lists of most Americans.[4] Understandably, most of us worry more about issues that directly affect our lives—issues such as the economy, taxes, education, health care, and crime—than we do about organized interest reform.[5] This is not likely to change, occasional scandal notwithstanding. As such, true reform will come only when courageous public officials exercise leadership on the issue. There is evidence that more and more leaders are willing to exercise such leadership. During his brief run for the Republican presidential nomination in 2000, for example, John McCain made campaign finance reform one of the centerpieces of his campaign. He did not prevail, but he did show that the public is responsive to calls for change. Perhaps momentum for change is building.

A FINAL THOUGHT

The overriding goal of this book has been to inform you about organized interests and the role they play in American politics. This said, it is important for you to remember that American politics in general and organized interest politics in particular changes quickly. Fifteen years ago, for example, soft money was not an issue in election campaigns. Today it is everywhere. Similarly, election issue advocacy was virtually unheard of until the early 1990s. Now organized interests of all stripes see such advocacy as an important way to affect public policy. In sum, things change quickly. So keep your eyes and ears open.

Notes

1. James Q. Wilson, *Political Organizations* (Princeton, NJ: Princeton University Press, 1995), p. xx.
2. Lydia Saad, "No Public Outcry for Campaign Finance Reform," *Gallup Poll Releases* (February 22, 1999), accessed at *www.gallup.com/poll/releases/pr970222.asp;*

"Testimony of Common Cause President Scott Harshbarger Before the Senate Rules Committee," *Common Cause News* (April 5, 2000), accessed at *www.commoncause.org/publications/april00/04505test.*

3. James Madison, "Federalist #10," in Randall B. Ripley and Elliot E. Slotnick, eds., *Readings in American Government and Politics* (3rd ed.) (Needham Heights, MA: Allyn and Bacon, 1999), p. 20.

4. CNN/USA Today/Gallup Poll, (March 10–12, 2000), accessed at *www.gallup.com /poll/surveys/2000/topline000310/q16.asp,* April 13, 2000.

5. Frank Newport, "Tax Cuts Have a Generic Appeal, But Are Not Voters' Highest Priority," *Gallup Poll Releases* (June 27, 1999), accessed at *www.gallup.com/poll /releases/pr990626.asp,* April 13, 2000.

Glossary

Access. The ability to see and speak with policymakers. Most organized interests value access highly.

Amateur lobbyist. A lobbyist who lobbies voluntarily.

Amicus curiae brief. "Friend of the court" brief. Amicus curiae briefs are often prepared by organized interests and submitted to courts. Submitting amicus briefs is one way that organized interests lobby the judiciary.

Association lobbyist. A lobbyist who works for and is employed by a single organization.

Back-end premium. Something that a new member will receive in addition to regular membership benefits, should he or she decide to join an organization. Many direct mail packages promise recipients back-end premiums.

Board of directors. A small group of people who are the ultimate source of formal authority for an organization.

Bundling. Collecting checks from individual contributors and then turning them over to a candidate or candidates. Some political action committees bundle.

Charity. An organized interest engaged in the free assistance of the poor, the suffering, or the distressed.

Church. An organized group of worshippers. A type of organized interest.

Citizen group. An organized interest that is open to any citizen.

Coalition. A loose collection of organizations and individuals that cooperates to accomplish common objectives. A type of organized interest.

Collective benefits. Benefits that accrue to an organized interest's members as well as to nonmembers. Most membership organized interests work for collective benefits.

College. An institution of higher learning. A type of organized interest.

Corporation. A business enterprise that exists primarily to make money. A type of organized interest.

Cost. One of the barriers to organized interest formation and survival.

Direct lobbying. Lobbying that entails face-to-face contact with public officials.

Direct mail advertising. A technique of indirect lobbying in which organized interests contact ordinary citizens through the mail.

Direct mail package. The parcel that contains an organized interest's direct mail appeal.

Direct telephone marketing. Contacting people over the telephone. One of the ways that organized interests raise money and recruit members.

Disturbance theory. A theory that societal change is responsible for organized interest proliferation.

Domestic governmental entity. An organized interest that lobbies one layer of American government on behalf of another.

Election issue advocacy. Spending that advocates particular positions on issues rather than the election or defeat of particular candidates, but nonetheless is intended to affect the outcome of an election. One of the means by which organized interests lobby with campaign money.

Elitists. Scholars who believe that political decisions are made by a narrow group of privileged elites.

Expressive benefit. An intangible benefit derived from working for a cause. A type of selective benefit.

Federal Election Campaign Act (FECA). The primary federal campaign finance law. Congress passed FECA in 1971 and amended it in 1974, 1976, and 1979. FECA mandated contribution limits, a disclosure regime, and a system of public financing for presidential election campaigns, and it created the Federal Election Commission. FECA also clarified the role of organized interests in campaign finance by banning direct contributions to candidates and political parties from all organized interests other than political action committees.

Foreign governmental entity. A governmental body that lobbies the U.S. government on behalf of the government of another country. A type of organized interest.

Formal direct lobbying. Lobbying that entails contact with public officials in their offices or at formal governmental proceedings.

Free-rider problem. The tendency for individuals not to join organized interests that work on their behalf. One of the barriers to organized interest formation and survival.

Front-end premium. A small gift sent as part of a direct mail package.

Hard money. Money donated to political parties that is given and spent within the confines of the Federal Election Campaign Act.

Hired gun. A lobbyist who has a number of clients and works for any organization that hires him or her.

Honorarium. A stipend given to a policymaker for a speech to an organized interest.

"In and outers." Government officials who become lobbyists after they leave government office.

Indirect lobbying. Lobbying aimed at citizens rather than public officials.

Informal direct lobbying. Lobbying that entails unceremonious contact with policymakers outside formal governmental processes.

Initiative. A proposed law that is placed directly on a ballot for citizen approval.

In-kind campaign contribution. A gift other than money that a political action committee gives to a candidate.

Institution. A nonmembership organization—for example, corporations, universities and colleges, and hospitals.

Interest. An attitude, value, or preference with some relevance to public policy.

Iron law of oligarchy. A "law" that within all organizations, a relatively small group of professionals dominate decision making.

Issue niche. A narrow, highly specific issue identity that allows an organized interest to avoid competition and conflict with other organized interests.

Junket. A free trip.

Labor union. A group of workers joined together for the purpose of collective bargaining with employers. A type of organized interest.

Legal analysis. Information about the legal ramifications of a proposed or existing policy or program. One of the types of information that lobbyists provide to policymakers.

Lobbying. Any attempt to influence public policy.

Lobbying Disclosure Act of 1995. A comprehensive piece of federal lobbying legislation that requires federal lobbyists to register with the federal government, disclose their activities, and refrain from giving expensive gifts to legislators.

Lobbying for contact. A type of indirect lobbying that encourages citizens to contact policymakers.

Lobbying law firm. A law firm that employs a number of lobbyists.

Lobbying to affect public opinion. A type of indirect lobbying that attempts to shape attitudes and opinions about an issue or series of issues.

Lobbyist. An individual who represents an organized interest before government.

Material benefits. Selective benefits that have tangible economic value.

Monitoring. Keeping track of what government is up to.

Nonaffiliated political action committee (PAC). A PAC without a parent organization.

Office of Public Liaison. An official White House entity that maintains contact with organized interests.

On-line computer solicitation. A method of fund raising in which organized interests solicit contributions on-line.

Organizational maintenance. Doing what it takes to keep the organization viable.

Organized interest. Any organization that engages in political activity.

Paradox of organized interests. The fact that while most of us are sympathetic to some organized interests, we also say we distrust organized interests.

Patron. An individual or organizational benefactor that contributes substantial resources to an organized interest.

Peak association. A trade association that represents broad business interests. A type of organized interest.

Personal solicitation. A method by which organized interests raise money and recruit members, in which organized interests make direct contact with individuals.

Pluralists. Scholars who hold that organized interests are active and influential in most major policy decisions and that this is not a bad thing.

Policy analysis. Detailed and often technical information about the economic and social effects of a proposed or existing policy or program. One of the types of information that lobbyists provide to policymakers.

Policy domain. A well-understood and established policy area or a community of players who work to make policy in a given issue area.

Political action committee (PAC). An organization set up solely to collect and spend money on electoral campaigns. A type of organized interest.

Political analysis. Information about the political effects of a policy decision. One of the types of information that lobbyists provide to policymakers.

Political efficacy problem. The widespread tendency for people to think that one person cannot make a difference. One of the barriers to organized interest formation and survival.

Political party. An organized group of individuals that nominates candidates for election to public office and proposes policies for implementation.

Private foundation. A nonprofit institution that exists solely to make grants to individuals and nonprofit organizations. A type of organized interest patron.

Professional association. An organization that represents the interests of people in a specific profession. A type of organized interest.

Professional lobbyist. A lobbyist who lobbies for a living.

Public interest. An interest held in common by all members of society.

Referendum. A proposed law that has been passed by the legislature but requires citizen approval before it can be implemented.

Selective benefits. Benefits that accrue only to an organized interest's members.

Self-governance. The process by which an organized interest makes decisions about how it goes about its business.

Single-industry trade association. A trade association that represents businesses in a specific industry. A type of organized interest.

Soft money. Money contributed outside the guidelines of the Federal Election Campaign Act, that is, money contributed by individuals and organized interests to political party committees.

Solidary benefits. Social rewards such as meetings, outings, and group gatherings. A type of selective benefit.

Staff. The people who perform day-to-day organizational activities such as monitoring, organizational maintenance, and lobbying and who are answerable to the organization's leader.

Subgovernment. A limited number of organized interests, legislators, and key bureaucrats who interact on a stable, ongoing basis to produce policy outcomes in a particular issue area.

Subgovernment theory. A theory that American government is characterized by a large number of subgovernments.

Survival. The ability to remain in business as an organized interest over the long term.

Teapot Dome affair. A famous scandal in the early twentieth century in which Interior Secretary Albert B. Fall received over $400,000 for his work on behalf of wealthy oil barons. Eventually Fall was tried and convicted of graft.

Think tank. A nonprofit institution that conducts and disseminates research. A type of organized interest.

Trade association. An organized group of businesses. A type of organized interest.

Universe of organized interests. The myriad organizations that fit the definition of *organized interest*.

University. An institution of higher learning. A type of organized interest.

Voter guide. A brief tract that presents candidates' positions on issues of concern to organized interests and their supporters.

Suggested Readings

Adams, Gordon. *The Iron Triangle*. New York: Council on Economic Priorities, 1981.

Ainsworth, Scott. "Regulating Lobbyists and Interest Group Influence." *Journal of Politics* 55 (1993): 41–56.

Alexander, Herbert, and Monica Bauer. *Financing the 1988 Election*. Boulder, Colo.: Westview Press, 1991.

Alterman, Eric. *Sound and Fury: The Washington Punditocracy and the Collapse of American Politics*. New York: HarperCollins, 1992.

Ansolabehere, Stephen, and Shanto Iyengar. *Going Negative: How Attack Ads Shrink and Polarize the Electorate*. New York: Free Press, 1995.

Athearn, Ronald G. *Union Pacific Country*. Lincoln: University of Nebraska Press, 1976.

Bachrach, Peter, and Morton S. Baratz. "Two Faces of Power." *American Political Science Review* 56 (1962): 947–952.

Bashevkin, Sylvia. "Interest Groups and Social Movements." In Lawrence LeDuc, Richard G. Niemi, and Pippa Norris, eds., *Comparing Democracies: Elections and Voting in Global Perspective*. Thousand Oaks, Calif.: Sage, 1996.

Bauer, Raymond A., Ithiel de Sola Pool, and Lewis A. Dexter. *American Business and Public Policy: The Politics of Foreign Trade*. New York: Atherton Press, 1963.

Baumgartner, Frank R., and Beth L. Leech. *Basic Interests: The Importance of Groups in Politics and in Political Science*. Princeton, N.J.: Princeton University Press, 1988.

Baumgartner, Frank R., and Jack L. Walker, Jr. "Survey Research and Membership in Voluntary Organizations." *American Journal of Political Science* 32 (1988): 908–928.

Beck, Paul Allen. *Party Politics in America.* 8th ed. New York: Longman, 1997.

Bentley, Arthur. *The Process of Government.* Chicago: University of Chicago Press, 1980.

Berry, Jeffrey M. *Lobbying for the People.* Princeton, N.J.: Princeton University Press, 1977.

———. "Subgovernments, Issue Networks, and Political Conflict." In Richard A. Harris and Sidney M. Milkis, eds., *Remaking American Politics.* Boulder, Colo.: Westview Press, 1989.

———. *The New Liberalism: The Rising Power of Citizen Groups.* Washington, D.C.: Brookings Institution Press, 1999.

Berry, Jeffrey M., and Kent E. Portney. "Centralizing Regulatory Control and Interest Group Access: The Quayle Council on Competitiveness." In Allan J. Cigler and Burdett A. Loomis, eds., *Interest Group Politics.* 4th ed. Washington, D.C.: Congressional Quarterly Press, 1995.

Berry, Jeffrey M., Kent E. Portney, and Ken Thomson. *The Rebirth of Urban Democracy.* Washington, D.C.: Brookings Institution, 1992.

Birnbaum, Jeffrey H. *The Lobbyists.* New York: Times Books, 1992.

Birnbaum, Jeffrey H., and Alan S. Murray. *Showdown at Gucci Gulch.* New York: Basic Books, 1987.

Blanchard, Dallas A. *The Anti-Abortion Movement and the Rise of the Religious Right: From Polite to Fiery Protest.* New York: Twayne, 1994.

Bosso, Christopher J. *Pesticides and Policy.* Pittsburgh: University of Pittsburgh Press, 1986.

Bowman, Ann O'M., and Richard C. Kearney. *State and Local Government.* 3rd ed. Boston: Houghton Mifflin Company, 1996.

Browne, William P. *Private Interests and Public Policy.* Lawrence: University of Kansas Press, 1988.

———. "Organized Interests and Their Issue Niches: A Search for Pluralism in a Policy Domain." *Journal of Politics* 52 (1990): 477–509.

———. *Cultivating Congress: Constituents, Issues, and Interests in Agricultural Policymaking.* Lawrence: University of Kansas Press, 1995.

———. *Groups, Interests, and U.S. Public Policy.* Washington, D.C.: Georgetown University Press, 1998.

Browne, William P., and Allan J. Cigler, eds. *Agriculture Interests.* Westport, Conn.: Greenwood Press, 1991.

Browne, William P., and Won K. Paik. "Beyond the Domain: Recasting Network Politics in the Post-Reform Congress." *American Journal of Political Science* 37 (1993): 1054–1078.

Cantor, David. "The Sierra Club Political Committee." In Robert Biersack, Paul S. Hernnson, and Clyde Wilcox, *After the Revolution: PACs, Lobbies, and the Republican Congress.* Needham Heights, Mass.: Allyn and Bacon, 1999.

Carpini, Michael X. Delli, and Scott Keeter. *What Americans Know About Politics and Why It Matters.* New Haven, Conn.: Yale University Press, 1996.

Cater, Douglas. *Power in Washington.* New York: Vintage Books, 1964.

Chazan, Naomi. "Engaging the State: Associational Life in Sub-Saharan Africa." In Joel S. Migdal, Atul Kohli, and Vivenne Shue, eds., *State Power and Social Forces.* New York: Cambridge University Press, 1994.

Choate, Pat. *Agents of Influence.* New York: Knopf, 1990.

Chong, Dennis. *Collective Action and the Civil Rights Movement.* Chicago: University of Chicago Press, 1991.

Chubb, John E. *Interest Groups and the Bureaucracy.* Stanford, Calif.: Stanford University Press, 1983.

Cigler, Allan J. "Interest Groups: A Subfield in Search of an Identity." In William Crotty, ed., *Political Science: Looking to the Future.* Vol. 4: *American Institutions.* Evanston, Ill.: Northwestern University Press, 1991.

Cigler, Allan J., and Dwight C. Kiel. *The Changing Nature of Interest Group Politics in Kansas.* Topeka: Capitol Complex Center, University of Kansas, 1988.

Cigler, Allan J., and Burdett A. Loomis. "Contemporary Interest Group Politics: More Than 'More of the Same.'" In Allan J. Cigler and Burdett A. Loomis, eds., *Interest Group Politics.* 4th ed. Washington, D.C.: Congressional Quarterly Press, 1995.

————. "From Big Bird to Bill Gates: Organized Interests and the Emergence of Hyperpolitics." In Allan J. Cigler and Burdett A. Loomis, eds., *Interest Group Politics.* 5th ed. Washington, D.C.: Congressional Quarterly Press, 1998.

Clark, Peter B., and James Q. Wilson. "Incentive Systems: A Theory of Organizations." *Administrative Studies Quarterly* 6 (1961): 129–166.

Commons, John R., E. B. Mittelman, and Henry W. Farnam. *History of Labour in the United States.* New York: Macmillan, 1918.

Conway, M. Margaret. "PACs in the Political Process." In Allan J. Cigler and Burdett A. Loomis, eds., *Interest Group Politics.* 3rd ed. Washington, D.C.: Congressional Quarterly Press, 1991.

Conway, M. Margaret, and Joanne Connor Green. "Political Action Committees and the Political Process in the 1990s." In Allan J. Cigler and Burdett A. Loomis, eds., *Interest Group Politics.* 4th ed. Washington, D.C.: Congressional Quarterly Press, 1995.

Corrado, Anthony. "Financing the 1996 Elections." In Gerald M. Pomper, Walter Dean Burnham, Anthony Corrado, Marjorie Randon Hershey, Marion R. Just, Scott Keeter, Wilson Carey McWilliams, and William G. Meyer, eds., *The Election of 1996.* Chatham, N.J.: Chatham House, 1997.

Costain, Anne N. *Inviting Women's Rebellion.* Baltimore: Johns Hopkins University Press, 1992.

———. "Social Movements as Interest Groups: The Case of the Women's Movement." In Mark P. Petracca, ed., *The Politics of Interests*. Boulder, Colo.: Westview Press, 1992.

Dahl, Robert A. *Who Governs?* New Haven, Conn.: Yale University Press, 1961.

———. *Dilemmas of Pluralist Democracy*. New Haven, Conn.: Yale University Press, 1982.

Davidson, Roger H., and Walter J. Oleszek. *Congress and Its Members*. 4th ed. Washington, D.C.: Congressional Quarterly Press, 1994.

———. *Congress and Its Members*. 7th ed. Washington, D.C.: Congressional Quarterly Press, 2000.

DeGregorio, Christine. "Assets and Access: Linking Lobbyists and Lawmakers." In Paul S. Herrnson, Ronald G. Shaiko, and Clyde Wilcox, eds., *The Interest Group Connection: Electioneering, Lobbying, and Policymaking in Washington*. Chatham House, N.J.: Chatham House, 1998.

DeGregorio, Christine, and Jack E. Rossotti. "Campaigning for the Court: Interest Group Conformation in the Bork and Thomas Confirmation Process." In Allan J. Cigler and Burdett A. Loomis, eds., *Interest Group Politics*. 4th ed. Washington, D.C.: Congressional Quarterly Press, 1995.

Diamond, Edwin, and Stephen Bates. *The Spot: The Rise of Political Advertising on Television*. Cambridge, Mass.: MIT Press, 1992.

Dwyre, Diana. "Spinning Straw into Gold: Soft Money and U.S. House Elections." *Legislative Studies Quarterly* 21 (1996): 409–424.

Dye, Thomas R. *Politics in States and Communities*. 9th ed. Englewood Cliffs, N.J.: Prentice Hall, 1997.

Epstein, Lee, and C. K. Rowland. "Interest Groups in the Courts: Do Groups Fare Better?" In Allan J. Cigler and Burdett A. Loomis, eds., *Interest Group Politics*. 2nd ed. Washington, D.C.: Congressional Quarterly Press, 1986.

Fesler, James, and Donald Kettl. *The Politics of the Administrative Process*. Chatham, N.J.: Chatham House, 1991.

Fiorina, Morris P. *Retrospective Voting in American National Elections*. New Haven, Conn.: Yale University Press, 1981.

Foreman, Christopher H., Jr. "Grassroots Victim Organizations: Mobilizing for Personal and Public Health." In Allan J. Cigler and Burdett A. Loomis, eds., *Interest Group Politics*. 4th ed. Washington, D.C.: Congressional Quarterly Press, 1995.

Freeman, J. Leiper. *The Political Process: Executive Bureau-Legislative Committee Relations*. Rev. ed. New York: Random House, 1965.

Frendreis, John P., and Richard W. Waterman. "PAC Contributions and Legislative Behavior: Senate Voting on Trucking Deregulation." *Social Science Quarterly* 66 (1985): 401–412.

Fritschler, A. Lee. 1989. *Smoking and Politics: Policymaking and the Federal Bureaucracy*. 4th ed. Englewood Cliffs, N.J.: Prentice Hall, 1989.

Garrow, David J. *Protest at Selma*. New Haven, Conn.: Yale University Press, 1978.

Garson, G. David. *Group Theories of Politics*. Beverly Hills, Calif.: Sage, 1978.

Gaventa, John. *Power and Powerlessness.* Urbana: University of Illinois Press, 1980.

Gengler, Charles E., and Thomas J. Reynolds. "A Structural Model of Advertising Effects." In Andrew A. Mitchell, ed., *Advertising Exposure, Memory, and Choice.* Hillsdale, N.J.: Erlbaum, 1993.

Gimpel, James G. "Grassroots Organizations and Equilibrium Cycles in Group Mobilization and Access." In Paul S. Herrnson, Ronald G. Shaiko, and Clyde Wilcox, eds., *The Interest Group Connection: Electioneering, Lobbying, and Policymaking in Washington.* Chatham House, N.J.: Chatham House, 1998.

Gleeck, Lewis E. "96 Congressmen Make Up Their Minds." *Public Opinion Quarterly* 4 (1940): 3–24.

Godwin, R. Kenneth. *One Billion Dollars of Influence.* Chatham, N.J.: Chatham House, 1988.

———. "Money, Technology, and Political Interests: The Direct Marketing of Politics." In Mark P. Petracca, ed., *The Politics of Interests: Interest Groups Transformed.* Boulder, Colo.: Westview Press, 1992.

Goldstein, Kenneth M. "Tremors Before the Earthquake: Grassroots Communication to Congress Before the 1994 Election." Paper presented to the annual meeting of the American Political Science Association, Chicago, 1995.

Golembiewski, Robert. "The Group Basis of Politics: Notes on Analysis and Development." *American Political Science Review* 54 (1960): 962–971.

Goodnow, Frank. *Politics and Administration: A Study in Government.* New York: Macmillan, 1900.

Goodsell, Charles. *The Case for Bureaucracy: A Public Administration Polemic.* 2nd ed. Chatham, N.J.: Chatham House Publishers, 1985.

Gray, Virginia, and David Lowery. *Population Ecology of Interest Representation: Lobbying Communities in the American States.* Ann Arbor: University of Michigan Press, 1996.

Grenzke, Janet. "Shopping in the Congressional Supermarket: The Currency Is Complex." *American Journal of Political Science* 33 (1989): 1–24.

Griffith, Ernest. *Impasse of Democracy.* New York: Harrison-Hilton Books, 1939.

Guth, James, and John C. Green. "Political Activists and Civil Liberties: The Case of Party and PAC Contributions." Paper presented at the annual meeting of the Midwest Political Science Association, Chicago, 1984.

Haines, Herbert. "Black Radicalization and the Funding of Civil Rights." *Social Problems* 32 (1984): 31–43.

Hall, Richard, and Frank W. Wayman. "Buying Time: Moneyed Interests and the Mobilization of Bias in Congressional Committees." *American Political Science Review* 84 (1990): 797–820.

Hansen, John Mark. *Gaining Access: Congress and the Farm Lobby, 1919–1981.* Chicago: University of Chicago Press, 1991.

Harris, Richard A. *Coal Firms Under the New Social Regulation.* Durham, N.C.: Duke University Press, 1985.

———. "Political Management: The Changing Face of Business in American Politics." In Richard A. Harris and Sidney Milkis, eds., *Remaking American Politics*. Boulder, Colo.: Westview Press, 1989.

Hayes, Michael T. *Lobbyists and Legislators*. New Brunswick, N.J.: Rutgers University Press, 1980.

———. "The New Group Universe." In Allan J. Cigler and Burdett A. Loomis, eds., *Interest Group Politics*. 2nd ed. Washington, D.C.: Congressional Quarterly Press, 1986.

Heclo, Hugh. "Issue Networks and the Executive Establishment." In Anthony King, ed., *The New American Political System*. Washington, D.C.: American Enterprise Institute, 1979.

Hedge, David M. *Governance and the Changing American States*. Boulder, Colo.: Westview Press, 1998.

Heinz, John P., Edward Laumann, Robert L. Nelson, and Robert H. Salisbury. *The Hollow Core: Private Interests in National Policy Making*. Cambridge, Mass.: Harvard University Press, 1993.

Herring, E. Pendleton. *Group Representation Before Congress*. Baltimore: Johns Hopkins University Press, 1929.

Herrnson, Paul S. "The National Committee for an Effective Congress: Liberalism, Partisanship, and Electoral Innovation." In Robert Biersack, Paul S. Herrnson, and Clyde Wilcox, eds., *Risky Business?* Armonk, N.Y.: M. E. Sharpe, 1994.

———. "Parties and Interest Groups in Postreform Congressional Elections." In Allan J. Cigler and Burdett A. Loomis, eds., *Interest Group Politics*. 5th ed. Washington, D.C.: Congressional Quarterly Press, 1998.

Hershey, Marjorie Randon. "Direct Action and the Abortion Issue: The Political Participation of Single-Issue Groups." In Allan J. Cigler and Burdett A. Loomis, eds., *Interest Group Politics*. 2nd ed. Washington, D.C.: Congressional Quarterly Press, 1986.

Hertzke, Allen. D. *Representing God in Washington*. Knoxville: University of Tennessee Press, 1988.

Hirschman, Albert O. *Exit, Voice, and Loyalty*. Cambridge: Harvard University Press, 1970.

Holt, Marianne. "The Surge in Party Money in Competitive 1998 Congressional Elections." In David Magleby, ed., *Outside Money: Soft Money and Issue Advocacy in the 1998 Congressional Elections*. Landham, Mary L.: Rowman and Littlefield, 2000.

Hrebenar, Ronald J., Matthew J. Burbank, and Robert C. Benedict. *Political Parties, Interest Groups, and Political Campaigns*. Boulder, Colo.: Westview Press, 1999.

Hrebenar, Ronald J., and Clive Thomas. *Interest Group Politics in the Southern States*. Tuscaloosa: University of Alabama Press, 1992.

———. *Interest Group Politics in the Midwestern States*. Ames: Iowa State University Press, 1993.

Hula, Kevin. "Rounding Up the Usual Suspects: Forging Interest Group Coalitions in Washington." In Allan J. Cigler and Burdett A. Loomis, eds., *Inter-*

est Group Politics. 4th ed. Washington, D.C.: Congressional Quarterly Press, 1995.

Hunter, Floyd. *Community Power Structure.* Chapel Hill: University of North Carolina Press, 1953.

Hyman, Herbert, and Charles Wright. "Trends in Voluntary Association Membership of American Adults." *American Sociological Review* 36 (1971): 191–206.

Iheany, Chris Enyinda. *An Econometric Analysis of Multimedia Effects on Consumers' Purchase Decisions at the Supermarket Level Using Scanner-Derived Data.* Ph.D. dissertation, University of Tennessee, 1995.

Imig, Douglas R. *Poverty and Power: The Political Representation of Poor Americans.* Lincoln: University of Nebraska Press, 1996.

Jackson, Brooks. *Honest Graft: Money and the American Political Process.* New York: Knopf, 1988.

———. "Financing the 1996 Campaign: The Law of the Jungle." In Larry J. Sabato, ed., *Toward the Millennium: The Elections of 1996.* Needham Heights, Mass.: Allyn and Bacon, 1997.

Jacobson, Gary C. *Money in Congressional Elections.* New Haven: Yale University Press, 1980.

Jenkins, J. Craig. *The Politics of Insurgency: The Farm Worker Movement in the 1960s.* New York: Columbia University Press, 1985.

Johnson, Paul Edward. "Organized Labor in an Era of Blue-Collar Decline." In Allan J. Cigler and Burdett A. Loomis, eds., *Interest Group Politics.* 3rd ed. Washington, D.C.: Congressional Quarterly Press, 1991.

Jones, Woodrow, Jr., and K. Robert Keiser. "Issue Visibility and the Effects of PAC Money." *Social Science Quarterly* 68 (1987): 170–176.

Kateb, George. "The Value of Association." In Amy Gutman, ed., *Freedom of Association.* Princeton, N.J.: Princeton University Press, 1998.

Key, V. O., Jr. *Politics, Parties, and Pressure Groups.* 5th ed. New York: Crowell, 1964.

Kiewiet, D. Roderick. *Macroeconomics and Micropolitics: The Electoral Effects of Economic Issues.* Chicago: University of Chicago Press, 1983.

King, James D., and Helenan S. Robin. "Political Action Committees in State Elections." *American Review of Politics* 16 (1995): 61–77.

Kingdon, John W. *Congressmen's Voting Decisions.* 2nd ed. New York: Harper and Row, 1981.

Kollman, Kenneth. 1998. *Outside Lobbying: Public Opinion and Interest Group Strategies.* Ann Arbor: University of Michigan Press, 1998.

Langbein, Laura I. "Money and Access: Some Empirical Evidence." *Journal of Politics* 48 (1986): 1052–1062.

Latham, Earl. *The Group Basis of Politics.* Ithaca, N.Y.: Cornell University Press, 1952.

Loomis, Burdett A. "A New Era: Groups at the Grassroots." In Allan J. Cigler and Burdett A. Loomis, eds., *Interest Group Politics.* 5th ed. Washington, D.C.: Congressional Quarterly Press, 1998.

Loomis, Burdett A., and Allan J. Cigler. "Introduction: The Changing Nature of Interest Group Politics." In Allan J. Cigler and Burdett A. Loomis, eds., *Interest Group Politics*. 5th ed. Washington, D.C.: Congressional Quarterly Press, 1998.

Loomis, Burdett A., and Eric Sexton. "Choosing to Advertise: How Interests Decide." In Allan J. Cigler and Burdett A. Loomis, eds., *Interest Group Politics*. 4th ed. Washington, D.C.: Congressional Quarterly Press, 1995.

Lowi, Theodore. *The End of Liberalism*. New York: Norton, 1969.

MacKenzie, G. Galvin. *The In and Outers: Presidential Appointees and Transient Government in Washington*. Baltimore: Johns Hopkins University Press, 1987.

Madison, James. "Federalist #10." In Randall B. Ripley and Elliot E. Slotnick, eds., *Readings in American Government and Politics*. 3rd ed. Needham Heights, Mass.: Allyn and Bacon, 1999.

Magleby, David, ed. *Outside Money: Soft Money and Issue Advocacy in the 1998 Congressional Elections*. Landham, Md.: Rowman and Littlefield, 2000.

Mansbridge, Jane J. *Why We Lost the ERA*. Chicago: University of Chicago Press, 1986.

Mayhew, David R. *Congress: The Electoral Connection*. New Haven, Conn.: Yale University Press, 1974.

McCool, Daniel. "Subgovernments and the Impact of Policy Fragmentation and Accommodation." *Policy Studies Review* 8 (1988): 264–287.

McFarland, Andrew S. *Public Interest Lobbies*. Washington, D.C.: American Enterprise Institute, 1976.

———. *Common Cause: Lobbying in the Public Interest*. Chatham, N.J.: Chatham House, 1984.

McGann, James G. "Academics to Ideologues: A Brief History of the Public Policy Research Industry." *PS* 4 (1992): 733–740.

Meyer, Jane, and Jill Abramson. *Strange Justice*. Boston: Houghton Mifflin Company, 1994.

Michaels, Judith E. *The President's Call: Executive Leadership from FDR to George Bush*. Pittsburgh: University of Pittsburgh Press, 1997.

Michels, Robert. *Political Parties*. New York: Free Press, 1958 [1915].

Milbraith, Lester W. *The Washington Lobbyists*. Chicago: Rand-McNally, 1963.

———. *Political Participation*. Chicago: Rand-McNally, 1965.

Mills, C. Wright. *The Power Elite*. New York: Oxford University Press, 1956.

Moe, Terry M. "A Calculus of Group Membership." *American Journal of Political Science* 24 (1980): 593–632.

———. *The Organization of Interests*. Chicago: University of Chicago Press, 1980.

Moore, Stephen, Sidney M. Wolfe, Deborah Lindes, and Clifford Douglas. "Epidemiology of Failed Tobacco Control Legislation." *Journal of the American Medical Association* 272 (1994): 1171–1175.

Mucciaroni, Gary. *Reversals of Fortune.* Washington, D.C.: Brookings Institution, 1995.

Nelson, Candice J. "Money in the 1996 Elections." In William Crotty and Jerome E. Mileur, eds., *The Election of 1996.* New York: Dushkin/McGraw Hill, 1997.

Nelson, Robert L., John P. Heinz, Edward O. Laumann, and Robert Salisbury. "Private Representation in Washington: Surveying the Structure of Influence." *American Bar Foundation Research Journal* (Winter 1987): 141–200.

Neuman, Russell. *The Paradox of Mass Politics: Knowledge and Opinion in the American Electorate.* Cambridge, Mass.: Harvard University Press, 1986.

Norton, Philip. "The United Kingdom: Parliament Under Pressure." In Philip Norton, ed., *Parliaments and Pressure Groups in Western Europe.* London: Frank Cass, 1999.

Nownes, Anthony J. "The Other Exchange: Public Interest Groups, Patrons, and Benefits." *Social Science Quarterly* 76 (1995): 381–401.

———. "Solicited Advice and Lobbyist Power." *Legislative Studies Quarterly* 24 (1999): 113–123.

Nownes, Anthony J., and Allan Cigler. "Corporate Philanthropy in a Political Fishbowl: Perils and Possibilities." In Allan J. Cigler and Burdett A. Loomis, eds., *Interest Group Politics.* 5th ed. Washington, D.C.: Congressional Quarterly Press, 1998.

Nownes, Anthony J., and Patricia Freeman. "Interest Group Activity in the States." *Journal of Politics* 60 (1998): 86–112

Nownes, Anthony J., and Grant Neeley. "Public Interest Group Entrepreneurship and Theories of Group Mobilization." *Political Research Quarterly* 49 (1996): 119–146.

O'Connor, Karen. *Women's Organizations' Use of the Courts.* Lexington, Mass.: Lexington Books, 1980.

Odegard, Peter H. *Pressure Politics: The Story of the Anti-Saloon League.* New York: Columbia University Press, 1928.

Olson, Mancur. The *Logic of Collective Action.* Cambridge, Mass.: Harvard University Press, 1965.

———. *The Rise and Decline of Nations.* New Haven, Conn.: Yale University Press, 1982.

Olson, Susan. "Interest Group Litigation in Federal District Courts: Beyond the Political Disadvantage Theory." *Journal of Politics* 52 (1990): 854–882.

Orren, Karen. "Standing to Sue: Interest Group Conflict in the Federal Courts." *American Political Science Review* 70 (1976): 723–741.

Patterson, Kelly. "The Political Firepower of the National Rifle Association." In Allan J. Cigler and Burdett A. Loomis, eds., *Interest Group Politics.* 5th ed. Washington, D.C.: Congressional Quarterly Press, 1998.

———. "Political Firepower." In Robert Biersack, Paul Herrnson, and Clyde Wilcox, eds., *After the Revolution: PACs and Lobbies in the Republican Congress.* Needham Heights, Mass.: Allyn and Bacon, 1999.

Peters, B. Guy. *American Public Policy: Promise and Performance.* 3rd ed. Chatham, N.J.: Chatham House Publishers, 1993.

Peterson, Mark A. "The Presidency and Organized Interest Groups: White House Patterns of Interest Group Liaison." *American Political Science Review* 86 (1992): 612–625.

Peterson, Mark A., and Jack L. Walker. "Interest Groups and the Reagan White House." In Allan J. Cigler and Burdett A. Loomis, eds., *Interest Group Politics.* 2nd ed. Washington, D.C.: Congressional Quarterly Press, 1986.

Petracca, Mark P. "The Rediscovery of Interest Group Politics." In Mark P. Petracca, ed., *The Politics of Interests: Interest Groups Transformed.* Boulder, Colo.: Westview Press, 1992.

Pika, Joseph A. "Reaching Out to Organized Interests: Public Liaison in the Modern White House." In Richard W. Waterman, ed., *The Presidency Reconsidered.* Itasca, Ill.: F. E. Peacock Press, 1993.

Piven, Frances Fox, and Richard Cloward. *Poor People's Movements.* New York: Pantheon, 1978.

Postman, Neil. *Amusing Ourselves to Death.* New York: Penguin Books, 1985.

Pratt, Henry J. *The Gray Lobby.* Chicago: University of Chicago Press, 1973.

Quirk, Paul J. *Industry Influence in Federal Regulatory Agencies.* Princeton, N.J.: Princeton University Press, 1987.

Rauch, Jonathan. *Government's End: Why Washington Stopped Working.* New York: Public Affairs Press, 1999.

Rich, Andrew, and R. Kent Weaver. "Advocates and Analysts: Think Tanks and the Politicization of Expertise." In Allan J. Cigler and Burdett A. Loomis, eds., *Interest Group Politics.* 5th ed. Washington, D.C.: Congressional Quarterly Press, 1998.

Riker, William H. *Liberalism Against Populism.* Prospect Heights, Ill.: Waveland Press, 1982.

Rosenthal, Alan. *The Third House: Lobbyists and Lobbying in the States.* Washington, D.C.: Congressional Quarterly Press, 1993.

Rothenberg, Lawrence S. "Putting the Puzzle Together: Why People Join Interest Groups." *Public Choice* 60 (1989): 241–257.

———. *Linking Citizens to Government: Interest Group Politics at Common Cause.* New York: Cambridge University Press, 1992.

Rozell, Mark J., and Clyde Wilcox. *Interest Groups in American Campaigns: The New Face of Electioneering.* Washington, D.C.: Congressional Quarterly Press, 1999.

Rubin, Alissa. "Interest Groups and Abortion Politics in the Post-Webster Era." In Allan J. Cigler and Burdett A. Loomis, eds., *Interest Group Politics.* 3rd ed. Washington, D.C.: Congressional Quarterly Press, 1991.

Sabatier, Paul A. "Interest Group Membership and Organization: Multiple Theories." In Mark P. Petracca, ed., *The Politics of Interests: Interest Groups Transformed.* Boulder, Colo.: Westview Press, 1992.

Sabato, Larry J. *PAC Power: Inside the World of Political Action Committees*. New York: Norton, 1984.

Sabato, Larry J., and Glenn R. Simpson. *Dirty Little Secrets*. New York: Times Books, 1996.

Salisbury, Robert H. "An Exchange Theory of Interest Groups." *Midwest Journal of Political Science* 13 (1969): 1–32.

———. "Interest Representation: The Dominance of Institutions." *American Political Science Review* 87 (1984): 64–76.

———. "Washington Lobbyists: A Collective Portrait." In Allan J. Cigler and Burdett A. Loomis, eds., *Interest Group Politics*. 2nd ed. Washington, D.C.: Congressional Quarterly Press, 1986.

———. "The Paradox of Interest Groups in Washington—More Groups, Less Clout." In Anthony King, ed., *The New American Political System*. 2nd ed. Washington, D.C.: American Enterprise Institute, 1991.

Salisbury, Robert H., John P. Heinz, Edward O. Laumann, and Robert L. Nelson. "Who Works with Whom? Interest Group Alliances and Opposition." In Robert Salisbury, ed., *Interests and Institutions: Substance and Structures in America Politics*. Pittsburgh: University of Pittsburgh Press, 1987. [1994].

———. "Iron Triangles: Similarities and Differences among the Legs." Paper presented at the annual meeting of the American Political Science Association, Washington, D.C., 1988.

Salisbury, Robert H., and Paul E. Johnson, with John P. Heinz and Edward O. Laumann. "Who You Know Versus What You Know: The Uses of Governmental Experience for Washington Lobbyists." *American Journal of Political Science* 81 (1989): 1217–1234.

Schattschneider, E. E. *The Semisovereign People: A Realist's View of Democracy in America*. New York: Holt, Rinehart, and Winston, 1960.

Schaper, William A. "What Do Students Know About American Government?" *Proceedings of the American Political Science Association* 2 (1905): 207–228.

Schlozman, Kay Lehman. "Representing Women in Washington: Sisterhood and Pressure Politics." In Louise A. Tilly and Patricia Gurin, eds., *Women, Politics, and Change*. New York: Russell Sage, 1990.

Schlozman, Kay Lehman, and John T. Tierney. *Organized Interests and American Democracy*. New York: Harper and Row, 1986.

Schriftgiesser, Karl. *The Lobbyists: The Art and Business of Influencing Lawmakers*. Boston: Little, Brown, 1951.

Scotch, Richard. *From Goodwill to Civil Rights: Transforming Federal Disability Policy*. Philadelphia: Temple University Press, 1985.

Scott, Andrew M., and Margaret A. Hunt. *Congress and Lobbies: Image and Reality*. Chapel Hill, N.C.: University of North Carolina Press, 1965.

Shaiko, Ronald G. "Lobbying in Washington: A Contemporary Perspective." In Paul S. Herrnson, Ronald G. Shaiko, and Clyde Wilcox, eds., *The Interest Group Connection: Electioneering, Lobbying, and Policymaking in Washington*. Chatham House, N.J.: Chatham House, 1998.

Shuldiner, Allan, and the Center for Responsive Politics. *Influence Inc.: The Bottom Line on Washington Lobbying*. Washington, D.C.: Center for Responsive Politics, 1999.

Smith, Martin J. *Power, Pressure, and Policy: State Autonomy and Policy Networks in Britain and the United States*. Pittsburgh: University of Pittsburgh Press, 1993.

Sorauf, Frank. *Inside Campaign Finance: Myths and Realities*. New Haven, Conn.: Yale University Press, 1992.

Stedino, Joseph, with Dary Matera. *What's in It for Me?* New York: Harper-Collins, 1992.

Tatalovich, Raymond. *The Politics of Abortion in the United States and Canada: A Comparative Study*. Armonk, N.Y.: M. E. Sharpe, 1997.

Thomas, Clive S., and Ronald J. Hrebenar. "Nationalization of Interest Groups and Lobbying in the States." In Allan J. Cigler and Burdett A. Loomis, eds., *Interest Group Politics*. 3rd ed. Washington, D.C.: Congressional Quarterly Press, 1991.

———. "Political Action Committees in the States: Some Preliminary Findings." Paper presented at the annual meeting of the American Political Science Association, Washington D.C., 1991.

———. "Changing Patterns of Interest Group Activity: A Regional Perspective." In Mark P. Petracca, ed., *The Politics of Interests*. Boulder, Colo.: Westview Press, 1992.

———. "Interest Groups in the States." In Virginia Gray and Herbert Jacob, eds., *Politics in the American States: A Comparative Analysis*. 6th ed. Washington, D.C.: Congressional Quarterly Press, 1996.

Thompson, Margaret Susan. *The Spider Web: Congress and Lobbying in the Age of Grant*. Ithaca, N.Y.: Cornell University Press, 1985.

Tierney, John T., and Kay Lehman Schlozman. "Congress and Organized Interests." In Christopher J. Deering, ed., *Congressional Politics*. Chicago: Dorsey Press, 1989.

Truman, David R. *The Governmental Process*. New York: Knopf, 1951.

———. *The Governmental Process*. 2nd ed. New York: Knopf, 1971.

Twentieth Century Fund Task Force on the Presidential Appointment Process. *Obstacle Course*. New York: Twentieth Century Fund Press, 1997.

Verba, Sidney, Kay Lehman Schlozman, and Henry E. Brady. *Voice and Equality: Civic Voluntarism in American Politics*. Cambridge, Mass.: Harvard University Press, 1995.

Vogel, David. *Lobbying the Corporation*. New York: Basic Books, 1978.

———. *Fluctuating Fortunes*. New York: Basic Books, 1989.

Walker, Jack L. "The Origins and Maintenance of Interest Groups in America." *American Political Science Review* 77 (1983): 390–406.

———. *Mobilizing Interest Groups in America: Patrons, Professions, and Social Movements*. Ann Arbor: University of Michigan Press, 1991.

Weaver, R. Kent. "The Changing World of Think Tanks." *PS* 3 (1989): 563–578.

Welch, William P. "Campaign Contributions and Legislative Voting: Milk Money and Dairy Price Supports." *Western Political Quarterly* 35 (1982): 478–495.

West, Darrell M., and Burdett A. Loomis. *The Sound of Money: How Political Interests Get What They Want.* New York: Norton, 1999.

West, Darrell M., Diane J. Heith, and Chris Godwin. "Harry and Louise Go to Washington: Political Advertising and Health Care Reform." *Journal of Health Policy Politics, and Law* (Spring 1996): 35–68.

Wiggins, Charles W., and William P. Browne. "Interest Groups and Public Policy Within a State Legislative Setting. *Polity* 14 (1982): 548–558.

Wiggins, Charles, Keith Hamm, and Charles G. Bell. "Interest Group and Party Influence Agents in the Legislative Process: A Comparative State Analysis." *Journal of Politics* 54 (1992): 82–100.

Wilcox, Clyde. "The Dynamics of Lobbying the Hill." In Paul S. Herrnson, Ronald G. Shaiko, and Clyde Wilcox, eds., *The Interest Group Connection.* Chatham House, N.J.: Chatham House, 1998.

Wilcox, Clyde, and Wesley Joe. "Dead Law: The Federal Election Finance Regulations, 1974–1996." *PS: Political Science and Politics* 30 (1998): 14–17.

Wilson, Graham K. *Unions in American National Politics.* London: Macmillan, 1977.

———. *Business and Politics.* Chatham, N.J.: Chatham House, 1985.

———. *Interest Groups.* Oxford: Basil Blackwell, 1990.

Wilson, James Q. *Political Organizations.* New York: Basic Books, 1973.

———. *Political Organizations.* Rev. ed. Princeton, N.J.: Princeton University Press, 1995.

Wilson, Woodrow. *Congressional Government.* Boston: Houghton Mifflin Company, 1885.

Wolfinger, Raymond, and Steven J. Rosenstone. *Who Votes?* New Haven, Conn.: Yale University Press, 1980.

Wolpe, Bruce, and Bertram J. Levine. *Lobbying Congress: How the System Works.* 2nd ed. Washington, D.C.: Congressional Quarterly Press, 1996.

Wright, John R. "PACs, Contributions, and Roll Calls: An Organizational Perspective." *American Political Science Review* 79 (1985): 400–414.

———. "Contributions, Lobbying, and Committee Voting in the U.S. House of Representatives." *American Political Science Review* 84 (1990): 417–438.

———. *Interest Groups and Congress: Lobbying, Contributions, and Influence.* Boston: Allyn and Bacon, 1996.

Wyant, Rowena, and Herta Herzog. "Voting Via the Senate Mailbag." *Public Opinion Quarterly* 5 (1941): 359–382.

Index

Internal Revenue Service (IRS), 99, 225
International Union of Brick Layers and
 Allied Craftworkers, 2
Internet, 183
Iron law of oligarchy, 80–81, 230
Issue advocacy, 145. *See also* Election
 issue advocacy
Issue niches
 explanation of, 230
 importance of seeking, 206–207

Jackson, Brooks, 152
Jackson, Jesse, 1
Jefferson, Thomas, 220
Jim Crow Laws, 103
Joe, Wesley, 148
John Birch Society, 2
Johnson, Lyndon, 3, 123
Johnson, Paul, 50, 78
Jordon, Vernon, 194
Judicial appointments, 104–105
Judicial hearings, 94
Judiciary. *See* Court system
Junkets
 CNMI, 115–116
 explanation of, 115, 230
 restrictions on, 117, 118
 value of, 115

Keating, Charles, 131, 157
Kenney, Don, 87
King, Martin Luther, 210
Kinsley, Michael, 181
Kondracke, Morton, 181

Labor unions
 Clinton impeachment and, 2
 coercion by, 50
 direct mail advertising and, 73
 examples of prominent, 13
 explanation of, 12, 230
 as organized interests, 12–13, 25
 as patrons, 51
 public sector, 12–13
 sale of goods and services by, 76
 self-governance within, 81
Leadership, 58–61
Leadership Council on Civil Rights,
 105

Leech, Beth, 28
Legal analysis
 explanation of, 92, 230
 knowledge regarding, 122
 value of, 92–93
Legislative hearings, 94–95
Legislators/legislative staff, 95–96
Levine, Bertram, 124, 205
Liaison offices, 98–99
Liddy, G. Gordon, 182
Light, Paul, 97
Limbaugh, Rush, 182
Litigation, 103–104
Lobby agents, 119
Lobbying. *See also* Direct lobbying;
 Formal direct lobbying; Indirect
 lobbying; Informal direct lobbying
 to affect public opinion, 145,
  172–173, 176, 208–209, 230
 bureaucracy, 99–102
 with campaign money, 131–161 (*See
  also* Campaign finance)
 chief executive, 97–99
 for contact, 230, 173–176
 corrupt practices in, 110–113
 courts, 102–105
 explanation of, 8, 87–88, 117, 230
 government, 88–90
 legislature, 93–96
Lobbying Disclosure Act of 1946, 117
Lobbying Disclosure Act of 1995,
 117–118, 230
Lobbying law firms, 120–121, 230
Lobbying strategies
 monitoring to provide information
  about, 77
 types of successful, 205–209
Lobbyists
 characteristics of, 121, 122
 for corporations, 11
 explanation of, 10, 230
 guidelines for successful, 124–126
 income of, 121
 informal meetings with, 114
 information provision to policymakers
  by, 90–93, 105–106, 110, 154
 legal analysis provided by, 92–93
 legislative restrictions on, 117–119
 monitoring government by, 78